Charles Marius Dozy

The Pilgrim Fathers

Vol. 3

.

Charles Marius Dozy

The Pilgrim Fathers
Vol. 3

ISBN/EAN: 9783337292355

Printed in Europe, USA, Canada, Australia, Japan

Cover: Foto ©Lupo / pixelio.de

More available books at **www.hansebooks.com**

„Ziet tot het moederland de zonen wederkeeren....."

DA COSTA.

Year Book of The Holland Society of New-York, 1888-1889

Edited by the Secretary.

YEAR BOOK OF

THE HOLLAND SOCIETY OF NEW-YORK.

1888–1889.

THE event in the history of The Holland
Society in the year from Pinkster, 1888,
to Pinkster, 1889, was the trip to Holland, which was suggested by the secretary, and undertaken by a party of about fifty,
which included a few friends and relatives of those
members of the Society who made this journey of
twice thirty-five hundred miles solely from a desire
to see the land of their ancestors. When it was
determined upon each took money in his purse,
and, while hoping that they would be welcome,
not one even dreamed of the more than hospitable
greeting and entertainment of which they were the
recipients from the time when they landed at Rotterdam till the last hour of their stay. The story of
this pilgrimage now follows, the first part in the words
of Mr. Sheldon T. Viele of Buffalo, N. Y., and the
latter part in those of the Rev. J. Howard Suydam,

D. D., who were duly elected the historians of the party. The expedition was authorized at the annual meeting of the Society, held May 22, 1888, when the Rev. J. Howard Suydam, D. D., offered the following resolution:

"WHEREAS, a number of our members propose to visit Holland during the summer according to the arrangements made by the secretary. Therefore,

"*Resolved*, that they be declared representatives of The Holland Society of New-York, and that a record of their visit be published in the next issue of the Year Book."

This was carried unanimously, over two hundred members being present.

THE NARRATIVE OF

THE VISIT OF THE HOLLAND SOCIETY

TO THE NETHERLANDS.

PART I.

BY SHELDON T. VIELE.

I.—BONJER'S PILGRIMS' PROGRESS.

THE morning of July 28, 1888, was bright, sunny, and sparkling, in beautiful contrast with the rain and dampness of the preceding twenty-four hours.

The good ship *Amsterdam*, in gala attire, decked with flags, and with her cabins filled with flowers, awaited the coming of the pilgrims. These soon began to arrive, accompanied by friends and relatives to see them off, and the decks quickly filled with the expectant voyagers. All were interested and excited at the prospect. Most of them were strangers to each other and to the ocean, but all felt a more than common interest in the occasion, and a sense of friendliness for their fellow passengers, growing out of the unusual circumstances attending the trip. Soon came the hour for departure. The whistle and bells drove all but the voyagers on shore, and promptly at 9:30 the gang-plank was hauled in and the ship left the wharf.

The sail down the bay was beautiful, and the magnificent harbor of New-York never appeared to better advantage than beneath the bright skies and in the crisp atmosphere of the perfect summer day. All were absorbed in the beauty of the scene until about noon when the pilot was to depart. With a few hurried words, hastily written in letters to be taken by him as last messages to the friends left behind, he swung over the side and our voyage was fairly begun.

Up to this time the opportunities for acquaintance were few, but all at once began the interchange of names, and thus was initiated the good comradeship of the party which was so noticeable a feature of the whole expedition.

The first event after the departure of the pilot was the sounding of the breakfast bell about 12 o'clock, and the members of The Holland Society made a hungry rush for the dining saloon. Confusion reigned supreme for a few moments until the genial Van Sielen brought order out of chaos, and all were soon assigned to the places that they were to occupy more or less successfully for the next twelve days. The tables were filled, every place taken, the novelty of the situation was exciting, and everybody was happy through the first meal.

Here was the first opportunity to call the roll of the pilgrims, and it resulted as follows:

MEMBERS OF THE HOLLAND SOCIETY,

VISITING HOLLAND, JULY, 1888.

Dr. John Van Duyn, and wife . . . . . Syracuse, N. Y.
Peter V. Fort, and daughter . . . . Albany, N. Y.
Mrs. Delahanty, and grand-daughter
Miss Delahanty . . . . Albany. N. Y.
Frank I. Vander Beek, and son
Frank I. Vander Beek, Jr. . . . . Jersey City, N. J.
Jas. A. Van Voast . . . . Schenectady, N. Y.
Dr. Harman W. Veeder . . . . . . Schenectady, N. Y.
Isaac E. Ditmars . . . . N. Y. City.
Robert A. Van Wyck . . . . N. Y. City.
G. Y. Vander Bogart . . . . Schenectady, N. Y.
Hon. Edw. Elsworth, Mayor of Poughkeepsie, N. Y., and
   daughter
Miss May Elsworth . . . . Poughkeepsie, N. Y.
Eugene Elsworth . . . . Irvington, N. Y.
Jas. H. Blauvelt, and son
Harry R. Blauvelt . . . . Nyack, N. Y.
Rev. J. Howard Suydam, D. D. . . . . Jersey City, N. J.
John H. Voorhees . . . . Washington, D. C.
Frank Hasbrouck, Treasurer of city of Poughkeepsie, N. Y.
Dr. Chas. H. Voorhees, and wife . New Brunswick, N. J.
H. B. Hubbard, and son . . . . Brooklyn, N. Y.
Rev. J. Elmendorf, D. D., and wife . . . . . N. Y. City.
Sheldon T. Viele . . . . Buffalo, N. Y.
Menzo Van Voorhis . . . . Rochester, N. Y.
W. H. Vredenbergh, and son . . . . . . Freehold, N. J.
Judah B. Voorhees, Deputy Surrogate, and wife, and
Miss Barkaloo, and
Mrs. Geran . . . . Brooklyn, N. Y.
Hon. L. L. Van Allen, and sister
Miss Agnes Van Allen . . . . N. Y. City.
Geo. W. Van Siclen, Secretary of The Holland Society,
                                          N. Y. City.
Theo. V. Van Heusen, and son
William Manning Van Heusen . . . . . Albany, N. Y.
Chas. E. Lydecker . . . . N. Y. City.
John L. Swits . . . . Schenectady, N. Y

Guests Accompanying Them.

H. B. GATES, and sister
MISS GATES . . . . South Orange, N. J.
FRANK PEARSON . . . . Jersey City, N. J.
LEE W. CASE . . . . Schenectady, N. Y.
GEO. H. HOWARD . . . . Washington, D. C.
ALEX. J. THOMSON . . . . Schenectady, N. Y.
LEHMAN ISRAELS,
        Special Correspondent of the " N. Y. Herald."

As soon as this breakfast was over all began to talk genealogy, as the most common ground for acquaintance on this peculiar trip.

It may be remarked in passing that for the next three days, whenever the party were not otherwise occupied, they all talked genealogy. Each had an intense interest in the particulars relating to his own family, with a somewhat languid concern for the families of the others.

The afternoon was bright, the sea was calm and smooth; everyone thought nothing could be pleasanter than a sea voyage. About 5 o'clock came the welcome sound of the dinner-bell. Again all the seats were filled, all were happy. Soon, however, began to be felt the long roll of the ocean, and one by one the pilgrims left the table and sought seclusion, until only about one-half of the number remained at the conclusion of the first dinner.

The first night at sea has been so often described, and is so familiar to all from the vivid sketches of more experienced travelers, that it is hardly worth while to attempt to portray the emotions that filled the breasts of our pilgrims as the night wore on.

The morning of Sunday was cloudy and cold, and the sea rather rough. Most of the pilgrims contrasted the glories of the previous morning with the discomforts of this first Sunday, and found the reverse side of the picture their imaginations had presented of the beauties of a sea voyage. There was no thought of any attempt to hold any religious exercises. We however struck the Gulf Stream in the evening, and the weather became warmer and the sea smoother.

Monday, July 30, was clear and much warmer, the water smooth. As soon as all who were able had finished their morning coffee the first edict of the voyage was promulgated. We were directed to prepare, forthwith, and hand to Mr. Israels, the versatile special correspondent of the "Herald," who accompanied us, a succinct account of our Dutch descent; and we were particularly instructed to insert therein any romantic incidents or legends that occurred in our family traditions. "But," said Van, "suppose we have n't any." "Then," said the autocrat, "invent some. If you are not sure of the proper name of your great-grandfather give him a good sounding one, and be sure to get in the romance. The enterprise of the great American newspaper *must* be rewarded."

Accordingly all went to work, and at intervals "our special correspondent," in whom we took much pride, was presented with our effusions. With these he retired to the recesses of his special stateroom, on the main deck, where secure from interruption he prepared several huge packages. These we saw mailed on our arrival, but their contents we were not to ascertain for many days after. Nothing else of interest occurred during the day, except that we passed a French steamboat, about 5 P. M., bound for New-York. This was the only steamship we passed on the voyage, and Van observed that we probably would not have passed her if she had been going the other way.

Tuesday, July 31, was clear, warm, and beautiful all day. Those of the pilgrims whose descent from the beggars of the sea was best proved by their immunity from seasickness thoroughly enjoyed the day. The others, who heretofore had been struggling through all the miseries of their situation, now began to revive and appear on deck, to think that life was worth living, and to manifest some interest in what was going on. The evening will long remain vividly impressed on the memories of all who were on deck by the beautiful display of the starry sky, and one good dominie was sufficiently recovered from his ills to walk the deck, gaze upon the scene with emotion, and softly murmur to himself: "The heavens declare the glory of God, and the firmament showeth his handiwork."

Wednesday, August 1, gave us a clear morning and a quiet sea. All had by this time recovered their equilibrium, all were acquainted, all had become accustomed to the routine of the existence, and as the subject of genealogy had become worn out everybody began to thirst for new excitement. So, with that originality of idea that always strikes a ship's company about this time on a voyage, a mock trial was arranged of which Van Sielen was the victim, and this served to pass away the morning. The pictures taken by the pictoriographer of the expedition will give a more vivid idea of this amusement than can any words of the historian. This day was also signalized by the formation of the "Quartette"; an organization which added greatly to the pleasure and profit of every occasion when the pilgrims came together afterwards during the voyage. The quartette was composed of Dr. Elmendorf, Mr. Van Sielen, and Mr. Lydecker of the Society, and Mr. Leopold Von Lindau, a fellow voyager, and a most agreeable gentleman and charming musician.

Thursday, August 2, was only marked in the morning by the first concert of the quartette, which was received with great applause. In the evening after dinner the great American spirit innate in all Anglo-Saxon blood asserted itself. After being repressed by stress of circumstance for nearly a week, it finally broke out with force and energy. A public meeting was held with all due form and ceremony, and various parliamentary proceedings were gone through with, with great zest and pleasure. At this meeting Dr. Suydam and Mr. Viele were appointed historians of the expedition, Dr. Van Duyn was appointed pictoriographer, and Mr. Robert A. Van Wyck was elected to fill the difficult and onerous position of marshal for the rest of the voyage. An assessment of $3 was also laid upon each member for the purpose of procuring funds for the pictoriographer to obtain a collection of photographs for the archives of the Society. This meeting was the result of a discussion that had been going on for the preceding two days among the various groups on the deck and in the smoke-room. It was felt by all that in some way an expression should be made of the fact that this was only a jaunt for pleasure and sentiment, and that there was no "business" in any way to be associated with it, either in our minds or in the minds of those with whom we might come in contact in Holland; that it was a "sentimental journey" and not a business venture. This was the fundamental spirit of the expedition, unanimously concurred in, and every occasion was taken afterwards to emphasize this in every way. Incident to this feeling, and as a sort of side issue, came up the question of any attempt on our part to reciprocate at this time any hospitalities that might be shown us. After a somewhat heated discussion, which was carried on with true parliamentary vigor, the question of the dinner was satisfactorily settled by a resolution which was passed, that "it is inexpedient on this trip to give a dinner in Holland." The rest of the evening was passed most pleasantly in listening to a concert from the quartette, and to the uproar of college glees sung with great spirit by the improvised choir of the Society, which now first put in its appearance as an auxiliary to the quartette. It had been found that there were representatives in the company from many of the leading colleges in the country, and that they all had some slight idea of tune and an abundant capacity for noise; so the choir became also an established institution.

Friday, August 3, was rainy and unpleasant; there was little to occupy the minds of most of the members, and so the spirit of mischief entered into the brains of the choir. A number of them put their heads together and worked out a little surprise for the evening's amusement. The informal meeting, after dinner, of the Society had now become an institution, and so, after the quartette had given us their music with great pleasure, the choir produced their first effusion, which was received with much more enthusiasm than its *merits* warranted. It is here given as the first original chant of the expedition, and to mark the first steps of our progress in the poetical line. It was "The Son of a Van," and ran about as follows:

THE SON OF A VAN.

(Air: "Son of a Gambolier.")

WRITTEN FOR THE CLUB BY MESSRS. VAN HEUSEN AND VIELE.

We came from Jersey City,
 For Rotterdam we steer,
And ancient Neptune's drunken reel
 Made some of us feel queer;
But now we're getting better
 And courage Dutch display
As in our corporations big
 We jam eight meals a day.

CHO.—I 'm a Van of a Van, of a Van, of a Van,
 Of a Van of a way back line,
Like every honest burgher
 I 'd rather gin than wine;
And Edam cheese and Heinneker bier,
 I bed you dot vas fine;
I 'm a Van of a Van, of a Van, of a Van,
 Of a Van of a way back line.

Our gallant Secretary,
 His whiskers blow about,
And daily to our vision clear
 He 's growing wondrous stout.
And our serio-comic tenor,
 One Elmendorf, D. D.,
Just opes his throat and a silvery note
 Floats o'er the deep blue sea.

Now G. Y. Van, the tired man,
 Again re-tired feels,
As the Mayor of Poughkeepsie
 Pulls wires from his heels;
And Jim Van Voast eats eggs on toast,
 And frozen coffee drinks;
But Harman Veeder saves his Case
 And with the purser winks.

3

Now Doc. Van Duyn, he pulls the twine,
　　Drops a nickle in the slot,
And photographs the fleeting grin
　　Instanter — on the spot;
Now Swits, the "Marvel-to-himself,"
　　Can keep his dinner down,
But Thomson from mock-trials runs,
　　His troubles for to drown.

There 's Fort who hates his dinner,
　　And our marshal who *won't* drink,
While Hasbrouck and Van Allen
　　Of naught but girlies think;
While Voorhees, John, J. M., and C.
　　Frisk happily about,
And with their coy voluptuous gaze
　　They cut the mashers out.

It is here appropriate to say something about the ship. Certainly if our experiences were in any way a sample of the voyages of the Netherlands American Line this Company can safely be recommended to the traveling public. The ship was commodious and steady. The officers were obliging and polite, and at the same time thoroughly attentive to their duty in every way. The discipline was good and every possible attention was paid to the safety of the ship. This seemed to be the first essential rather than the rapidity of the voyage, and it is a characteristic that is calculated to inspire confidence. The fittings of the ship were new, clean, and neat. The ladies' room on the upper deck was very handsome, with its Dutch tile; while the smoke-room was fully appreciated both for its comfort and its quaint panels illustrating Dutch life and character. We all had plenty of room, which is not often the case on the larger lines. The table was excellent, and the service good. The meals were served in courses, and were abundant in variety and quantity. A sample dinner in the middle of the voyage is here given:

MENU.

S. S. *Amsterdam*, 5th August, 1888.

DINNER.

Soup Royale.
Petit pâtés de veau.
Roast beef, spinach.
Calf's head, sauce Hollandaise.
Roast ham, green peas.
Roast pigeons, stewed pears.
Pastry.
Fruits.   Coffee.

Saturday, August 4, was cloudy and damp, and at dinner we had our first experience of the most dismal feature of ocean travel, the fog whistle. This was then heard for the first time and took away much of the pleasure of the meal. However, after dinner the choir assembled and did their best to cheer the spirits of the passengers, and then was heard for the first time the second effusion. This was by Mr. Charles E. Lydecker, and was the "Pilgrimage to Holland, July, 1888."

THE PILGRIMAGE TO HOLLAND.

(Air: "Oranje boven al.")

Across the bounding dark blue sea
    Goes forth our Holland Society
On a rollicking, novel kind of a spree
    To the ancestral home ;
To land of dykes and dunes and mills,
    To land of pure Genever stills,
To land of resolute strong Dutch wills,
    We come, we come, we come.

CHO.—To land of dykes and dunes and mills, etc.

We have Vans, and Hoos, and Hees, and Huys,
   En Dorfs, en Dams, en Duyns, En Lys,
En Veeders, Vieles, Voasts and Forts,
   And various other sorts;
We have Beeks and Bogarts, Swits and Velts,
   Hasbroucks, and Hubbards, and eke Van Pelts,
And Waerths and Loos and Spaders (not Celts)
   To storm the old Dutch ports.—CHORUS.

Met metworst, eien en aspersie
   Snij boonen, erwten, en olie
Eendvogel, komkommer, spinazie,
   We get there all the same;
Tuinbonje, ossenvleesch, Schnapps, Schiedam,
   Aardappelen, Lamsbout, Visch, Edam,
Frambozen, Beycheville, Amsterdam,
   We get there all the same.—CHORUS.

When dark the sky, and waves run high,
   And spray with sting blinds every eye,
We ever try to wet our dry
   Below the cabin stair;
For home and loved ones left behind,
   The toast comes ever to the mind,
And to ourselves we must be kind,
   And all the same get there.—CHORUS.

This was received with such enthusiasm that the fog arose about 9 P. M. and everybody went to bed happy.

Sunday, August 5, found the weather still cloudy and misty, but the sea was calm, and the entire party felt the appropriateness of celebrating divine service. Service was accordingly held at 10 A. M. and was a very impressive occasion, led with good taste and effectiveness by Dr. Suydam and Dr. Elmendorf. The sermon preached on that occasion by Dr. Elmendorf was so striking and so appropriate, that many of the hearers asked that it be preserved in the records of the expedition. It is accordingly herewith inserted with great satisfaction and pleasure by the historian.

PRE-DESTINATION NOT FATALISM.

A sermon preached in the saloon of the steamer Amsterdam, Sabbath, August 5, 1888, on the excursion of The Holland Society of New-York to Holland, by Rev. J. Elmendorf, D. D.

Paul said to the Centurion and to the Soldiers, Except these abide in the ship ye cannot be saved.

The Acts, xxvii:31.

PAUL the prisoner had become the acknowledged master of the situation. His warning,—" sirs, I perceive that this voyage will be with injury and much damage, not only of the lading and ship, but also of our lives,"— with which he endeavored to prevent the officers of the ship from leaving their anchorage at Crete, in the face of equinoctial storms, had doubtless been remembered with bitter regret, because it was unheeded, and with growing conviction of his superior wisdom. When, therefore, he stood forth and declared to his despairing companions, " I exhort you to be of good cheer, for there shall be no loss of any man's life among you, but of the ship," and then gave the words of the angel of God to him as the ground of his promise, we may be sure they were all ready to receive his communication with unspeakable gratitude, and to regard him as their great deliverer.

Their awakened confidence and gratitude were not to be accepted as a tribute to himself, but were to be used in effecting their escape. God would not deliver them by a miracle, but by their most careful and energetic employment of the means at hand.

Two instances of Paul's asserted authority are given in the narrative. When by soundings the sailors found that the vessel was driving toward a rocky coast, knowing that the crisis of their peril was near, they selfishly determined to take their chances of escape in the ship's boat and leave their companions to their fate. The pretext by which they tried to do this was in an attempt to cast anchors out of the fore ship. But the alertness of Paul detected their scheme, and his prompt words to the centurion and soldiers were: "Except these abide in the ship, ye cannot be saved." Help for their deliverance would be needed, which only these experienced sailors could render, and if this was not secured, themselves would yet be lost. No one doubted his word now; so at once the soldiers cut the ropes of the boat and let her fall into the sea.

Then another want was more vigor and endurance than their long toil and fast had left them, for the hardships yet before them; and so, with reviving and inspiriting cheerfulness, they must take food. This they did from the force of Paul's advice and example.

These two recorded facts prove Paul's careful regard for and attention to the *natural conditions* of escape from their encompassing dangers.

But this important question quite certainly arises in every thoughtful mind: How could one who had made the unqualified declaration by divine authority, "There shall be no loss of any man's life among you," afterward consistently assert, "Except these abide in the ship ye cannot be saved"?

He could do this, my friends, through being an intelligent predestinarian instead of a fatalist.

This difference, which we really need clearly to see and remember, Paul radiantly exemplified through all his Christian career.

While other inspired authors most clearly and resistlessly declare the doctrine of God's decrees, it is in the writings of Paul that the most numerous and most significant references to it are found. He is pre-eminently the establisher and expounder of the truth of divine foreordination. In the IXth of Romans he fully states the doctrine and answers objections to it until he reaches the sovereign will of God as the final and sufficient reason for his decrees. "Nay, but, O man, who art thou that disputest with God?"

In another place he gives this concise and comfort-ing view of the relations of believers to God's provi-dence and purpose of grace: "We know that all things work together for good to them who are the called according to his purpose. For whom he did fore-know he also did predestinate to be conformed to the image of his Son, that he might be the first-born among many brethren. Moreover, whom he did pre-destinate them he also called: and whom he called them he also justified: and whom he justified them he also glorified."

In writing to the Ephesians he accounts for their great spiritual blessing in this way: "According as the Father of our Lord Jesus Christ hath chosen us in him, before the foundation of the world, that we should be holy and without blame before him in love, having predestinated us unto the adoption of children by Jesus Christ to himself, according to the good pleasure of his will."

In his letters to the Colossians, to Timothy, and to Titus, he speaks again and again of the "elect." It is abundantly manifest that this truth is fundamental in his convictions, and that it could hardly pervade his thoughts more thoroughly if the sublime words of the Lord by Isaiah were ever uppermost in his mind: "Remember the former things of old, for I am God, and there is none else; I am God, and there is none like me.

"Declaring the end from the beginning, and from ancient times the things that are not yet done, saying, My counsel shall stand, and I will do all my pleasure."

But while the proof abounds in all Paul's writings that his belief in the purposes of God and his reliance upon His providence were in him forces of tireless energy and sources of exhaustless strength and consolation, we look in vain for his slightest approach to presumptuousness in either secular or spiritual matters. His conviction was as clear and deep and constant that the *means* were divinely appointed, as that the end was certain; and that in all human experience the *use of the means* was *indispensable to the securing of the end.*

We find among others this striking instance of his constraining sense of responsibility in accomplishing an event which God had just told him must occur.

In one of the violent disturbances between the Sadducees and Pharisees in Jerusalem over Paul's preaching, the chief captain, fearing they would pull him in pieces, commanded the soldiers to rescue and bring him into the castle. In the following night, "The Lord stood by him and said, Be of good cheer, Paul: for *as* thou hast testified of me in Jerusalem, *so must* thou *bear witness also at Rome.*"

On the very next morning Paul learned through his nephew that forty Jews had entered into a conspiracy to kill him, and had sworn not to eat or drink until they had done this. How natural would have been the answer — Oh, God will take care of this. He has just told me that I must witness for him in Rome, and he will see that I get there. Did he do this? No, indeed. He immediately sent the young man by a centurion to the chief captain with his statement. And by means of the information thus given his destruction was prevented and his safety secured.

Now why did not the apostle quietly and without effort leave the matter to his Almighty Lord, from whose mouth he had the fullest assurance that he should see Rome? Because he was not a fatalist; because he did not believe *only half* of the doctrine of the divine decrees. He knew, as we know, and as another has concisely said, "God makes use of the *prudence* with which he has endowed man, as an *agent* in the very providence" that befriends him. Paul knew, as we all ought to, "that to neglect the natural means of safety with which God provides us is to tempt and dishonor him, and induce him in judgment to employ those means against us which in his mercy he had designed for our comfort and salvation." So he at once used his best wisdom and the means at hand to save his own life.

In all his religious course, also, the same broad, practical consistency marks his thoughts, words, and acts.

While referring his conversion and Christian hope wholly to the sovereign grace and electing love of God, and cherishing unshaken confidence that "He who had begun a good work in him would finish it until the day of Jesus Christ," yet he gave the most

4

earnest "diligence to make *his calling and election sure.*" He was stimulated to the most energetic and best adapted religious efforts, as if by a constantly apprehended possibility that he might yet lose the prize in the Christian race, fail of reaching the victor's crown in the Christian warfare, or fall short of the final plaudit of his Lord. His own intense words were, "I therefore so run, not as uncertainly; so fight I, not as one that beateth the air: But I keep under my body, and bring it into subjection: *lest* that by any means, when I have preached to others, I myself should be a castaway."

In the discharge of every duty, in every place, at every time, in every relation, Paul strove as if *there were no decree,* all the while believing and feeling that his striving would be futile, except as it harmonized with and accomplished the divine purpose. Or better, he strove as one who knew that his *striving* was as *essentially a part of the decree* as was the *end* it was to effect.

The critical worldly reason sees only contradiction in the mental state of one who trusts God implicitly to do something, and yet feels that it will not be done unless he does it himself. Is not the reconciliation found in the view that God makes the man his *voluntary instrument* in doing what he will have done?

Paul brings this out with ever enduring sublimity and sufficiency in his appeal to the Philippian Christians: "Wherefore, my beloved, work out your own salvation with fear and trembling. For it is God which worketh in you, both to will and to do of his good pleasure."

This was Paul's mind as he stood forth on the drifting wreck before that panic-stricken, despairing company. His words were: "There stood by me this night the angel of God, whose I am and whom I serve, saying, Fear not, Paul; thou must be brought before Cæsar: and lo, God hath given thee all them that sail with thee. Wherefore, sirs, be of good cheer: for I believe God, that it shall be even as it was told me."

But, as he accepted the providential information that forty Jews had conspired to kill him *as God's warning* that he must do what he could to thwart their murderous scheme, so now, he accepted God's cheering purpose and promise as a reason for taking new and confident courage, and making their best efforts to escape the threatening destruction. He did not expect *God* to do for them what he had given them the power and encouragement to do for themselves.

So, when the only competent and appointed workers were about to desert them, he said: "Except these abide in the ship, ye cannot be saved."

There was much to be done, which only these experienced sailors could do. The ship was to be farther lightened; the anchors must be taken up; the rudder bands must be loosed; the mainsail must be hoisted up to the wind; all that skillful seamanship could dictate and effect must be done, until the vessel should strike the shore and go in pieces, as it had been foretold she should. Then, when all this had been done, as the bow grounded immovably, and the hinder part of the ship was broken with the violence of the waves, some by swimming and some on fragments of the wreck reached the land, and *all,* according to the promise, were saved.

All this working was a clear discharge of duty, because it was according to the dictates of sober reason and the promptings of practical common sense. How unreasonable and wicked, in the light of Paul's example, would have been the advice of a fatalist; *i. e.*, one who holds that all things take place by necessity, irrespective of means. His counsel, under the words of the angel of God, must have been, "Do nothing, but wait and see what God will do for our deliverance." When he saw one in the water striking out for the shore, his command must have been, "Stop exhausting yourself by swimming, God is pledged to bring us to the land!" And to those frantically clinging to their supports he must have shouted, "Don't weary and bruise yourselves in holding on to your boards and beams, but cling to the divine promise: there shall be no loss of any man's life among you."

Consistent fatalism must forbid or neglect the use of means for the accomplishment of any end, whether of recognized slight or great importance. Holding the view that these *ends* are absolutely predetermined, and that nothing done or left undone can change them, the employment or the omission to employ agencies amounts to the same thing. Therefore, the fatalist who purposes and tries to do anything is contradicting his faith. If he would like to be in a distant place, at a particular time, it is entirely useless for him to look after the means of accomplishing the journey; for, according to his faith, if he is fated to be there, nothing need help, as nothing can hinder, the event. If he desire to possess something he has only to wait and see whether it is decreed that he shall have it. Eating is useless except as an enjoyment,— and even that ought to come without eating, if one is to have it; better, therefore, eating is use-

less except as a habit, for one's life must continue to
its appointed end whether he eat or not. So prepos-
terous is this belief when reduced to practice. Yet
some may be found in well nigh every Christian community who claim to hold this view. Their busy
lives contradict their own words, and show how
superficial and insincere is their profession.

The great majority of reasonable people, however,
who believe in the revealed perfections of God, hold
the doctrine of decrees,—at least, concerning all
worldly matters,—as Paul believed it, and act accordingly. If they wish to go anywhere, to possess
or effect anything, to defeat any harmful project,
however confidently they believe that the omniscient
God knows what the issue is to be,—and that therefore it must be determined according to and in order
to that knowledge,—they exercise their best wisdom
in selecting their means and methods, and energetic-
ally and persistently use these to achieve the desired
end. Had they been or were they in peril as Paul
was from those murderous conspirators; had they
been with him on the endangered vessel, they would
have done, they would do, as he and his companions
did. Reasonable beings instinctively, and by principles which deepen and strengthen in their life
experiences, employ the powers with which their
Creator has endowed them, and the agencies he has
made subject to them, in effecting the things that
seem to be desirable and right. Their lives everywhere and ever, whether with or without any regard
to the subject, prove that he who knows the end from
the beginning *includes the means which are to accomplish it* as certainly as the end to be accomplished
in his decree. Any other theory of foreordination,

reduced to practice, results in the folly of expecting something from nothing.

But it is only in worldly matters that this wide conformity of action to conviction is found. Many who illustrate it everywhere else, when they come to the religious life and interests turn fatalists, and by their words sometimes, and oftener by their conduct, say, "If I am to be saved, I shall be saved without my own efforts; but if I am to be lost, I cannot help it." And some who are unwilling to echo this bald view reach the same ground through modified forms of erroneous thought and speech: "God must save me, therefore I can do nothing to save myself." "Faith is his gift, and until he bestows it I cannot believe. The Holy Spirit must quicken me, and until he does this I cannot move spiritually." These, like the fatalist's decrees, are only half-truths. God must save us; but instead of teaching us that we can do nothing toward this, he declares just the opposite truth: "Except *ye repent*, ye shall all likewise perish." "Believe on the Lord Jesus Christ and thou shalt be saved."

Faith is God's gift, but the act of believing is ours; and how shall any know whether He has bestowed the gift until himself tries to believe? While men profess to be waiting for the quickening power of the Holy Spirit, God says to them, "Ye do always resist the Holy Ghost."

The cause of all these erroneous pleas is forgetfulness of the fact that in religious matters as in all the duties and experiences of life God deals with us as reasonable and moral beings. Many seem to think that God must save their souls, as men save an ox or an ass that has fallen into a pit, by lifting or forcing it, without its coöperation, or against its resistance, from a place of danger to one of safety. But God saves men's *souls* by moving them through the same intellectual and moral powers by which he saves their endangered bodies, and with the same kind of motives. When menaced by murderous conspirators, or exposed to destruction on a foundering ship, the value men set on their earthly existence, and a sense of their obligation to continue it, make them use with greatest promptness and persistence the best available means for their deliverance. So, if men believe that their immortal souls are periled by their roaring and devouring enemy, and that they are in danger of sinking into the depths of eternal anguish and despair, they must put forth efforts for their own salvation by the use of the means which God hath appointed to effect this.

Thus did Paul. When, under the flashings of the heavenly vision that arrested his persecuting way to Damascus, he learned his danger, his first cry was, "Lord, what wilt thou have me *to do?*" And from that moment until he could say, "I have finished my course," he exemplified how doing God's will, or obeying God's word, demonstrates to the doer its divine origin and authority, and makes him the conscious subject of his saving power.

Is it said, surely, when we enter the sphere of true and saving religious experience, we are subject to and dependent upon a peculiar, mysterious, and incomprehensible influence of the Holy Spirit? Yes, indeed! In this life we can hardly hope to be able to comprehend how God can work within a soul both to will and to do of his good pleasure, and yet leave that soul wholly free and responsible in its own will-

ing and doing. Yet both these things are facts; for
the divine scriptures assert the first, and equally with
human consciousness affirm the other. But they are
no more facts in the *religious* than they are in the
other experiences of life. Men while freely willing
and doing in their worldly projects are as directly
fulfilling the divine plans and making "his counsel
to stand," as they are by their religious efforts. And
clearly we are no more dependent upon God for
spiritual life, than we are for that which animates
body and mind in our worldly activities.

The providence of God and his management of the
world, so that he is "doing all his pleasure" by the
free and responsible acts of men, is as profound a
mystery as is the great economy of grace by which
he is gathering an elect people unto himself. But
we have nothing to do with the mysteries. "Secret
things belong to God: but those things which are
revealed belong unto us and to our children, forever,
that we may do all the words of his law."

For the individual soul the way is plain. Step by
step it must follow the path of duty at the time
before it. "Then shall we know if we follow on to
know the Lord." Act after act of obedience to the
command *now* heard fulfills to the soul Christ's
words, "He that hath my commandments and
keepeth them, he it is that loveth me: and he shall
be loved of my Father, and I will love him, and will
manifest myself to him."

And when one knows that he is a sinner, and that
unless he repents, and believes in the Lord Jesus
Christ, he will perish in his sins, he is no more
authorized to delay the discharge of his duty by
raising the question of the relation of his salvation

to the decrees of God, than is the man who has taken poison, accidentally, and who holds in his hand the antidote, to delay swallowing it by the inquiry, "Is it decreed that I shall live or die?" There is but one reply for such. Swallow the antidote or die! Believe on the Lord Jesus Christ or perish!

After dinner the choir again assembled, but in deference to the day confined their efforts to psalms and hymns and spiritual songs, which were given by the efficient aid of the quartette with good effect. Van remarked that it spoke well for the general bringing up of the company that so many of them seemed familiar with so many hymns.

The fog whistle, by this time grown almost too familiar, accompanied us as we went to bed.

Monday, August 6, was more clear and pleasant in the morning, and the entire party were on deck. Then occurred the trial of Dr. Suydam for the alleged theft of certain necessary wearing apparel from his room-mate. Unfortunate as it may seem this was founded upon an actual fact, and the historian can only draw a veil over the details of the occurrence. Our friend, the fog whistle, put in its usual appearance at dinner and accompanied us during part of the evening; but the choir, nothing daunted, gave their usual evening medley, and produced, for the novelty of that evening, a rhyming account of the voyage, by Dr. Suydam, entitled "The Departure":

5

THE DEPARTURE.

The time, it was the summer, and the year was eighty-eight,
And Jersey was the city, and Jersey **was the State,**
Where the Dutchmen came together **with gripsack in the hand,**
To make the start for Holland, the dear old Motherland.

They bade good-bye to mothers, to wives, and **children dear,**
The smile was forced, the voice was low **that spoke the words of cheer;**
And the face that once was lion, assumed the phase of lamb,
As it faded in the distance on the deck of the *Amsterdam.*

'T was beautiful to look upon as downward through the bay
From cities dense, 'twixt islands green, the good ship
plowed her way;
Old ocean in his mildest mood received her to his arms,
Which caused the timid passengers to banish all **alarms.**

The night **was** passed, the morning came, the **sun rose**
bright and clear,
The call to break the matin fast was welcomed without fear
By only a **few of that** Dutchmen crew, since Neptune 'gan
to roll;
While the others lay in their berths below to pay the exact-
ing toll.

The world had rolled but three times round and then the festal board
Received anew the absent ones, again with strength restored;
Since then, at every call of bell, they 're waiting at the door;
Five times a day they eat, and eat, and still they cry for more.

On deck it 's quite amusing, and quite instructive, **too,**
To note the themes of converse 'mong this peculiar crew,
'T is talk of years of long ago when o'er this same wide sea
Their fathers sailed, unto our land, to plant the family tree.

The Mohawk Vans were there, and the Vans from Jersey shore;
From the Hudson came the Huguenots, and other Vans a score.
While others still, of blood as pure, from old Long Island
came.
And Northern lake, and Southern clime, still added to the same.

All cousins in their native land, across the sea they're borne
To see from whence their fathers came two hundred years
  agone:
To recall the deeds of valor, and the battles that they won,
Whence came the boon of freedom to the land of setting
  sun.

Good fortune all attend them, may gods of sea and land
Give favoring gales, send balmy air, in forest and on strand,
And the God on high, who rules in sky, his lesser powers
  retain
To guard these genial Dutchmen, and bring them home
  again.

Tuesday, August 7, came in with the fog still attending us. The fog whistle blew almost all day, and in the evening, until everybody was fatigued and nervous from the monotonous repetition. In the afternoon the excitement grew intense at what was supposed to be the first glimpse of land. Off on our left, as the fog lifted a moment, the captain said that a little patch of what looked like mist to the pilgrims was really the first land of our outward voyage. We were by this time so accustomed to put full faith in everything that he did and said that we accepted his statement with gratitude, but were unable to verify it by our own senses. We passed the Scilly Islands in a dense fog and our signals were unsuccessful. Quiet was necessary on the ship, in order that any approaching danger might easily be heard; so the evening meeting in the saloon was not held, and the choir were obliged to have a few songs in an undertone in the recesses of the smoke-room. The ship made but little progress during the entire day and night, sounding and feeling her way through the fog into the dreaded English Channel with caution and discretion that proved the able seamanship of her commander.

Wednesday, August 8, found us still in the fog, which seemed to grow denser and denser. The sounds of life could now and then be heard through the mist, but nothing could be seen through the almost darkness that surrounded us. At 11.15 in the morning we dropped anchor to await the rising of the fog. It was a striking illustration to the historian of the exact nature of the seamanship of to-day that was then by accident afforded him. Just before the anchor was dropped the historian was standing where he could watch the captain at work in the chart-room over the charts and logs spread around him. A sailor brought to him the last soundings, the water mark indicating on the line the depth of water, and the tallow at the bottom of the lead showing the soil. The captain cut the latter out, looked at it a moment, saw the depth indicated by the line, and then looking up, and happening to catch the historian's eye, he pointed to a spot on the chart as indicating our position. This was just off Brighton, in a narrow part of the Channel. Then came the order to drop anchor. Absolute quiet was necessary in order that careful watch could be kept on all sides; all the officers were on the bridge and the crew at their posts. The unusual circumstance of a stoppage being necessary at this stage of our journey cast a gloom over the entire party, and the hours were passed in as comfortable a state as could be until long after dinner. About 9 P. M. the fog suddenly lifted. The lights of England shone all round us; and there we were, just where the captain had indicated, immediately off Brighton, and the electric lights of the watering places showed clearly through the evening skies. The stars came out, all fog disappeared, the spirits of the passengers arose with a bound, the ship started at full speed, and all on board were again happy.

Then came the last meeting of the Society on the boat. This was held in the cabin, Vice-President Hasbrouck in the chair. After a solo by Van Siclen, in his fine bass voice, Mr. Van Heusen, Sr., offered the following resolution:

"Resolved, That we, members of The Holland Society, here assembled on board the good ship *Amsterdam*, bound for Rotterdam, and quite near our destination, do most earnestly out of our hearts thank Secretary Geo. W. Van Siclen for his earnest, intelligent, and persevering efforts to promote and insure our comfort and pleasure on this voyage. 'God zeegene hem.'"

This was seconded, and carried with enthusiasm. Then the Rev. Mr. Suydam offered the following resolution:

"Resolved, That The Holland Society place upon record its grateful appreciation of the treatment received during the present voyage from the representatives of the Netherlands American Steam Navigation Company, and from Captain Bonjer and the officers of the *Amsterdam;* especially for retaining the cabin for our accommodation, for the variety and abundance of provisions skillfully prepared, for the unexcelled service, for the uniform courtesy manifested by officers and subordinates, for the constant anticipation of our necessities, and our comfort.

"Success to the Company! Peace and safety to officers and crew in the discharge of their perilous duties!

"And every blessing upon their wives and children at home!"

Which was carried unanimously, with the addition by Van Siclen that it be spread on the ship's book, and the further addition by Lydecker that all cabin passengers desiring to unite with us in this expression of our feelings on the ship's book be requested to so unite in the signing of the resolution. It was then resolved that Mr. Van Siclen be appointed the representative of the Society to respond for the Society to any addresses of welcome that might be received after landing in Holland. Mr. Van Wyck then moved that we resolve ourselves into a glee club. This was carried with enthusiasm, and all of the old songs were resung; and the crowning ebullition of the poetic muse of the voyage was then produced from the graceful pen of Dr. Elmendorf, as follows:

THE HOLLAND SOCIETY OF NEW-YORK TO OLD HOLLAND.

(Air: "Integer Vitæ.")

Land of our fathers, we thy shores are seeking,
　Drawn by thy glory, driven by filial love;
O'er each famed spot where waves as famed are breaking,
　Now we would fondly rove.

Earth has no land more full of moral wonders;
　No names are brighter on history's radiant page;
Symbols of peace, or echoing war's dread thunders —
　From age to following age.

Liberty's champions, truth's most willing martyrs,
　Here taught the world how sweet it is to die
For one's dear country; for one's hope more precious
　Of immortality.

Good men are better for the men of Holland;
　Nations are nobler whose lives received her life;
Valor is firmer from the strength each right hand
　Gains from her holy strife.

Come we with reverence to the graves of grandsires;
  Lay our heart offerings on their hallowed ground ;
Go with the purpose their nobleness inspires,
  And worthy sons be found.

God of our fathers, who their nation founded,
  Keep thou the people great, and strong, and pure;
In love of country, truth, and brethren grounded,
  While nations shall endure.

After the adjournment all again went on deck.
The beautiful night and the excitement of being again
under way under such auspicious circumstances, with
the certainty that our voyage was almost ended, kept
all from sleeping. There was much to be seen in the
constant succession of lights on the English coast.
The number of vessels continually passing, and the
evidences all around us of human life, were in striking
contrast with the isolation through which we had
been traveling for so many days. At 11.30 we passed
a large lighthouse station, with telegraphic communication to London, and accordingly we signaled
our presence. This was done by a man in the bow
with a green roman candle, a man in the center of
the ship with a white, and another in the stern with
a green, thus showing the colors of the Company.
At the word of command these were all ignited at
once and the effect was most pleasing. In a few
moments came the answering signal from the tower;
and we knew that the next instant electric messages
would be conveying the intelligence of our safety
both to Holland and to America.

Here ends the record of the voyage. It has been
made as brief as mention of its principal events
would allow. To those who participated in its pleasures this epitome of what happened will recall many
happy hours and pleasant incidents. Although in a

measure overshadowed by the unexpected grandeur and warmth of our reception in Holland, yet the voyage of the *Amsterdam* on that memorable expedition, and the kindness and seamanship of the gallant Bonjer and his associates, will ever remain most pleasing memories in the minds and hearts of the Pilgrims to Holland.

II.—THE RECEPTION.

THE morning of Thursday, August 9, found us in the North Sea, with clear sky and smooth water. Our curiosity and interest were strung to the highest pitch in the certainty that our long voyage was about over, and that the land of our forefathers soon would be before us. Crafts of every description were continually passed, and all eyes were strained for the first glimpse of land. A most foreign looking vessel bore down upon us, and the Dutch pilot of the North Sea came on board. He was a most thorough specimen of an old salt, rather above the medium height, but massive and broad in construction, with a weather-beaten face, surrounded by a fringe of whiskers. Clad in a half naval uniform, he walked the bridge, intent only on his duty, and with no regard to the many curious eyes upon him. Soon on our port bow could be seen a long strip of what at first seemed like a thin cloud, but which rapidly assumed form and stability, and was seen to be low stretches of sand with banks and little hillocks built up by the wind and waves. This was our first glimpse of Holland. We noted with surprise the clear line of demarkation between the dark blue waters of the

North Sea, and the greenish, yellow-tinted waters of
the Maas and Scheldt rivers. This at first appeared
almost like a long narrow needle, in the clear water of
the sea, but gradually became broader and wider and
darker in color until it extended north and south as
far as the eye could reach at the distance of six miles
from shore. Then a great church with a massive
tower appeared, rising apparently out of the sand,
with nothing around it, and here and there a few
lighthouse towers; and these were the only prominent
features of the landscape. In a few moments we
entered the canal or Nieuw Waterweg at the Hoek of
Holland. Our steamer was then decked with flags,
the officers in full uniform, all in readiness for the
welcome which awaited us. As we fairly entered the
canal we began to see the distinctive characteristics
of the Dutch scenery. Standing on the deck of the
steamer, fifteen feet above the level of the canal, we
seemed to be able to overlook the greater part of
Holland. On the banks of the canal on either side
were seen the tops of willows and birch trees, planted
closely, with regularity, and trimmed so as to have no
undergrowth. The land on both sides was much
below the level of the banks of the canal, so that we
looked down upon the land, which lay far below us.
Hidden in clusters of green were seen the tops of
houses, and in the fields, unmarked by fences, but
really separated by low small ditches, were black and
white cattle peacefully grazing. Soon the windmills
began to appear on all sides; some quiescent, some
lazily moving their arms, others rapidly waving their
great limbs. Presently a most business-like little
steam yacht approached the vessel, and the custom-
house officers came on board, accompanied by a small

6

reception committee. Then was given the first evidence of the many courtesies to be showered upon us. A gentleman appeared with a large number of tags on which were printed, Mr. ——, Member of The Holland Society of New York. Each of us was asked how many pieces of baggage he had; and to each was given the requisite number of tags, with instructions to write his name on the tag, and place one on each piece of baggage. Every piece that bore one of these tags was passed without examination by the custom-house officers. This was an act of governmental courtesy as unexpected as it was graceful. Another tug decked with flags then appeared, steaming rapidly towards us, bearing a delegation from Rotterdam, who came on board and were introduced to many members of the party. The brass band who accompanied them escorted us on our way, playing American airs in honor of the visitors. All the shipping that we passed were decked with flags, and salutes and cheers were frequent. The pilgrims, excited by the occasion, and enthusiastic and patriotic to the highest degree, over and over again gave their cheer, which they had carefully prepared for the occasion, viz., Rah, Rah, Rah; Rah, Rah, Rah; Rah, Rah, Rah; B-o-n-j-e-r; Bonjer. In this way we passed Maasluis, Vlaardingen, and Schiedam, three smaller places on the river, and at length approached the wharves of Rotterdam. The city rose before us, full of life, and with many imposing structures. As we neared the wharf, about four o'clock in the afternoon, we could see the long gang-plank ready to be swung on board, and near by an immense mastiff watching every movement with intense interest. The moment the ship was fast and the plank moved the dog bounded forward and was the first on board. He was the noble animal of the captain awaiting his return and manifesting in every way his joy at the arrival of his master.

Here at the wharf we were met by a committee representing Rotterdam, among whom besides Mr. J. V. Wierdsma, director of the Netherlands American Steamship Co., were Jhr. Otto Reuchlin, Mr. Hendrik P. H. Muller, Hzn., and many prominent gentlemen of the city.

We were speedily placed in carriages and told to have no concern for our baggage. In a long procession we were quickly transported through the town to a large railway station; there we disembarked, and for a few moments were left to ourselves to recover our composure after our exciting welcome. With characteristic American adaptability, we all fell to investigating the station, buying papers, light refreshments, and cigars, for the sake of having our first transactions in a foreign currency. Our greatest surprise in this line was experienced when we found that really fair cigars cost about two cents apiece. Shortly afterwards a special train drew into the station, and we were quickly aboard. The foreign cars, with their divisions into three carriages, running crosswise, seemed novel, and added to the general foreign feeling we all experienced. As a special mark of honor the King's railway carriage was placed at the disposal of the ladies of the party. We started about five o'clock and were rapidly carried, with few stops, to our destination. On either side, as we looked out, the distinctive features of the Dutch scenery presented themselves; a broad low country, with dark gray clouds in the sky; flat meadows cut into regular

parallelograms by small canals; farm-houses surrounded by trees planted closely, and in straight lines,
forming a square around the house; black and white
cattle everywhere; well kept roads higher than the
fields, traversing them at almost regular intervals;
windmills everywhere, ranging from the baby wind-
mill, about two feet high, at the end of minute ditches,
up to the enormous towers wherein were pumps
driven by steam. As we approached Amsterdam it
almost seemed like the approach to the upper end of
New York when coming in on the railroad; blocks of
houses a few squares off just being completed, and
between them and the railroad a half-made and half-
filled street stretching out, with its pavement yet
unfinished. Amsterdam was reached about seven
o'clock in the evening. Quickly disembarking we
were met at the station by a reception committee,
Messrs. Cazaux van Staphorst, J. Voûte, Czn., and A.
J. van Eeghen, with open carriages, and were driven
in a sort of informal procession through the crowded
streets to the hotel. Salutations were given us on
every side, and as we approached the hotel the American flag waving over its portal showed the welcome
beneath its doors. The quickly arriving crowd of active Americans proved almost too much for the rather
slow-moving temperament of the proprietors, but we
were soon assigned to our rooms. The overflow were
provided for in the Hotel Rondeel close by, and about
nine o'clock we sat down to our first dinner. The
hotel, which was the headquarters of the visitors
while in Holland, was the Bracks Doelen, on Kloveniersburgwal Gracht, a fairly comfortable hostelry,
chosen for its central position. One or two of the
party, who had made the journey before, had given

PLATTE GROND

VAN

AMSTERDAM in 1888

MET SITUATIE

van het Vondelspark, in verband met het

nieuw aangelegde Willemspark, Natura Artis Magistra

EN ALLE VERDERE NOODZAKELIJKE AANWIJZINGEN

VOOR VREEMDELINGEN

Herzien voor het jaar 1888

DOOR

A. J. VAN DER STOK Jr

Prijs

60 Cent

AMSTERDAM — Tj. VAN HOLKEMA

PLATTE GROND

VAN

AMSTERDAM in 1888

MET SITUATIE

van het Vondelpark, in verband met het

nieuw aangelegde Willemspark, Natura Artis Magistra

EN ZEER VEIRLEI PERSONAARLIER AANWIJZINGEN

VOOR VREEMDELINGEN

Herzien **voor het jaar 1888**

Prijs
60 Cent

A. J. VAN DER STOK Jr.

AMSTERDAM   J. VAN HOLKEMA

AMSTERDAM

Hôtels, Restauraties, Café's, enz.

VOORNAAMSTE LOGEMENTEN:

Amstel-Hôtel (aan de Hooge Sluis).
Brack's Doelen (Doelenstraat).
Hôtel des Pays-Bas (Doelenstraat).
Bible-Hôtel (Warmoesstr. en Damr.)
Rondeel (Doelenstraat).
Hôtel Neuf (Kalverstraat).
Mille Colonnes (Rembrandtplein).
Hôtel American (Leidscheplein).
Hôtel Adrian (Kalverstraat.
Poolsche Koffiehuis (Kalverstraat).
Hôtel Kleintjes (Kalverstraat).
Hôtel Oude Graaf
Hôtel Suisse (Kalverstraat).
De Haas (Papenbrug).
Stadt Elberfeld (O. Z Achterburgw.)
Hôtel Oldewelt (Nieuwendijk).
Wapen van Friesland (Warmoesstr.)
Hôtel Rembrandt (Rembrandtplein).
Palais Royal (Paleisstraat).
Hôtel Hollanda's (Leidscheplein).
Hôtel Handelskade (Czaar Peterstr.)
Hôtel Krasnapolsky (Warmoesstr.)
Hôtel Kloppenburg (Leidscheplein).
Hôtel du Passage (Prins Hendrikk.)
Hôtel Français (Rokin).
Hôtel de l'Europe (Singel).
Het wapen v. Holland (P. H. kade).
Hôtel Garni Plantage Fransche laan.

VOORNAAMSTE RESTAURATIES:

Krasnapolski (Warmoesstraat).
Mille Colonnes (Rembrandtplein).
Die Port v. Cleve (bij 't Postkantoor)
Café Restaurant Ned. Panopticum.
Het Vosje (Rokin).
De Pool (Rokin).
American Bar (Rokin).
Café Suisse (Kalverstraat).
De Karseboom (Kalverstraat).
Hôtel American (Leidscheplein).
Palais Royal (Paleisstraat).
Café Willemsen (Heiligenweg).
Café Roseamm (Damrak).
Restaurant Riche (Rokin).

In bovenstaande restauraties eet men
van 's middags 2—7½ uur naar keuze
volgens de spijskaart van den dag; bo-
vendien is er in alle hôtels gelegenheid
tot deelname aan de table d'hôte, des
middags tusschen 5—6½ uur. In de Koffie-
en Bierhuizen kan men zich van 's mor-
gens vroeg tot den avond laten bedienen
met biefstuk, eieren en brood. Oester-
winkels vindt men in de Kalverstraat,
Reguliersbreestraat en in de Paleisstraat.
Banket- likeur- en chocoladewinkels in
de Kalverstraat en in eenkele hoofdstraten.
De vermaarde likeurwinkel van Wijnand
Fockink is in de Pijlsteeg, toegang
Damstraat, en die van Lucas Bols in
de Kalverstraat.

MANÈGES.

Vondelkade.
Nieuwe Kerkstraat.

VOORNAAMSTE KOFFIEHUIZEN:

Poolsche Koffiehuis (Kalverstraat).
Café Suisse (Kalverstraat).
Die Port van Cleve (bij 't Postkantoor).
N. Amsterd. Koffiehuis, (Kalverstr.)
Café Français (Kalverstraat).
Café Neuf (Kalverstraat).
Café Kleintjes (Kalverstraat).
De Oude Graaf (Kalverstraat).
Caves Français (Kalverstraat).
Café Roseamm (Damrak).
Café Restaurant Panopticum.
Café Londres (Amstelstraat).
Mille Colonnes (Rembrandtplein).
Café Continental (Sarphatistraat).
Hôtel American (9 biljards).
De Roode Leeuw (Vijgendam).
Café Beursplein (Rokin).
De Koncet (Gravenstraat).
Café Zincken (de Ruyterkade.)
Unions des producteurs (Doelen-
straat en Rokin).
Bodega Comp. (Kalverstraat).
Frieke en Co. (Rokin).
Munchener Kindl (Rokin).
Wiener Café (Rokin).
Kroonbier-divan
Krasnapolsky
   met 19 biljards.} Warmoes-
Munchener Kindl   straat.
Löwenbrau
Palais Royal (Paleisstraat).
De Stad Sidney (Pijpenmarkt).
Café Settels (Prins Hendrikkade).
Rembrandt (Rembrandtplein).
Café des Pays-Bas (Rembrandtplein).
Café Flora (Weteringschans).
Café de Pool (Rokin).
Paviljoen (Vondelspark).
Casino (Waterlooplein).
Café Restaurant de Poort v. Mui-
den (Commelin-straat).
Café Restaurant Handelskade.

BADHUIZEN:

Koude en Warme, Zee en Rivier-
baden, Rokin over de Ned. Bank.
Koude, Warme en Dampbaden.
Heerengracht bij de Leliegracht.
Koude en Warme Baden, Wester-
doksdijk. (Barendszkade).
Koude en Warme Baden, de Ruy-
terkade (Th v. Heemstede Obelt).
Koude en Warme Baden, Amstel-
dijk, hoek Jan v. d. Heidenstraat.
Badplaats Buiten-Amstel bij Schol-
lenbrug.
Openb. Zwemplaats bij de Westelijke
Doksluizen.
Openb. Zwemplaats in de Dijkgracht.

HOOFDBUREAU DER POLITIE.

Spinhuissteeg.

Stoomdrukkerij van Roeloffzen & Hubner

us many stirring accounts of the glories of the Kalverstraat at midnight, and accordingly, at a moderate estimate, about ninety per cent. of the expedition made their way to this famous street at the time when they had understood its glories were the greatest. They found a narrow street, not very long in extent, with sidewalks about a yard wide, and the roadway paved with asphalt. It was lined on both sides with shops and restaurants, all ablaze. No vehicles are allowed in the street after ten o'clock; and with both roadway and sidewalk filled with pedestrians passing to and fro, all life and gaiety, it certainly was a scene strange to American eyes, and one not entirely consonant with our ideas of Dutch phlegm and decorum.

AMSTERDAM.

THE morning of Friday, August 10, found the entire party well, in good spirits, and eager for the novelties before them. On arriving at the hotel the evening before, each member of the party was presented with a huge envelope. This contained a large map of Amsterdam, an elegantly gotten-up guidebook of the city, specially prepared for the use of the members of The Holland Society, cards of invitation to several clubs and societies, and tickets for the various trips prepared for us by the Amsterdam committee. This was a most complete surprise and showed the care and liberality which had been displayed in preparing for our welcome. We felt indeed that we were welcome guests in a most hospitable land.

VOORNAAMSTE LOGEMENTEN:

VOORNAAMSTE KOFFIEHUIZEN:

VOORNAAMSTE RESTAURATIES:

LIJST van STRATEN, GRACHTEN enz., die in dit plan te vinden zijn.

MIDDELEN VAN VERVOER.

GEBOUWEN EN INRICHTINGEN.

SCHOUWBURGEN, LOCALEN VOOR CONCERTEN, ENZ.

rs van Amsterdam.

To be retained.

THIS TICKET ADMITS A MEMBER

OF THE

„Holland Society of New-York"

to the **Reception** at the AMSTEL-HOTEL,

on **FRIDAY, AUGUST 10th 1888 at 8.30 p. m.**

and on Board the Steamer „WILLEM III"

Harlinger Pier, de Ruyterkade,

on **TUESDAY, AUGUST 14th 1888 at 8.30 a. m.**

for a Trip to MARKEN and HOORN.

KONINKLIJK ZOOLOGISCH GENOOTSCHAP
NATURA ARTIS MAGISTRA.
AMSTERDAM.

UITNOODIGING

voor den Heer

JUDAH B. VOORHEES,

of Brooklyn, N. Y.

tot een bezoek aan bovengenoemd Genootschap

L. G. VAN HOORN,
President.

J. M. B. BEUKER,
Secretaris.

Amsterdam, Augustus 1888.

G. F. WESTERMAN,
Directeur.

At the request of Mr. H. CAZAUX VAN STAPHORST and of

Mr. J. VOÛTE CZN. the Trustees of the „LEESMUSEUM", 102 Rokin

(Reading Club), will have much pleasure in extending the privileges

of the Club to Mr. GILES Y. VAN DER BOGART, of Schenectady, N. Y.

for two Weeks, from August 10th 1888.

We found that the committee, with kind intent to allow us an opportunity to recover from the fatigues of the journey, had left the first morning free for the pilgrims to get rested and accustomed to their novel surroundings. All therefore indulged in a little foreign shopping, and some promiscuous sight seeing.

The *Amsterdamsche Courant and Handelsblad* of August 10, 1888, in its City News thus spoke of our arrival :

OUR AMERICAN BRETHREN.

They have arrived ! They are within our walls, these descendants of our forefathers who crossed over to the New World and settled there. They are here, at Amsterdam, they who now, a great many of them at least, are residents of New York, the New Amsterdam of former years. And even if they have been compelled to replace the language of Holland with that of Albion, still they have not forgotten Holland, still they, the members of The Holland Society, consider it an act of piety to visit the country where their ancestors lived, to view the spot where stood the cradle of their forefathers.

And therefore they came to Holland in a Dutch steamer, a ship of a Dutch company, the *Amsterdam.* This morning a member of our editorial staff had an interview with Mr. Geo. W. Van Siclen, the actual projector of this trip, one might say the president of that section of The Holland Society which is now in our midst. The reception our reporter met with was most polite. Mr. Van Siclen, who has been in Holland before, considered it a pleasure to be interviewed by an Amsterdam newspaper-man. Of course the first question was about the sea-voyage. "How has it been ? "

"Charming. We had a splendid vessel, and above all an excellent commander; everybody on board was kindness itself. Good weather favored us, but for that matter," Mr. Van Siclen added with a smile, "we members of The Holland Society always have fine weather. We met some fog in the Channel which delayed us a few hours. But otherwise

A

GUIDE

THROUGH

AMSTERDAM

offered to the members of the

HOLLAND SOCIETY OF NEW-YORK

ON THE OCCASION OF THEIR VISIT TO THIS CITY

AUGUST 1888.

THE

RECEPTION COMMITTEE

on the occasion of a visit of Members of the „Holland
Society" of New-York to the city of Amsterdam in August,
1888, includes the following gentlemen:

F. A. ANKERSMIT, member of the firm of Jacob Ankersmit
& Son, merchants.

C. D. ASSER, Junr., L.L. D.

Professor T. M. C. ASSER, L.L. D.

CHARLES BOISSEVAIN, Editor of the „Algemeen Handelsblad".

J. M. VAN BOSSE, member of the firm of Wed. J. van
Bosse & Son, underwriters.

H. CAZAUX VAN STAPHORST.

C. E. DUTILH, Junr., General Agent of the Netherlands
American Steam Navigation Company.

J. H. VAN EEGHEN, member of the firm of H. Oyens &
Sons, Bankers.

W. HEIJBROEK, Jr., member of the firm W. Heijbroek, Jr.
& Co.

Dr. H. F. R. HUBRECHT, Director and Manager of the
Bell-Telephone Company.

Rev. P. H. HUGENHOLTZ, Junr.

R. R. H. TOE LAER, Director of the „Equitable" Life
Insurance Company of New York.

H. J. DE MAREZ OYENS, member of the firm of H. Oyens
& Sons, Bankers.

J. L. PIERSON, member of the firm of Adolph Boissevain
& Co., Bankers.

AUG. RAPP, Jr., Director of the „New York" Life Insurance Company.

A. ROELVINK, member of the firm of B. W. Blijdenstein
& Co., Bankers.

3

Amsterdam, the capital of the Netherlands,*) has a population of nearly 400,000 inhabitants. Its history begins in the early part of the XIIIth century, when the Lord of Amstel built a castle at the mouth of the Amstel-river, and laid a dyke, which is now the Dam. Hundred years later the city was united with the county of Holland and gradually extended its trade, especially with Germany and the Scandinavian kingdoms. In 1452, when the greater part of the city was burnt, Amsterdam was considered the largest market of the Northern Netherlands. In the beginning of the XVIth. century its merchants and shipowners extended their operations to the Canary-islands and to the Mediterranean. During the period of religious dissensions and of the war with Spain, Amsterdam sided for a long time with the Spaniards to the great detriment, bordering on ruin, of its mercantile and shipping interests. In 1578, the magistrates who had favored the Spanish cause having been expelled, a new aera begins in the history of the city. All the merchants, who had left on account of their allegiance to the Prince of Orange, returned, and when some years later Antwerp fell into the hands of the Spaniards, a large part of the population of the latter city settled in Amsterdam. In 1597 the first ships sailed from this port direct for India. The East-India-Company was incorporated in 1602, the West-India-Company in 1621. But half a century before, Amsterdam and other Dutch vessels had already reached Guiana, called „ the wild coast", and fetched salt from there, which Holland required in large quantities for its herring-trade. North America was visited by Amster-

---

*) The seat of the government is at the Hague, which is also the King's residence.

5

dam merchants some years before the West-India-Company
was incorporated.

Having the key to the East- and the West-Indies, treasures
flowed to Amsterdam, which now became the great center
of trade of the whole of Europe, overshadowing the glory
of Venice and Antwerp. During this period the great
City-hall was built, in commemoration of the conclusion of
peace with Spain (1648), and adorned as well with all the
treasures that wealth could procure at that time in marble,
metals, and woods, as with the master-pieces of the best
artists of the Dutch school of painting and sculpture. It
is now used as a royal palace. The fine residences along
the Heeren- and Keizersgrachten date from the same period.

Whilst the XVIIth. century had been one of action and
industry, the XVIIIth. was one of rest and quiet enjoyment
of the treasures amassed by former generations. Nevertheless the trade of the city continued to be very considerable,
but several wars with England, which caused the loss of
many thousands of ships with their rich cargoes, the revolution of 1795, and the domination of the French (till 1813),
with its heavy war contributions and the reduction of the
interest on the national debt to one third of the original
figure, ruined a great many people. The population of
Amsterdam was reduced to 120,000. With the return of
the house of Orange a revival soon became apparent. The
„Nederlandsche Handel Maatschappij" was incorporated in
1824, a large canal running from Amsterdam northward to
the sea was made in 1819-24, and new docks on both sides
of the city were built 1828-32.

About the middle of this century, however, it became
evident that all these works would only enable Amsterdam to compete with other ports, provided, a shorter communication with the sea was established. This led to the
construction of the North-sea-canal, and of the port of
Ymuiden. The canal was opened in 1876.

The consequent increase of trade is shown by the following table:

Year.	Ships having passed the Locks at Ymuiden (North-Sea).						Ships having passed the locks (Zuider Zee.)
	Out-ward.	Cub. Meter.	In-ward.	Cub. Meter.	Both ways.		
					Ships.	Cub. Meter.	
1875	Opening 1st November 1876.						68,905
1876	147	132,662	96	99,361	243	232,023	80,664
1877	1706	1,462,178	1670	1,421,598	3376	2,883,776	90,868
1878	1655	1,581,504	1587	1,601,369	3242	3,182,873	80,648
1879	1919	1,857,833	2094	1,953,980	4013	3,811,813	73,879
1880	2214	2,107,188	2281	2,157,744	4495	4,264,962	87,763
1881	2266	2,320,927	2337	2,269,397	4603	4,590,324	78,399
1882	2321	2,580,370	2353	2,595,325	4674	5,175,695	81,568
1883	2773	2,742,049	2821	2,695,242	5594	5,437,291	91,253
1884	2776	2,979,764	2660	2,952,598	5436	5,932,362	84,629
1885	2744	3,022,977	3067	3,031,295	5811	6,054,272	86,033
1886	2852	{ 2,401,055* 718,719†	3090	{ 2,428,920* 704,431†	5942	{ 4,829,975* 1,423,150†	86,033 85,239
1887	3019	4,077,128†	3237	4,137,604†	6256	8,214,732†	89,437

In connection with this canal the port of Amsterdam itself was considerably improved. The city constructed the Suez-piers, cattle-piers, wood-harbour, eastern tradequay, hydraulic-engines, petroleum-harbour, and several other quays and piers. The Dutch government built a railroad with its station close to the port, whilst a new canal to the Rhine is now in course of construction. Many millions of guilders have been spent for the improvement of the port of Amsterdam during the last ten years.

Steamers and sailing vessels, drawing 24 feet can reach Amsterdam at all times. The Locks, now in use, can accommodate vessels of a length of 400 feet, and the construction of locks for the accommodation of even longer vessels is in a fair way of being realized. Along the „ Commercial Quay" the canal has a depth of 26 feet.

* Net; † Gross.

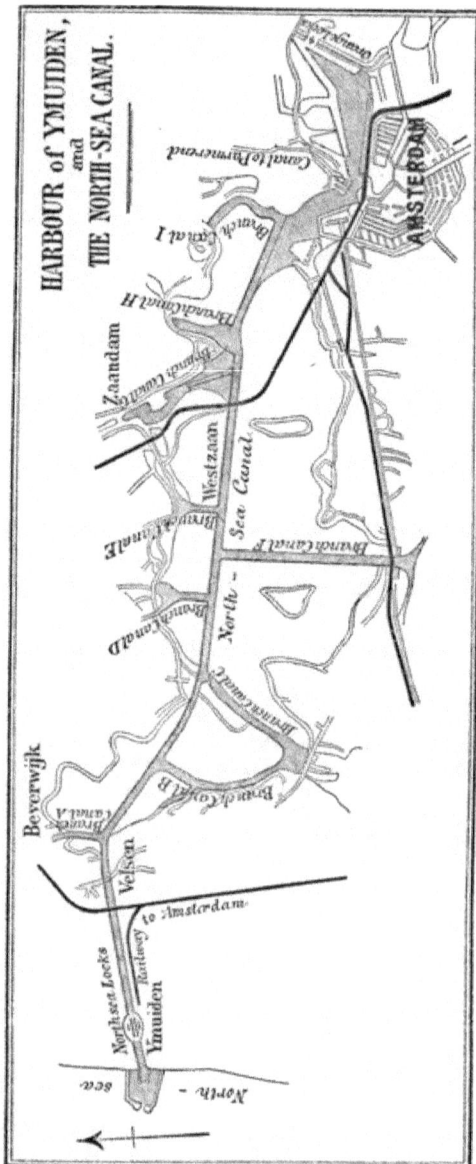

HARBOUR of YMUIDEN, and THE NORTH-SEA CANAL.

Scale = 1 à 160.000

Cabs at the Stations and at the Cabstands. The driver is
bound to give his number and a table of fares. Drive of
$\frac{1}{2}$ hour, or less, 70 cts.; of more than $\frac{1}{2}$ hour, but not
exceeding 1 hour, 1 fl. Every additional $\frac{1}{4}$ hour 25 cts.
After midnight: $\frac{1}{2}$ hour, or less, 1 fl. 20; every additional
$\frac{1}{4}$ hour, 40 cts. No charge for light luggage carried inside,
and no gratuity may be exacted.

Table of fares for Carriages hired at the Livery Stables :
Closed carriage, per drive, 80 Cts., per hour, 1 fl.
One horse open carriage, per drive 1 fl., per hour, 1 fl. 50.
Two horse carriage, per drive 2 fls., per hour 2 fls. 50.

Tramways. Fare 12$\frac{1}{2}$ cts.; tickets can be obtained at the
kiosks for 10$\frac{1}{2}$ cts., and from some booksellers per package
of 25 for 2 fls. 50. Transfer tickets, only obtainable from
the conductors 12$\frac{1}{2}$ cts.

PRINCIPAL LINES : Dam — Plantage — Linnaeusstraat :
Dam 8.20 a.m. to 11—30 p.m.; Linnaeusstraat 7.55 a. m. to
11.10 p.m. At night, *green* light.

Dam — Sarphatistraat: Sarphatistraat 8 a.m. to 11.10
p.m. Dam 8.15 a.m. to 11.30 p.m. At night, *red* light.

Tulpplein — Weesperzijde : Tulpplein 8.30 a.m. to 11.45
p.m. Weesperzijde 8 a.m. to 11 p.m. At night, *red*
light.

Dam — Vondelstraat—P. C. Hooftstraat: Vondelstraat
and P. C. Hooftstraat 8 a.m. to 11.10 p.m.; Dam 8.15
a.m. to 11.30 p.m. At night, Dam — Vondelstraat, *red*
light. Dam — P. C. Hooftstraat, two *red* lights.

Leidscheplein — Plantage : Leidscheplein 8 a.m. to
11.10 p.m. Plantage 8.20 a.m. to 11.30 p.m. At night,
green light.

Leidscheplein — Marnixstraat : Leidscheplein 8 a.m. to
11.10 p.m. Marnixstraat 8.20 a.m. to 11.30 p.m. At
night, *red* light.

Leidscheplein — Overtoom : Overtoom 8 a.m. to 11.10
p.m. Leidscheplein 8.30 a.m. to 11 p.m. At night, *green*
light.

Dam — Prins Hendrikkade : Dam 8 a.m. to 11.20 p.m.
Prins Hendrikkade 8.15 a.m. to 11.30 p.m. At night, *red*
light.

2

Kadijk — Czaar Peterstraat: Kadijksplein 8.15 a.m. to 11.45 p.m. Czaar Peterstraat 8 a.m. to 11.10 p.m. At night, *red* light.

Dam — Haarlemmerplein: Haarlemmerplein 8 a.m. to 11.30 p.m. Dam 8.15 a.m. to 11.30 p.m. At night, two *green* lights.

Dam — Central Station: A car runs for every train arriving at the Central Station or leaving it, on the lines Dutch Railway C⁰. or Eastern Railwy C⁰. At night, *green* light.

Dam — Rhenish Railway Station: A car runs for every train arriving at the Station or leaving it. At night, two *red* lights.

Dam — Amsteldijk: Amsteldijk 8 a.m to 11.10 p.m. Dam 8.20 a.m. to 11.30 p.m. At night, *green* light.

Steam-tram. See: trips.

Steamboats. Dam — Schulpbrug (Station Rokin, near the Beursstraat) every ¼ hour; fare 7½ cts. (Tickets at the kiosks 5½ cts.) Other lines: Schreierstoren — Handelskade — Koninginnedok, every hour, and every ½ hour; Amsterdam to Nieuwendam, to Oostzaan, to Ouderkerk, etc. Ferryboat to the *Tolhuis* from the de Ruijterkade 4 cts.

Restaurants: *Riche* on the Rokin: *Panopticum* * (cost 900,000 fl. to built), Amstelstraat; *Krasnapolsky* * (largest establishment of Europe, summer- and winter-gardens; 20 billiard tables; lighted by electricity), Warmoesstraat; *Hollandais* *; *American Hotel* * (fine view of the city from the top), both Leidsche plein; *Artis* (Zoölogical Gardens); *Milles Colonnes* *, Rembrandtsplein; *Willemsen* *, Heiligenweg; *Café Neuf* *, *Oude Graaf* *, *Français* *, *Reinsberg* *, *Suisse* *, *Bavaria* *, *Löwenbräu* *, *de Karseboom*, all in the Kalverstraat; *Port van Clere* *, N. Z. Voorburgwal; *Concordia* *, St. Luciensteeg; *Palais Royal* *, Paleisstraat; *'t Vosje*; Rokin (Billardroom); in the Warmoesstraat German and Bavarian beershops; *Maison Strouken* *, Leidsche Kade; *Londres* *, Amstelstraat, etc.

Coffee-houses. The restaurants marked thus * are also coffeehouses; among others may be mentioned; *Continental*, Tulpplein; *Poolsche Koffiehuis*, Kalverstraat; *Pariljoen*, Vondelpark; *Nieuwe Amsterdamsche Koffiehuis*, Kalverstraat (old gin); *Roode Leeuw*, Vijgendam; *Flora*, Weteringschans; *Vondel*, Vondelstraat; *Komeet*, Gravenstraat, etc.

Bodegas, Bars and Refreshment Rooms. *Wijnand Fockink*, Passage, Damstraat; (very interesting; it has remained in the same condition as in the former century) *'t Lootsje*, Kalverstraat (old style); *Bodega Continental*, Kalverstraat; *Bodega Amsterdam*, Damrak; *Bodega Port van Clere*, Voorburgwal; *Union des Producteurs*, Rokin and Doelenstraat; *Caves de France*, Kalverstraat.

Oyster Rooms. *van Laar*, Damrak, Kalverstraat, and Reguliersbreestraat; *Saur*, Reguliersbreestraat. **Confectioners** etc., *Figi* and *van Giesen*, Kalverstraat.

Post and Telegraph. The Main Office: N. Z. Voorburgwal, at the back of the Palace. Branch offices in P. C. Hoofstraat and other parts of the City; a Telegraph Office at the Exchange.

The Messengers' C⁰. (uniform cap, marked in front, D. V. M. and number.) Main Office: 82, N. Z. Voorburgwal; branch offices in some parts of the City. Tariff: 10 cts. per ¼ hour. 15 cts. per ½ hour, etc. (without handcarts, etc.)

Bathing Establishments: Rokin, opposite the Bank of Netherlands. 60 cts. per bath; 158 Heerengracht, 50 cts. per bath; 117 Amstel, 35 cts. per bath; Amsteldijk, 30 cts. per bath. *Swimming and Private Baths*, de Ruijterkade, 40 cts. per bath.

Exchange Offices: Auspach & Donk, 188 N. Z. Voorburgwal; Joh. Kramer & C⁰. 17 Dam; Twentsche Bank, 144 Spuistraat; Sanders & C⁰., Paleisstraat and Nieuwendijk; Levie Brothers, Kalverstraat.

Bankers. Adolph Boissevain & C⁰., 237 Heerengracht. Twentsche Bank, 144 Spuistraat; Hope & C⁰., 579 Keizersgracht; Succ. Banque de Paris et des Pays-Bas, 539 Heerengracht; Amsterdamsche Bank, 597/9 Heerengracht; Determeyer, Weslingh & Son, 518 Heerengracht; Lipmann, Rosenthal & C⁰., 6 Nieuwe Spiegelstraat; Becker & Fuld, 452 Keizersgracht; Wertheim & Gompertz, Amstelstraat.

Antiquities. Speijer, near the Dam; Boas Berg; Etienne Delaunoy, all Kalverstraat; van Galen, N. Z. Voorburgwal; Salomons, Sophiaplein.

Depôt of Delftware. Tognacca en Cossa, Kalverstraat.

Painting and engravings. Buffa en Co., Kalverstraat; Van Gogh, Keizersgracht.

Booksellers iu nearly every street. Fred. Muller & C⁰.,
the celebrated antiquarians, make a speciality of books
of American History, Doelenstraat near Brack's Doelen
Hotel. Another very good store is R. W. P. de Vries
Warmoesstraat.

Stands with second hand books for sale in the University
Passage (Oudemanhuisport).

The best and largest **stores** are in the Kalverstraat,
Nieuwendijk, Leidschestraat and Reguliersbreesstraat,
which thorough-fares are crowded every evening.

Theatres, Concerts, etc.

(consult the Newspapers.)

Municipal Theatre (Stadsschouwburg), Leidsche Plein ;
Sculptures of Bart van Hove. Seldom open in summer.

Paleis voor Volksvlijt (Industrial Palace), concert, or ballet.

Zoological Gardens (Natura Artis Magistra), concert every
Wednesday evening and every Monday afternoon, in
summer.

Parkschouwburg (Theatre of the Park), opperettas, (Thursday and Sunday in the Hall, the other evenings in the
garden).

Grand Théatre van Lier, Amstelstraat, Dutch, English and
German Plays.

Théâtre van Lier, Plantage, Dutch Plays.

Park, concerts.

Frascati (Prot & Son, proprietors). Plantage, Operettas.

Salon des Variétés, Amstelstraat, Comedies.

Tivoli, Music Hall, Nes (in the summer relache).

Tolhuis, across the Y, by ferryboat, Concerts Sunday.

Music Halls, Nes and Warmoesstraat.

Circus of Carré, Binnen Amstel, closed in summer.

Principal Churches.

Dutch Reformed, Nieuwe Kerk, Oude Kerk, Nooder Kerk,
Zuider Kerk, Wester Kerk, Ooster Kerk, Amstel Kerk,
Eilands Kerk, Koepel Kerk, Oude-Zijds Kapel, Nieuwe-
Zijds Kapel.

Evangelical Lutheran, Spui and Singel ; Reformed Lutheran,
Kloveniersburgwal.

Christian Reformed, Keizersgracht and Plantage.

Dutch Reformed (Dolens), Keizersgracht, in course of construction.

French or Walloon, O.Z. Achterburgwal (Walenpleintje), and Keizersgracht.

English Episcopal, Groeneburgwal.

English Presbyterian, Bagijnhof.

Free Church, Weteringschans.

Reformed Remonstrant, Keizersgracht.

United Baptist, Heerengracht.

Scotch Mission, Binnen Amstel.

Scandinavian, Prins Hendrikkade.

Roman Catholic, Mozes en Aaron, Houtgracht; De Boom, Kalverstraat; het Duifje, Prinsengracht; De Posthoorn, De Zaaier, both Keizersgracht; de Krijtberg, Singel; Petrus en Paulus, N.Z. Voorburgwal; De Papegaai, Kalverstraat; Heilige Willebrordus, Amsteldijk; Hart van Jezus, Vondelstraat.

Synagogue of the Dutch Jews, Jonas Daniel Meijerplein.

Synagogue of the Portuguese Jews, Muiderstraat.

For a **trip through the City** and taking the Main office of the Dutch Railway Co. as point of departure one finds (on the right), the Prins Hendrikkade (bust of Prince Henry of the Netherlands, by Stracké) the river Y, East and West docks (on the left). Following the tramway-line Damrak one sees on the left:

The „**Oude Kerk**" (Old Church) of the year 1300; shown every day on application to the sexton (Koster) (Gratuity 25 cts.). Stained glass windows representing, among other things, the death of Maria, beautiful work of XVIth century; the „Iron Chapel" (archives); a funeral chapel of the family de Graaf by Quellien; monuments of Heemskerk, van der Zaan, etc.

On reaching the **Dam**, one of the largest squares of Amsterdam, considered as the central point of the city one finds, on the left, **the Exchange**, built 1865; in the centre the

Monument commemorating the events of 1830—'31, by Royer. To the right the „**Nieuwe Kerk**" (New Church) rebuilt in 1648, after a fire in 1645; the pulpit is Vinckenbrincks masterpiece, fine organ, stained glass windows, monuments of de Ruijter, van Galen, van Speijk, Vondel, Da Costa, etc. To be seen daily on application to the sexton (koster). Gratuity, 25 cts.

The Palace (admission 50 cts.) of the middle of the 17ᵗʰ century, built by Jacob van Campen, sculptures by Quellien, decorative painting by Flinck, Ferdinand Bol, Jordaeus, de Wit, etc. bronzework by Hemony. The building rests on 13659 piles, is 80 metres long, 63 broad, 33 high, including tower, 51 metres. From the tower one enjoys a nice view of the city. The vane is in the form of a ship, the former seal of the city. The Palace is decorated, inside and outside, with numerous allegorical figures and emblems. Each corner of the roof, with its 18 stacks of chimneys, is ornamented with the Imperial crown, the Emperor Maximilian having given the City the privilege of using the Imperial crown in its armorial bearings in 1490. The front pediment contains an allegorical group, representing Amsterdam; on the border are statues of Peace, Providence and Justice. The pediment at the back of the Palace symbolizes Commerce; on the top stands Atlas bearing the globe on his shoulders; close by are statues of Watchfulness and Temperance. The building was used as a Town-hall till 1808. The principal apartments are: the Council Chamber, the Audience Chamber, the Throne-room, the Ball-room, formerly the Salle-des-pas-perdus.

Clubs: Zeemanshoop, (Seaman's Hope), and the Groote Club (Large Club) are on the corners, Doctrina et Amicitia near one end of the

Kalverstraat:

Burger Weeshuis (Municipal Orphan-Asylum), most curious to see, (interesting old regents room), **Nieuwe Zijds Kapel** (Church), built in commemoration of the miracle which happened on that spot 1345 **Bagijnhof** (a court) with the oldest wooden house.

On the right: Heiligenweg, **House of Detention;** Singel, on the right the **University Library.** Where in honor of the American visitors an exposition will be held of all books, maps, portraits concerning to the early history of America (admission free). Koningsplein, the bridge across the Heerengracht leads into the Leidschestraat.

Priusengracht : (on the right) the **Palais vau Justitie.** (Law courts).

Leidsche Plein : (on the right) the **Stadsschouwburg** (Municipal Theatre) on the left the „**Gymnasium**" (Latin School), the building of the free Church, Vondelstraat. On the left : the Girls' Orphan-Asylum of the Dutch Reformed Church. At the end of the Vondelstraat, the Roman Catholic Church Sacred Heart of Jesus.

In the Vossiusstraat : the „ **Instituut tot onderwijs van Blinden** " (Institution for teaching the Blind), opened in October 1885.

Vondelpark planned in 1865 and picturesquely laid out by a few distinguished citizens ; it now covers 100 acres ; statute of Vondel by Royer, Pavilion (restaurant), dairy.

Along the **Overtoom Canal** ; **Dutch Riding School.** (Hollandsche Manége) ; on the left : the Extramural Hospital, Return through the Vondelpark ; Stadhouderskade.

The **Museum,** built by the architect Cuijpers ; collection of paintings of the old Dutch and Flemish masters ; cabinet of prints and drawings, all formerly in the celebrated „Trippenhuis" ;

<small>Remarkable are : Rembrandts' masterpieces : the Nightwatch „De Staalmeesters", and the widow of admiraal Swartenhond ; van der Helsts' „Schuttersmaaltyd", and Roelof Bickers Company, and several other paintings of the celebrated masters. All the large pictures with portraits of Schutters (civic guards) belong to the city of Amsterdam.</small>

Collection of modern paintings, (formerly in the Pavilion „Welgelegen", at Haarlem) ; Museum van der Hoop (old dutch school pictures) ; Collection of modern paintings, planed in 1874 by C. P. van Eeghen Esq., loan collection of paintings ; Museum of antiquities (Entrance on the left) antiquities, and works of art partly belonging to the city Amsterdam and to the Royal Antiquarian Society.

<small>Rich collection of silver and gold works, pottery, wood carvings etc. This Museum has partly been classified in rooms representing the period, to which the articles belong.</small>

Museum of the Navy ;

<small>Remarkable is a part of „the Royal Charles" victoriously brought to Holland by admiral de Ruyter after the defeat of the english fleet near Chatham.</small>

Collection of Plaster Models ;

Close by : **Asylum for Blind Adults** and **Royal Academy of Plastic Arts.**

On the left: Frederiks Plein; **Paleis van Volksvlijt** (Industrial Palace) planned by Dr. Sarpathi, built by C. Outshoorn. At present generally used for concerts, ballets, etc.

On the left: Weteringschaus; **Public Playground for Children; Mechanics' School; the Free Church** (Vrije Gemeente); new **Gymnasium** (Latin School); **Industrial School for Girls**; the **Prison** (for solitary confinement only).

Return by the Leidsche Straat to the Heerengracht: on the corner of the Speigelstraat and Heerengracht, the Netherlands Trading Society (Handelmaatschappij); at n°. 511 Heerengracht **Museum Six,** (to be seen by permission).

Celebrated portraits of the Burgomaster Jan Six and his mother, by Rembrandt, and other paintings.

On the Keizersgracht at n°. 609, close to the Vijzelstraat **Museum Fodor,** (fee, week-days, 50 cts.; Sundays, 25 cts.; no admission on Tuesdays) paintings of modern Dutch and French schools, etc., bequeathed to the city by C. J. Fodor, a wealthy merchant, who died 24 Dec., 1860.

Vijzelstraat to Sophia Plein: **Munttoren,** a tower dating from 17th century; seat of the Royal Antiquarian Society.

On the Rokin: **The Bank of Netherlands;** almost opposite to it: **Leesmuseum** (Reading Rooms), open to the members of the Holland Society.

On the right: Doelenstraat to Kloveniersburgwal: Oudemanhuispoort, sculpture by Ziesenis: **The University;** Tower of the Southern Church (Zuider Kerk). Nieuwe Markt, with the old St. Anthonisgate late 15th century, Hall of the Masons' Guild, now Fire Brigade Station, but to be altered for the purpose of receiving the archives of the City. Fish Market.

Along St. Antonie-breestraat (2nd house from the bridge Rembrandt's dwelling). Jews' Quarter. Roman Catholic **Church Moses and Aaron, Synagogues,** most interesting is the old Portugese Hebrew Synagogue built 200 years ago in the figure of Solomon's temple. (with fine silverworks). **Diamond Cutting Factories,** of Boas Brothers, of A. E. Daniels & Son and of J. S. Metz, are all close by. Most interresting for visitors is that of Mr. Daniëls (Zwanenburgerstraat).

Following the Muiderstraat to the Plantage. **Hortus Botanicus** (Botanical Gardens), Theatres of G. Prot and Son, of the Park, and of van Lier.

Zoological Gardens (Natura Artis Magistra) admission free for the members of the Holland Society. Founded in 1838 by Dr. G. F. Westerman. Covers an area of upwards of 20 acres. World-renowned collection of animals, birds, plants, etc. Ethnological Museum. Japanese Museum. **Aquarium** (admission: visitors to Zoölogical Gardens, 25 cts.; other visitors, 50 cts.) Consists of tanks containing about 1000 cubic metres of fresh-water and sea-water. The sea-water is brought from Ymuiden, in a steamer built for the purpose. The upper tanks have a capacity of 230,000 liters. Behind the plate-glass, forming the front of the tanks, are specimens of the teeming population of sea and river.

Opposite the Zoological Gardens is the **Panorama** ; admission, 50 cts.) The building has an Art-Room for the Exhibition of paintings and sculpture.

Leaving the Panorama the way leads past the **St. Jacobs-Gesticht,** an asylum for aged poor Roman Catholics, to the **Muiderpoort** (Muiden-Gate), the only remaining gate of the former century. Outside the gate is the **Ooster-begraafplaats** (Eastern Cemetery).

To the left in the Linaeusstraat are the famous **Nursery-Grounds** of the firm of Groenewegen & Co.

Somewhat further is the **Rechthuis** of Watergraafsmeer, (at present a coffee-house), and the **Horticultural School „Linnaeus",** where instruction is given in gardening and botany, and whence the city draws its supply of trees and plants.

Returning to the Muiderpoort one sees on the right the Infantry barracks **Oranje Nassau.** Passing through the gate and turning to the left into the Sarphatistraat one finds the following buildings: The **Cavalry Barracks,** the **Army stores,** the **Military Hospital,** the **Children's Hospital,** and close by, on the right, in the Roetersstraat, the Main Office and Stables of the **Amsterdam Omnibus Co.**

Amstel. Amstel-Hotel. The bridge called „Hoogesluis", lately rebuilt.

Binnen-Amstel (Eastside), Prinsengracht : **Timber-Yard of the City.** Circus Carré.

Weesper-Kerkstraat: the **French Riding School,** the **Workhouse** (founded 130 years ago), the **Hebrew Alms Houses,** the **Hebrew Hospital,** and the **Alms Houses** of the Evangelical Lutheran Congregation.

3

Keizersgracht to the Binnen-Amstel (Eastside): **Asylum**
for the aged poor of the Dutch Reformed Church, an
institution of more than 200 years standing.

Zwanenburgerstraat: Diamond Cutting Factories; the
Hebrew Orphan-Asylum for boys; that for girls is in
the Rapenburgerstraat; **Orphan-Asylum** of the Dutch
Reformed Church in course of reconstruction.

Following the Staalstraat and Kloveniersburgwal one comes
to the Rembrandtsplein (Statue of Rembrandt) and
Thorbeckeplein (Statue of Thorbecke).

Amstelstraat: **Salon des Variétés** (theatre), **Grand Théâtre
van Lier, Panopticum** (admission, 50 cts.), a successful
imitation of Madame Tussaud's waxworks, but more particularly of the „Théâtre Castran," Berlin, which latter
artist is the talented maker of about 200 of the wax-works
exhibited: the likenesses are often striking, and the
dresses sumptuous. See especially the group of the
Royal Family, the Marken-chamber, from ten Kate,
the „Botermarkt," etc.

Crossing the new Blauwbrug, follow the Nieuwe Heerengracht to the **Entrepôt-dok** (Custom House and bonded
warehouse). Kadijksplein: **Zeemanshuis** (Sailors' Home),
founded in 1856.

's Rijks Werf (Royal Navy-Yard) (no fixed gratuity):
covers upwards of 32 acres of ground. Stocks for fourteen large vessels. The crane has a lifting power of
10000 kilos (about 90 tons). Docks for the construction
of iron-clad vessels, etc. Ask for the „Koningsloep"
(King's Sloop).

Koninklijke Fabriek van Stoom- en andere werktuigen
(Engineering Works).

Return to Prins Hendrik-kade. Training Ship **„ De Was-
senaer"** (shown on application). **Kweekschool voor de
Zeevaart** (Training School for the Mercantile Navy),
founded in 1785 (rebuilt in 1880) to commemorate the
naval battle off Doggersbank, allegorically represented on
the front; contains, among other things, many relics, busts
and curiosities of celebrated Dutch naval commanders.

On the Prins Hendrik Kade are also the offices of the **Royal
Steam Navigation Co., of the Netherlands** and of the
Steam Navigation Co., „ Nederland".

To the right: the **Oosterdok** (Eastern docks), and the
Handelskade (Commercial Quay); the latter is one of the

most important works undertaken of recent years by the Municipal Government; the inner harbor covers 1200 metres; the quay is 1882 metres in length with an 80 ton steam-crane, etc.

Returning to the Prins Hendrikkade and passing between the „Schreierstoren" (Weepers' Tower) from XV⁰ century and the „Semaphore" Office, which is a signal station in connection with Ymuiden, one approaches the new Central Terminus; going under the Railway Bridge one reaches the de Ruijterkade, where the coffee-houses offer an agreable restingplace, and whence one enjoys a fine view of the river Y, with its busy and interesting scenery.

On the opposite side of the river : **Koninginne-dok** (Queen's Dock), Petroleum Warehouses, **Tolhuis**.

Haarlemmerdijk, **Willemspoort**: Gas Works of the Imperial Continental Gas-Association, supplies gas from 1 Nov. 1885.

Marnixkade: **Tooneelschool** (Dramatic School).

Westertoren (Tower of the West Church), 85 metres high. Church, a master-piece of style and sculpture by de Keyser; decorative painting by de Lairesse.

Keizersgracht: „Huis met de hoofden" (House with the Heads), at present the Commercial School (Handels-school). Schoolmuseum (admission, 25 cts.)

Heerengracht: near the Leliegracht a picturesque house in the old dutch style of the beginning XVII⁰ century.

This house built by the rich merchant Bartolotti, as well as the „huis met de Hoofden" built by de Geer, may give an idea of the dwellings of wealthy inhabitants of Amsterdam at that time.

Keizersgracht near the Wolvenstraat: **Felix Meritis**, Concert Hall, collection of physical and mathematical Instruments.

Follow the Keizersgracht to the Leidschestraat, hence to the Koningsplein and Rokin: **Arti et Amicitiae** (Admission, 25 or 50 cts.) a society of artists founded in 1839; see the Historical Gallery; at times, collections of paintings and works of art.

The bridge opposite leads to the Bank of Netherlands already mentioned, and to the Hospital, or on turning to the left to the **Nes** (which, with the Warmoesstraat, forms the oldest part of the city). **Tivoli Theatre.** Through Lombardsteeg (**The Lombard**) to O. Z. Voorburgwal;

City Hall (Raadhuis), contains some paintings antiquities, the city archives (Municipal Statute books dating from 1465, Municipal Budgets from 1531, Books of Resolutions from 1536), Collection of manuscripts, coins, etc., etc.

The Burgomasters-cabinet to be seen before 10 o'clock with the master piece of Ferdinand Bol, pictures of van der Helst. Lingelbach, Zaenredam etc. The Burgomasters-waiting-room with portrait of Maria de Medicis by Honthorst and the armorial bearings of Burgomasters and Aldermen. The assemblyhall of the common council with the portraits of the kings, and paintings of J. and A. Backer, N. Elias, etc. In another room: the Dam as it was in 1604, painted by Adriaen van Nieuwland.

To show the American visitors the growth of the city a collection of old drawings and engravings concerning Amsterdam and its principal buildings has now been laid for inspection.

Carriage Drive.

Dam, Kalverstraat, Reguliersbreestraat, Rembrandtsplein, Utrechtschestraat, Frederiksplein, Hoogesluis. Sarphatistraat. Muiderpoort, the so called Nieuwe Wijk (New Quarter). Oostenburgergracht, Prins Hendrikkade, Westerhoofd, Nieuwendijk. Paleisstraat, Heerengracht, Leidschestraat. Vondelpark, Stadhouderskade. Amsteldijk, return to the Binnen-Amstel, Kerkstraat, Plantage, Muiderstraat, the so called Jodenkwartier (Hebrew Quarter), Nieuwmarkt. Kloveniersburgwal, Doelenstraat, Rokin, **Dam.**

Trips in the Vicinity.

Het Kalfje, by carriage, through the Vondelpark, along the shady Amstelveenschen Weg, Kalfjeslaan, and picturesque Utrechtschezijde (left side of the river) (Time: 2 hours).
Tolhuis on the river Y (ferryboat, 5 cts.). Frequent concerts, etc.
Sluices of **Schellingwoude, Zeeburg,** (by steamer), fine view of the City, the Harbour, and the Zuiderzee. At Zeeburg is the Pumping Station, with engines of 240 horsepower : for introducing fresh water into the canals of Amsterdam.

Café **Berebijt** and café **Maas** on the river Amstel (by
steamer).

Ouderkerk and other villages along the river Amstel,
by steamer.

Muiden, castle of Muiden, **Muiderberg** (bathing place, the
most remarkable echo of the world, fine site) **Naarden,**
etc., by Gooische Steamtram, which has two lines: Amsterdam to Laren, and Huizen to Hilversum — the first
line is divided into four sections, viz., Amsterdam to
Diembrug; Diembrug to Muiden; Muiden to Naarden,
or Muiden — Muiderberg; Naarden to Laren — the second
line is divided into two sections, viz., Huizen to Laren,
and Laren to Hilversum. Fare: 15 cts. per section,
tickets to be taken beforehand; otherwise, 20 cts. per
section. Ticket-office at the Station of the Rhenish Railway Co. (at the railing).

Sloterdijk by Steam-tram at Willemspoort, 15 cts. per ride;
if tickets are obtained beforehand, 12½ cts.

Haarlemmermeer, by carriage along the Overtoom, Sloo-
terweg, Slooten, part of Haarlemmermeer, return along
the canal and to the „Dubbele Buurt", and then through
the Vondelpark (Time: 2 hours).

Per Steamer, at the Y (Westerhoofd) to Nieuwendam,
Buiksloot, Purmerend, along the „Zaanstreek" (Zaan-
district), etc.

Haarlem, Zaandam, Alkmaar, etc., by Rail from the
Central Station.

Marken, a fishing village in the Zuiderzee, per steamer,
daily.

Zandvoort (one hour by rail), much frequented bathing-
place, fine arcade, villas, tram, Bath-Hotel with „Kurzaal".

Wijk aan Zee (one hour's journey: per rail to Beverwijk,
and then per steam-tram), a quiet bathing-place.

IJmuiden (by rail, or by steamer of Goedkoop Bros.)
Shortest route from Amsterdam to the North-sea. The
harbor was projected by the engineer Conrad, and exe-
cuted under the supervision of the Dutch engineer Dirks,
and of Sir John Hawkshaw; the work was begun in
1865, and completed in seven years. The place though
small, is of great importance on account of its excellent
harbour: it contains a couple of churches, the Hotel
„Willem Barents" etc.

everything went all right. The reception was most cordial; a great deal of trouble has been taken for it and we appreciate it highly."

"Has The Holland Society many members and has it any connection with the 'Dutch Club' at New-York?"

"We have over six hundred members, all descendants of those Dutchmen who first settled on that spot where New-York now stands. They all belong to the most respected New-York families. No native-born Dutchman can become a member of the Society. I do not know what the 'Dutch Club' is. We have no connection with it."

"And what is the object of your coming to Holland?" asked our reporter.

"Only an act of piety, a desire to visit the country and the people from which we are descendants; only that and nothing else."

"I have, however, heard it whispered around," our reporter ventured to say, "that your coming has something to do with the Holland Trust Company, just like the coming of the Transvaalers, not long ago, had to do with their railways."

"You will do me a great favor," said Mr. Van Sielen, "to contradict this in your paper in the strongest terms. I repeat, we have no ulterior objects; we come for pleasure only, to view the land of our forefathers. Besides, the members of our Society are all well-to-do, and do not solicit any money here for any enterprise."

We do not doubt for a moment that the members and their ladies will be hospitably received everywhere, and proof given them that their ancestors' virtue, hospitality, is still Holland's chief virtue.

At three o'clock in the afternoon came our first formal reception in the imposing old Town Hall. Under the guidance of Mr. Cazaux van Staphorst, Mr. de Roever, city archivist, and Mr. Le Jolle, general secretary, we were ushered in through many reception rooms filled with attendants in liveries, into a council room, or main room of the hall, where we were received by Mr. G. van Tienhoven, the Burgo-

7

master of Amsterdam, on behalf of the municipality.
He is a tall, dark-complexioned man of striking and
impressive features, intellectual in appearance, and
of pleasing address. He made an excellent speech of
welcome in English, and in conclusion invited our
attention to the collection, then displayed on tables
set for the purpose, of antiquities relating to the connection between Old Amsterdam and New Amsterdam, and all taken from the archives of the city. To
this address Mr. Van Siclen made a short and appropriate answer, and the "eerewijn," "wine of honor"
(champagne), an indispensable requisite to all such
ceremonies, was passed by the attendants. We then
turned our attention to the collection. Here were
prints, documents, maps, and books of the XVth,
XVIth and XVIIth centuries, illustrating all that
was then known of the history and growth of the
New World. Among them were letters and other
documents from the early settlers in New Amsterdam, and many things of interest to the antiquarian
and historian. Unfortunately our time was too short
to fully appreciate the treasures spread before us.
Our attention was attracted by the quaint pictures
on the walls, among them portraits of regents of
the old almshouses and hospitals. These contained
several names familiar to us in the ranks of the
Society.

In the evening we were invited to a full dress reception at the Amstel hotel, the finest in Holland.
The reception was held in a beautiful suite of rooms,
for some years occupied by the Empress Eugenie.
These were liberally decorated with the national
colors of Holland and America, blended in a most
tasteful manner, and the orange above all. The

flowers were beautiful and abundant, and there was
fine music in attendance. Here we met many of the
ladies and gentlemen of Amsterdam, and took great
pleasure also in greeting Robert B. Roosevelt, the
United States Minister to Holland, and a member
of our Society, who came from the Hague to join in
our welcome. During the evening an eloquent and
graceful speech of welcome on behalf of the city and
country was made by Professor J. M. C. Asser,
counsel to the Minister of Foreign Affairs, Advocate
and Professor of Law at the University of Amsterdam.
This was in English, and a most finished production in
style and delivery. This was appropriately responded
to by Van Siclen, and the warmth of our welcome
caused his enthusiastic nature to overflow with expressions of gratitude and affection, to which we all
gave a most cordial assent. An elegant collation was
served, and the hours were spent in social intercourse.
There was something of shyness on the part of our
Dutch friends in making advances, and something
of unusual timidity on ours in endeavoring to express
our sentiments, but the genuine feeling of hospitality
on the one part and of warm appreciation on the
other was unmistakably present. After the reception,
the party broke up into little groups, and under the
guidance of their new found friends saw something
of the evening life of Amsterdam. The historian can
only vouch for one party, who were pleasantly entertained at the Café Volksvlight, and afterwards at the
Café Krasnapolski, which is said to be the largest
beer garden in Europe. In this way we saw something of the social life of Amsterdam, and we were
most pleasantly impressed with its brightness and
with the moderation displayed.

A fuller account of this elegant reception is translated from the *Amsterdamsche Courant and Handelsblad* and from the *Nieuws van den Dag* of August 13, 1888:

The Reception in the Amstel Hotel.— In a worthy manner — a manner showing not only good taste, but also that hospitality of which we Hollanders are always boasting (and, as appeared again, not without cause) — the Americans who are within our walls were welcomed last night by the committee formed for that purpose.

The large hall on the Weesper side of the Amstel Hotel was profusely decorated. On entering the hall one faced a bust of William the Silent, Father of his Country, surrounded by green foliage, and over it along the ceiling the flags of the United States and Holland and Orange were to be seen. In the four corners of the hall stood flowers and plants, and in two corners were placed the Dutch and United States coats of arms. Hidden by plants, a band of music was placed at the right of the hall.

The visitors were received by the members of the committee, while we remarked among those present the Wethouders, Driessen, Coninck, Westenberg and Pet, Dr. Westerman, and about 10 o'clock the Mayor, Mr. G. van Tienhoven, made his appearance.

When, about 9 o'clock, all were present and the Dutch and American national airs had been played, Mr. Cazaux van Staphorst, member of the committee, addressed the foreigners in English. He said that it gave the committee pleasure to be allowed to receive the Americans in a city and a country for which they had so often shown their appreciation, in a country which is of both the cradle. It is, he continued, not customary in this city to present foreigners with the freedom of it, and we can therefore offer you only the hand of friendship and hope that this tie shall continue to grow stronger, and that, when you have returned to your country, you will have carried from here most pleasant recollections. Mr. Geo. W. Van Siclen, Secretary of The Holland Society, was the next speaker:

"Members of the Committee, Citizens of Amsterdam, I value it highly that I have the honor and privilege, for us all, to be the interpreter of our gratitude for all your

friendship and hospitality on our arrival here. The visit
we pay here is a visit of piety for our ancestors. We come
from a land rich in gold, silver, corn, wine and oil, but not
these articles of commerce bind us to you; but our country,
where principles of liberty reign, free instruction, free religion—that country was founded upon these principles by
people coming from this place.

"Here," the speaker continued, "on this sacred soil once
stood the houses of our fathers, here floated once our national colors, for the colors of Holland's flag are our colors
also, and this union of colors," he hoped, "would always be
the symbol of the union between the two nations." It goes
without saying that these words coming from the heart,
and spoken with force and fervor, were applauded to the
echo.

Professor Asser was the next speaker. Calling attention
to the difference in form of government between America
and the Netherlands, he said that this did not prevent both
nations from feeling themselves descendants from the same
forefathers. At an early date Amsterdam had wanted to
establish relations of friendship and of commerce with the
brethren across the ocean; and in a humorous and witty
manner he related the fact that, when the American people
was waging the War of Independence against England, it
was the city government of Amsterdam which wanted to
make a treaty of commerce with the Congress of the young
Republic. Now, and things went none the worse for it,
such treaties are concluded by the mutual ambassadors, to
whom this task may safely be entrusted. He then addressed, while those present cheered, the newly appointed
minister of the United States to our Government, Mr.
Roosevelt, in order to congratulate him with his appoint-
ment and thank him for his presence on this occasion.

The speaker said it had struck him, while not long ago
reading a report of the Society's annual meeting, that a
toast had been proposed to the memory of William the
Silent and another to that of John van Oldenbarneveldt,
men to whom we owe so much. He further recalled how
from that family of Orange our King had come, a King
who loves his country and his people above all.

Professor Asser concluded his stirring address with the
offer to conclude a treaty of cordial friendship, "for," he said,
"we have each a mutual respect for our traditions—we for

those of Washington, Lincoln, Franklin, and Edison; you
for our great men." Again loud applause was not lacking,
and the shaking of hands which followed showed plainly
the deep impression which these eloquent words had made
on all present.

We were joined on our arrival in Amsterdam by
Judge Henry W. Bookstaver and wife, and by Mr.
A. T. Clearwater, a member of the Society, and his
wife, so that our forces numbered about fifty during
the formal reception of the expedition.

Saturday morning, August 11, found the party
refreshed by a good night's sleep on shore, and eager
for new objects of interest. At 9.30, by special invitation, the Zoological Gardens were opened to us, and
the president and many of its officers were in attendance to do the honors of the place. Here is one of
the best collections of the kind in the world, and we
saw it all to the very best advantage. Each one of
the gentlemen connected with the institution took a
little group of the visitors in his charge, and everything was most carefully explained. It is a marvelous example of the work of one man. The director,
Dr. Westerman, has devoted fifty years of his life to
the development of this collection. He spends the
greater part of each day there, and has done so for
half a century. From small beginnings, under his
care and enthusiasm, it has grown to its present
magnificent proportions. The animals all show the
best of care, and the aquarium is one of the most beautiful sights of its kind in the world. At the conclusion
of this interesting circuit we were received in the large
hall of the institution, where a luncheon was served,
and a very kindly speech of welcome made by the venerable director, duly responded to by the Secretary;

Minister Roosevelt was also present on this occasion, and thoroughly enjoyed his pleasant surroundings.

At 2.30 in the afternoon we visited the library of the University. Professor Dr. H. C. Rogge, with his wife and daughters, received us with dignified and charming simplicity, and we were then conducted by the professor and by J. F. van Someren, Esq., through its treasures. Here is a library of 150,000 volumes, beautifully arranged, and rich in literary wealth. Great care had been taken to display books, documents, and maps relating to our early history, and the attendants were particularly attentive in pointing out the choicest of the treasures. The catalogue is arranged upon the card index system, and all the details of the library are conducted in the same manner as the best of our institutions in this country. We found a study room, a room devoted to books of reference, and other points of a well arranged modern library. The historian was particularly pleased with this library from having had some personal interest in a kindred institution on this side of the water, and was pleased to see that the institutions of both countries seemed conducted with the same spirit of intelligence. We noticed early atlases, crude maps, the finest portraits of the Princes of Orange, of the Burgomasters of Amsterdam, some political cartoons of our early political history, very rare now in this country, and many other objects of interest. Here, as in other collections in Holland, we noticed the Year Books of The Holland Society prominently displayed.

The *Nieuws van den Dag* of Amsterdam, thus described more fully this exhibition of historical antiquities:

The lively interest which our American brethren have manifested, especially in this country, in everything connected with the early history and development of the old New Netherlands and New Amsterdam, has been the cause that by far the greater majority of books, pamphlets, and other writings relating thereto have migrated to New-York years ago. Rare specimens have left Europe in that way. It is evident that this fact must prove an impediment when an effort is made in this city to show somewhat fully what has been preserved of these writings, prints, etc. Special appreciation should therefore be shown for what has been done in this line at our Amsterdam University Library to show the American visitors what we have left on this subject.

The oldest representation of the Nieuw-Amsterdam that was, is taken from a painted ship-board dating from 1651; and having belonged to the ship *Lydia*. This board was sold to an American some years ago by the late Frederik Muller, who had an excellent photograph made of it. This photograph may here be compared with two engravings, one of 1685 (from a collection of town views), the other of 1740, from which an idea can be obtained of the growth of this originally very small locality; in 1651, it was little more than a fortress with a few scattered houses outside of it.

The "Beschryving van Nieuw-Nederland," by Adrian van der Donk (1655), is one of the few Dutch books treating of our American colony. Dating from our century little can be found except the dissertation of D. T. van Alphen about the history of New Netherlands (1838), and three essays of the late Utrecht Professor O. van Rees (1855, when he was attorney at Amsterdam) about the history of the Dutch settlements in North America. Besides there are to be seen a couple of curious little books dating from the middle of the 17th century, one of 1656, containing the "conditions" upon which, with the consent of the Burgomaster of Amsterdam, one could settle in the American colonies, and one of about 20 years later in which different information is given about the best way of colonization, as to victuals, cultivation, etc.

A great part of the collection is occupied by the maps and charts of that part of the world. It is well known what a degree of excellence cartography had attained in our country in the 17th century, and the specimens shown here are most remarkable also in this respect.

A clear proof of the trouble taken and sacrifices made by the residents of New-York in order to get thoroughly acquainted with the ancient history of their city, is given by the collection of 14 splendid 4to volumes, "Documents relating to the Colonial History of the State of New-York," also by an edition in 4 volumes of the "Documentary History of New-York," which last work contains the history of the city only. Both have been published at government expense, and are embellished with maps and illustrations. The "Annals of Albany" are also here.

A curious contrast with these works forms the well-known "History of New-York by Diedrich Knickerbocker," by Washington Irving, in which the author ridicules the affection of many of his countrymen for their Dutch descent. The book for this reason caused quite some indignation when it appeared, but of course it belonged in this collection. The reminiscences of the church life of the Dutch settlers are also represented by several works (both in Dutch and English). In this connection the book about "The College of William and Mary," which was founded during the reign of our Prince Willem III., is remarkable.

That the Americans took some interest in our Dutch literature is shown by a translation by E. W. Hoskin, 1847, of "De Pleegzoon" ("The Adopted Son") by Van Lennep, and of Toller's "Overwintering in Nova Zembla" (by D. van Pelt, 1884).

The entire collection terminates with the head "Americana," presented last year by Van Eeghen & Co. to the library and mainly relating to the American War of Independence in the last century, and principally consisting of books, maps, caricatures, etc.

The exhibition, arranged with taste and judgment, contains plenty of features to make a visit pleasant, not only for our American brethren, who probably know much of it, but also for our citizens, who can learn much that is new and interesting.

In the evening, by invitation, we attended a concert at the Crystal Palace, or Paleis Voor Volksvlijt, by the military band of the regiment of Grenadiers and Jagers. The following was the programme:

8

ZATERDAG, 11 AUGUSTUS.

BUITENGEWOON CONCERT.

DOOR DE KON. MILIT. KAPEL VAN HET REG'M'T GRENADIERS
EN JAGERS.

Directeur, W. VAN DER LINDEN.

———

EERSTE DEEL.

1. Hochzeitsmarsch aus der Oper "Der Rattenfänger
   von Hameln". . . . . V. E. NESSLER.
2. Symphonie, No. 4 . . . . NIELS W. GADE.
   (a) Andante; allegro, vivace e grazioso.
   (b) Andante con moto.
   (c) Scherzo.
   (d) Finale; allegro, molto vivace . ARR. F. DUNKLER.
3. Adagio. . . . . WOLDEMAR BARGIEL.
   Euphonium Solo voor te dragen door den Heer
   K. Wilcke . . . . ARR. W. VAN DER LINDEN.
4. Groote Fantaisie uit de Opera "La Favorite," van
   Donizetti . . . . F. DUNKLER.

TWEEDE DEEL.

5. Ouverture "Guillaume Tell" . . . . ROSSINI.
6. Concert Fantaisie uit de Opera "Rigoletto," van
   Verdi. Gearrangeerd en voor dragen voor
   Alt, Saxophone, Solo, door den . Heer L. BENARD.
7. (a) Nordisches Volkslied en Brautmarsch . . HAMERIK.
   ARR. F. DUNKLER.
   (b) Ungarische Tänze, No. 5 . . . . . . JOH. BRAHMS.
   ARR. W. V. D. LINDEN.
8. Le Carneval de Venise Fantaisie burlesque, F. DUNKLER.

The City of Amsterdam presents a most striking picture of commercial activity and enterprise, and gives every indication of rapid and healthful progress.

Sunday, August 12, was clear and pleasant. It is a remarkable fact that the weather during our entire stay in Holland, with one trifling exception, was fine. This was in striking contrast with the inclement weather that had preceded our arrival, and gave occasion for many expressions of gratification that even the weather department joined with the rest of the country in giving us a cordial welcome. Most of the party visited the Rijks Museum, a most impressive and magnificent building. This covers nearly three acres of ground, and was erected in 1877–85 from the plans of P. J. H. Cuypers, and is in the so-called early Dutch renaissance style. Here all were impressed by the magnificent masterpiece of Rembrandt, the "Night Watch." Of particular interest to the pilgrims, were the guild and corporation pieces, a characteristic development of Dutch art. Many of these pieces are of enormous size and contain numbers of portraits, all taken from life and grouped around some central object. They are seen in every collection in Holland, and are mostly of the XVth, XVIth, and XVIIth centuries. Under each portrait is in most cases given the name of the subject, and here several of our party found their own names, undoubtedly signifying either an ancestor or some one of their kin. It became a favorite study for most of the party to examine these pieces in order to find, if possible, their own names; this study was also pursued in the churches on the slabs and tombstones, and in many instances the search was rewarded with success. The Rijks Museum is certainly an edifice worthy of a great city and a great people, and the collections therein worthy of the building.

Some of the party took the opportunity to make a hurried excursion to Haarlem for the sake of visiting the old church, and hearing the great organ. They returned delighted with their trip, which was a success in every way, and the historian gives it on information and belief that one of their chief sources of pleasure was that they had the opportunity of hearing two sermons in Dutch, of good old-fashioned length, during one service.

Another little party made an excursion to Zaandam, a thriving town of about 13,000 inhabitants, and thoroughly Dutch in appearance. Here they made the acquaintance of the 400 windmills which extend in an almost unbroken line along the banks of the Zaan. Their objective point, of course, was the hut of Peter the Great, and after several attempts it was at last reached. They reveled in the historical and mythical associations connected with the place and gazed reverently on all they saw. They found the tablets on the wall commemorating the various visits of the crowned heads, and viewed picture after picture of Peter the Great, in various costumes and attitudes, until they were thoroughly imbued with the idea, that certainly here was the spot where the Great Czar had spent many busy and useful days.

From their various excursions the party all gathered to a common center as night drew on, and the evening was passed by most of them quietly at the hotel.

The charities of Amsterdam, both public and private, are almost innumerable. Some of them are very ancient, and the quaint costumes of the beneficiaries, still to be seen on the streets, gave rise to many inquiries from the visitors. Among these charitable institutions was one of especial interest to some of our members, and the historian is indebted to Mr. John H. Voorhees of Washington, D. C., for the following account of

THE AMSTERDAM'S WELVAREN, JOHN WARDER INFANT SCHOOL.

Among the many institutions of a benevolent and educational character, for which Amsterdam is noted, is one which has a peculiar interest for American citizens in a historical point of view, and for some of The Holland Society because of its association with the family of one of its members.

The Amsterdam's Welvaren (Amsterdam's Welfare), is the name of an infant school, conducted in a quiet building at No. 7 Beeren Straat in that city, where 140 poor children of the neighborhood, between the ages of two and seven, have free daily instruction and care, provided from a fund arising in the following manner.

The *Amsterdam's Welvaren* was the name of a Dutch East Indiaman owned in Amsterdam, which was captured in 1781 by an English vessel, the *Nancy* of which John Warder, then of London, was part owner. Holland was then in treaty alliance with our young Republic, and her commerce was a prey to English privateers, and the captain of the *Nancy*, unknown to her owners, took out Letters of Marque and made lawful prize of the Dutch ship.

John Warder soon thereafter moved to Philadelphia, where his branch house operated for many years, and his descendants are still connected with business interests in this country. He was a member of the religious society of Friends, and his principles forbade him to avail himself of the share of the prize money which fell to him. He made diligent efforts to reimburse the Dutch owners, but complications arising from the condition of Europe, disturbed by the continental wars then raging, and the difficulty of adjusting the shares of different claimants, some of whom could not be found, prevented him from making the intended restitution, and so the money was invested until he finally distributed the fund, paying principal and interest. There being a small residue, this was reinvested, until in 1830, in conjunction with English Friends and Mr. John Mollet, a Friend residing in Amsterdam, a building was purchased and the present school opened in Beeren Straat as narrated. This was the first infant school established in Amsterdam. It is conducted by a resident female teacher and four assistants, and is under the charge of a board of Lady Directresses. The instruction is on the kindergarten principle, and the little ones, to relieve the institution from the name of a pure charity, pay each a penny a week to the educational fund.

The above facts were obtained in part from a tablet inserted in the wall of the principal school-room and from one of the Lady Directresses, to whom the writer is indebted for many courtesies, and, in her words,

"It is hoped that the school will long remain and be to the neighborhood as the name of the ship indicates, an Amsterdam's Welvaren."

A little incident will illustrate the interest taken by all classes in our visit. In Amsterdam, one evening, a few of us strolling about came across the fish market, and close by saw a building of the middle ages known as St. Anthonieswegg, which we found was now occupied by the fire-brigade. Our curiosity was excited by the difference in the apparatus from that used in our own country, and, as we began to examine it, the men in charge asked us if we were members of the American Holland Society. We replied that we were, and immediately all on duty did their best to point out to us every detail of the various devices, ending up by taking us to the neighboring canal and showing us the fire-tug lying there and its method of use.

LEYDEN.

ON Monday, August 13, we took a special train at 9.10 in the morning for our visit to Leyden as the guests of the Third of October Society. This had been anticipated with great interest and will ever remain a red-letter day in the memories of all who participated. The journey is a short one of about twenty-seven miles, and on the way we passed through Haarlem, only wishing that our days were long enough and many enough to allow a visit to that venerable town. The most of the journey lies along the Polder, which Dutch enterprise has made out of the old Haarlem Sea, and blooming fields and fertile grounds have taken the place of the tempestuous waters over which our forefathers fought the terrible struggle with Spain.

On arriving at the station we found an enormous crowd blocking up every approach. Cheers and exclamations filled the air as the train stopped. On alighting we were received in the waiting-room by the chairman of the reception committee, Mr. N. Brouwer, who spoke excellent English. To his speech Mr. Van Siclen made one of his tasteful responses, and the way was led to the carriages. Here the thoughtful care which distinguished all the arrangements of the various committees in Holland manifested itself. In each carriage was placed one of the ladies of the party and two of the gentlemen, and accompanying each three was an English-speaking member of the reception committee, who devoted himself during the day to the comfort of the three thus placed under his care. We were preceded by the band of the Trained Guards, a military organization descended in a direct line from the militia of the city who so bravely held their own in the memorable siege. When all had taken their places in the carriages, the procession started. The entire populace were on the streets in holiday attire, as the day had been given up by the whole community to our reception. All the streets were gaily decorated with flags and bunting. The cheering was incessant. The crowds were so thick that it was with difficulty that the procession could make its way, and each one of the party of fifty Americans felt that he or she was receiving such an ovation as would only be given in America to the most popular candidates in an exciting election. In this way, with cheers of welcome on every hand, we advanced as far as the students' club, "Minerva." Here we halted, and the president of the club, Baron Rudolph Six, advancing to the first carriage made a most charming little speech of welcome in behalf of the students of the University, and asked our acceptance of a memorial from the students expressive of their good-will. He then asked us to join him in drinking the health of the House of Orange, and at once servants bore to all the carriages wine glasses filled with orange bitters, and each one tied with a little bow of orange ribbon. This was done with great enthusiasm, and then we advanced to the Town Hall. This edifice is most striking in its appearance, and is dated from the close of the XVIth century. Over the side entrance on the north is the celebrated inscription:

"'nae s Warte hVnger-noot gebraCht had tot de doot bInaest zes-dVIzent MensChen, aLs' t god den heer Verdroot gaf hI Vns Weder broot, zo VeeL WI CVnsten

THE PROCESSION IN LEIDEN.

WeusChen." (When the black famine had brought to the
death nearly six thousand persons, then God, the Lord,
repented of it and gave us bread again as much as we
could wish.)

This inscription, which refers to the siege of 1574,
is a chronogram, the capitals (among which W is
reckoned as two V's) recording the date, and the 131
letters the number of days during which the siege
lasted.

Above the center of this Town Hall waved the
American flag. Up the lofty flight of steps we advanced to the Municipal Council Chamber. Here we
were received by the deputy mayor, Hon. M. L. J.
van Buttingha Wichers, and the members of the
Council with their old emblems of municipal authority prominently displayed. The acting mayor then
made us an address in English.

At the end of his address the wine of honor was
presented to the guests. Mr. Van Sielen called upon
the Rev. Dr. Suydam to respond for the Society. He
did this in the following eloquent oration:

*Response of Rev. J. Howard Suydam, D. D., to the
Address of Welcome to The Holland Society of New-
York by the Burgomaster of Leyden.*

Two years since, our fellow-member, Mr. Coykendall of Kingston, N. Y., invited The Holland Society
to a banquet at the Hotel Kaaterskill, situated on a
spur of the Catskill Mountains, 2500 feet above the
level of the sea.

The entertainment accorded us at that time has
been in constant remembrance during these days of

9

ovation tendered us by you, our kindred of former generations,—an ovation more adapted to royalty than to simple citizens of a Republic.

Upon that occasion the pleasant duty was assigned me to respond to a toast entitled, "The Relief of Leyden." I concluded my remarks with a resolution of cordial sympathy with the "Third of October Association" of this city. Although the hour was two in the morning, the members all remained in the hall, and by a unanimous vote the resolution was passed and ordered to be cabled across the ocean to you, the whole company rising to their feet in enthusiastic approbation.

We little thought that so many of our number, who were then together at midnight on that mountain height, would stand here in these Lowlands of Holland, face to face with those who then were so prominently in our thoughts, their welcomed guests, in the enjoyment of their lavish hospitality, and have our hearts stirred to their depths by treading the very soil upon which were enacted scenes which even yet cause the pages of history to glow with living fire.

Mr. Burgomaster and gentlemen of the Committee of the Third of October Association, we reciprocate your kind expressions. I wish it was in my power to respond in your language as clearly as you have addressed us in ours. We are profoundly grateful for your attention. We are aware that it is not to ourselves as individuals that these distinguished honors are rendered, but to the sentiment, which, as the product of the maintenance of a principle two hundred years since, abides with equal strength in your breasts and in ours.

Come and visit us in America, gentlemen, accompanied by your wives and your children, and permit The Holland Society to endeavor to make it manifest better than by words how much your present kindness is appreciated.

I find it impossible to entertain the thought of the Netherlands disassociated from the sea. Some of her large and ancient cities stand where the ocean once made its bed. Countless acres of her rich grazing lands have been rescued from beneath the depths upon which sanguinary naval battles were fought. As we look and wonder and meditate, our recollections of the old Grecian mythology appear dimly before the mental vision.

We are reminded of the story of Jason and the golden fleece. We recall the composition of that distinguished company in the "Argo," their long absence from home, the dangers they encountered, their contests, the temptations to which some in their weakness yielded, but which others manfully overcame; and as the outcome, how the stolen fleece was restored,— courage, perseverance, virtue, and a noble purpose having gained a complete triumph.

In all respects the analogy is not complete; yet there are a few salient points of resemblance between those adventurers on that vessel, guided by a divinity which expressed itself in prophecy through the wood of which its mast had been formed, as it made its way through the unknown waters of the Mediterranean, and the enterprise of our fathers, which carried them from these near-at-hand ports across the Atlantic to make their habitation in the wilds of North America.

It is true the golden fleece had not been stolen. Our fathers were not impelled in the search by a superstitious regard for a sentimental talisman. To them it signified what gold can procure. It signified a livelihood for themselves and their families; it signified a rapidly increasing population; it signified the evolution of the hamlet from the hovel, and of great cities from the hamlet. It included in its meaning, education, elevation, culture. It embraced all that which we will be pleased to exhibit to you, when you shall do us the honor to visit our shores as the welcome guests of The Holland Society of New-York. This is the meaning of the golden fleece for which our fathers, the Dutch Argonauts of these Northern Seas, made their expedition to the far-away land of the setting sun.

Accuse us not of sordid avarice because we did not return it, when found, to you; we retained it. And now after an absence of two hundred years we have returned to make our report.

Kindred of former generations, aye, may I not say, brothers of to-day, we have found the golden fleece and we have made good use of it.

I wish to emphasize this, *we have made good use of it*, and for the reason that our fathers, yours and ours, taught us how to utilize what we have in possession. They carried from this land the principles which constitute the present greatness of the United States of America. Few in number as were our colonial forefathers, they have left an indelible impression upon a land now comprising a population of more than sixty millions of inhabitants. This was deepened and expanded by those refugees for conscience' sake who fled from their homes in the British Islands to take

up their abode in this very city which now welcomes
us. They were men and women who sought and here
found freedom to worship God. What before was
ideal, here became a blessed experience; and having
drank deeply from the virtues of the Pierean spring
which flowed in such volume from these Lowlands,
they, too, sought a permanent home in the New
World. The remains of their leader, who intended
to follow the precious freight of the "Mayflower" and
the "Speedwell," now lie beneath the floor of yonder
cathedral,— a truly great man, removed in the prime
of a vigorous manhood. May I not suggest that
some movement be made towards erecting a suitable monument in this city to the memory of John
Robinson?

The Pilgrim and the Hollander departing from
the same soil, and affected by the same influences,
planted in America the principles which they drew
from the hearts of their mothers, or absorbed from
the surrounding atmosphere. From these were born
the great Republic of the West, now in its maturity,
the wonder of the wonders of the ages.

And this reminds me of another story in the old
mythology, learned in youth, but which, like other
classics, fades away as time passes and professional
duties demand attention.

You will recall, with me, that one of the numerous
offspring of Neptune, and because of his love for
Terra, was Antaeos, who proved to be a savage brute
in the form of a man. Around his primitive dwelling
in the wilderness in which he dwelt were monuments
composed of the bones of the victims he destroyed,
and he claimed as his proper prey all who came
within his reach.

No one was able to cope with him in personal combat. At length Hercules made the attempt, and though he often threw him to the ground, he immediately sprang up into new life and vigor. Hercules made the discovery that so long as Antaeos remained in contact with the earth he was invincible. He must be removed or he would retain his savage nature, and continue his merciless slaughter. Hercules therefore seized him and held the monster within the grasp of his mighty arms until he perished.

Suggestive as is this myth of valuable lessons not remote from the present occasion, I ask you to note this one as illustrated in ourselves, who have gone away and lived apart from our Motherland. It is this: that the aspirations and achievements of our Holland forefathers, inherited in our memories and engraven upon our hearts, have enabled us completely to overcome the cruel savagery of a pioneer civilization. You may see the bones of our leaders which mark a ghastly pathway from the rock-bound coast of New England to the golden gate of California. But you will also see at this present time that there has been a Hercules engaged in mortal combat with Antaeos. There has been a power exercised which has lifted the great giant of slavish toil above the earth and strangled him; so that the humanities are now in the ascendancy. This is the product of applied science indicated by inventions, and religion, compelling those comprising the race, each in the other, to recognize a man.

This Herculean influence came to us largely from this land. Your eighty years' struggle against un-

just oppression and for religious liberty; and that
love of learning which established this university of
Leyden, the acknowledged cradle of the sciences,
which to-day bestows such a wealth of benefit upon
mankind; and that dogged perseverance which knew
no master,— not among men, not even in nature,—
no master but the one God before whom we all bend
in reverent homage; these memories, these aspirations, these achievements, have possessed us, so that
the people of our country are living to-day, like
yourselves, in the upper atmosphere of the arts and
letters, philosophy and poetry, religion and philanthropy.

The Hercules born of science and religion has
conquered the savage Antaeos by lifting him above
the earth.

We also learned from this, your country and our
old home, the value of opportunity. You taught us
to choose the best gifts which time proffers; and you
also taught us not to yield, but to conquer circumstances.

The contest with circumstances makes or destroys
men. In this is ever illustrated the survival of the
fittest. It is not the quantity but the quality of
what we take to ourselves that constitutes the ele-
ment of growth in a true man.

As it is with the individual, so is it with the multitude which comprises a community or a nation.

Holland has given us examples of both — the choice
of the best, and the conquest of circumstances.

My meaning in this respect to the gifts of time is
forcibly expressed by our American sage, the late
Ralph Waldo Emerson. He says:

Daughters of Time, the hypocritic days,
Muffled and dumb like barefoot dervishes,
And marching single in an endless file,
Bring diadems and faggots in their hands.
To each they offer gifts after his will,—
Bread, kingdoms, stars, and sky that holds them all.
I, in my pleached garden watched the pomp,
Forgot my morning wishes, hastily
Took a few herbs and apples, and the day
Turned and departed silent. I, too late,
Under the solemn fillet saw the scorn.

Opportunity! The right choice of time's gifts! To take the greatest and the best as we may! She presents that which will develop our manhood. Shall we take only that by which we may exist?

In our blessed book of books it is written, that because Solomon asked wisdom, therefore there were added riches and honors. He chose the best. And here, where we now stand, two hundred and fourteen years ago the suffering inhabitants of this city were offered a choice of what should contribute to their immediate material advantage, or of that which should develop their higher manhood and result in greater blessing to their children. And hence your University, which gave your city a world-wide reputation as the Athens of modern times. You taught us how to choose. Our fathers gave us aspiration. The days brought their rich gifts, and those who chose, enjoyed them, so that your kindred across the sea are proud to hold up to your view the product of the seed taken from hence centuries agone.

Besides the best gifts of time, you also have equally and signally illustrated the subjugation of circumstances.

It is often said that the mountains develop the best form of manhood. An English nobleman, traveling our rocky State of Vermont, in company with the late ex-Vice-President of the United States, Henry Wilson, asked, "What can you raise here?" To which Wilson replied, "*Men.*"

It is true. The mountains develop the best form of manhood, but it is because men are there compelled to force a livelihood from an unremunerative soil.

It is not necessarily the mountain, but it is the contest and the triumph over difficulties of whatever character that forms the best type of manhood. This is here, in Holland, as it is yonder in Piedmont. Those of the Netherlands can successfully cope with those of the Pyrenees — Orange with Philip. Has it not been demonstrated?

Aye! It is the people who master circumstances who become great, and grow on all sides of their nature. And here we find a perpetual example in these dykes and dunes, in these wondrous waterways, in these flourishing cities, and in these beautiful, cleanly homes.

O friends, kindred, blood of our blood, we respond with equal warmth to your kindly greeting, and we say to you, that so long as the desire for liberty shall dwell within the breasts of man anywhere throughout the world; so long as men shall cherish the hope of a blessed immortality; so long as there shall be aspiration for individual elevation, and for that of the race; so long as conveniences and comforts of a material kind are desired and to be secured — so long must Old Holland be cherished in the memory; so long must gratitude, like the lights

10

in the temple of Vesta, burn upon the altar of human hearts for what she has done and for what she will ever continue to do for mankind.

With all this meaning that I have endeavored to include in my remarks cast into the words, and very much more, we join you in exclaiming, *Oranje boven, Oranje boven al.*

Here flowers were presented to all the ladies and gentlemen. We then took a hurried glance at the many antiquities in the Town Hall, and regretted that time was passing so fast that we could not longer enjoy their inspection. After this we went on foot to the Burg, that most interesting relic of prehistoric times. As we mounted to its top and looked over the scene, we could not help recalling how three centuries before the famine-wasted defenders of the city had looked from thence in eager hope that succor was at hand. Too soon we were recalled from the thoughts of the past to the pleasures of the present, and found our way to the Museum. There again we had a most appropriate little speech of welcome from Dr. W. Pleyte in behalf of the authorities of the Museum, and a card of admission to the special exhibition gotten up for us, representing the ancient city of Leyden; and one of the earliest views of New Amsterdam was presented to us as a memento of the occasion. Here again flowers were given to the ladies. We then proceeded next door, to one of the most magnificent exhibitions made for us in Holland. A two-story house had been specially procured for the occasion and cleared of its contents, and all the riches of the libraries and collections of Leyden, which related to the connection between

AUGUST. LEIDEN. 1888

EXHIBITION OF DOCUMENTS RELATING TO THE PILGRIM-FATHERS.

New Amsterdam.

Leyden and America, and the early Dutch settlements in North America, were laid out for our benefit, with learned attendants to point out their beauties. A printed book of twenty-eight pages (inserted facing p. 80), containing a catalogue of the treasures, had been especially prepared for the occasion.

After an inspection of these treasures, much too short to either gratify our curiosity or to repay the kindly zeal which had prompted their collection, we were forced by the shortness of our stay to proceed onward. We made a hurried visit to the University and a rapid survey of the various rooms, gazing with interest at the portraits of the professors in the senate room, and the historical treasures there displayed. We viewed with amusement the cartoons of the students on the walls of the passageways, paid a brief visit to the chapel, and then made a hurried inspection of the fine monument to Vandewerf, the heroic burgomaster under whose lead the defense of the siege was so long and successfully conducted. With appetites sharpened by all we had seen, we then proceeded to the most fashionable restaurant in the city, where was served in a room overlooking a fine garden an elegant and bounteous collation. The same arrangement that had been made for the carriages was here observed. Small tables were set for each party, and a Dutch host presided at each; a fine orchestra hidden behind banks of ferns discoursed pleasing music, and everything served to attract and cheer the somewhat fatigued visitors. Two of the courses were most appropriate to the occasion, being two of those which are always prepared for the banquets of the Third of October Society. One was the celebrated "Hutspot."

The tradition of this dish is, that this was the dinner which was cooking for the Spaniards at the time they were surprised by the attack of the relieving force, and was left by the Spaniards in their flight. Our genial Secretary has seen to it that all the members of the Society have the recipe for this famous dish. The other course was white bread, on which were served delicate small herring with a delicious sauce. This is always accompanied by a rhyming couplet, which signifies that as long as Leyden has white bread and herring she has nothing to fear. After full justice had been given to the luncheon and our hearts were warmed by wine, Mr. Brouwer made a most interesting speech; among other things, he said:

"Yes, we now see with our own eyes that this small acorn of liberty has at last brought out a great oak. Has not your great historian, John Lothrop Motley, made the remark that the resistance to England's despotism found its example in our resistance to Spain? The mother has not forgotten her children. Her example was the incitement to keep to the front the banners of liberty. The Republic of North America excites us. But, thank God, as honest children, you have not forgotten your mother. You and I and all of us feel that we are brothers and sisters, descending from the same grand old tree of past generations. May this grand oak, now in full bloom in America, never cease in growth. Ladies and gentlemen, please rise and drink to the toast of ' The great American Republic: Liberty above all.'"

This was received with enthusiasm and responded to by Van Sielen in Dutch. Then, as the time was drawing short, we took quite a long walk through the

VAN DER WERFF OFFERING HIS BODY AS FOOD.

pleasant park to the Society Musis Sacrum, a club delightfully situated at one end of the park, and which
is for the exclusive use of the members and their
families. Here Mr. J. J. van Masyk Huyser Van
Reenen, the president, gave a most charming little
address in which he said: "There may exist some differences of opinion upon the matter of religion as
well as that of politics, yet, in the reception of
foreigners every one is united and in full accord
when it relates to guests whose breasts are decorated
with tokens of love for the House of Orange, and
whose hearts beat warmly for the same. Mutual
friendship already exists, but now it is made stronger
by a social glass and by a brotherly shaking of hands."

Baron von Roell, in behalf of the students of the
University, then presented to the ladies an American
flag in silk, as a token of their gallant admiration for
their charms. Here our choir distinguished themselves by a rendition of most of the chants of the
voyage, which were given with effusion, and received
with enthusiasm. The students responded with several
of their songs, and a very jolly half hour was passed.
Making our way through the crowd which had again
assembled outside, we entered our carriages, and
started on our way to the station, but were again
stopped in front of the students' club, and pressed to
take one last taste of gin as a parting shot. As we
reached the station we passed through ranks of the
students, ranged on both sides of the door, who
gave us a parting salutation full of warmth and feeling. After we were within the doors, in deference to
the entreaties of our hosts, the choir came together
and sang "Yankee Doodle" as a farewell song. It
may here be remarked, that all through Holland, by

bands, and on organs and church-chimes, "Yankee Doodle" was played for us on every possible occasion. As the train moved off, Mr. Van Siclen taught us a cheer for the Leyden University in the original Dutch (Leve de Leidsche Universiteit), which we repeated, answering cheers and exclamations coming from all sides. Thus ended one of the most memorable days of the trip, ever to be pleasantly remembered by all who participated therein.

A better idea of the Dutch view of this magnificent reception may be gained from the following translation from the *Leyden Daily News* [*Leidsch Dagblad*], of August 14, 1888:

THE VISIT OF THE AMERICAN MEMBERS (LEDEN DONATEURS) OF THE THIRD OF OCTOBER ASSOCIATION TO LEIDEN.

Early in the morning our city wore a festive aspect, flags floating from all public buildings and many private residences in a gay manner, thanks to the strong breeze, and glittering in the rays of the sun, hidden too often this summer. Indeed, the sun shone on our streets and canals. Our city was about to enjoy the honor to receive our brethren from America, and if the storm and the rain of the night before had caused many fears, in the morning there was cause for contentment.

Not only the national tricolor, the orange, and the city colors, but also the American flag (red and white stripes, and silver stars) braved the gale; among others it adorned the City Hall, the Cotton Factory, and the middle of the Breestraat. When the train was due at the station, also ornamented with flags, a large crowd went there to witness the arrival.

These visitors, brethren from old New Amsterdam, seemingly forgotten for two hundred years, they reappeared, proud of being Hollanders. They came far from over the sea to see that old country from which their mighty republic sprang; they also came to Leiden.

And Leiden, or rather the Third of October Association, received them in a worthy manner; and if they have changed the tricolor for the starry banner, they have not been estranged; they are, as we are, descendants from those hardy sailors of the seventeenth century, who conquered the world by courage and force; we grasp their hands as relatives.

What wonder that we recall with a feeling of sadness how in 1615 the flag of the Dutch Republic was planted on that little fortress of Manhattan Island, out of which gradually grew powerful New-York. Shall we not remember that a Hollander, Pieter Stuyvesant, was the actual founder of that prosperity?

But here they are, the long-expected guests. The 10.40 train stops, and the band of the National Guard plays the American national air while the assembled multitude cheers.

The committee of the Third of October Association escorts the guests to the first-class waiting-room, where Mr. N. Brouwer, the president, addresses them in English as follows:

"*Ladies and Gentlemen:* Allow me to say a few words in the name of the Third of October Association. First, I welcome you to Leiden, and want to thank you for your visit to our city and to our Association. Brethren and sisters, descendants of the same Watergeuzen of the Sixteenth Century, separated by the Atlantic Ocean, but firmly bound together by the same principles of civil and religious liberty, it is for our Association a great honor to call you our guests to-day. Our special gratitude is due the ladies who will largely contribute to the pleasure of the day. Time being limited we will try to make the best use possible of it, and therefore I invite you to enter these carriages, which will convey you to the City Hall. If in each carriage one lady and two gentlemen will take seats, a member of our committee will join you, in order that each of us may enjoy your company. Allow me first to offer the ladies a small bouquet, as a testimonial of our feelings. May this bouquet be the omen of a fine day."

After this the members of the reception committee, consisting, besides the officials of the Third of October Associa-

tion, of Mr. C. M. Dozy, City Archivist; P. du Rieu, jr.,
Conservator of the Municipal Museum; Louis D. Petit, of
the Royal University Library; Dr. W. Pleyte, Conservator
of the Museum of Antiquities; James de Fremery, Consul
of the Netherlands at San Francisco, U. S., here temporarily;
Dr. E. A. O. Was, and P. J. van Wyngaarden, officials of the
Third of October Association; these gentlemen offered
their arms to the ladies, to escort them to the sixteen
carriages, in each of which a member of the committee
took a seat, and then the cavalcade went to the City Hall,
saluted by a large multitude with shouts and clapping of
hands.

In front of the Club "Minerva" a short stop was made;
there they were greeted by the students, who, while the
music played "Io Vivat," offered them a printed document
and a glass of Orange bitters.   The document read:

"1575 — 1888.

"ACADEMIA LUGDUNI–BATAVORUM.

"The Students of Leiden, sympathizing with the members of The Holland Society, U. S. A., but not able to receive
them at their club house at this moment, claim the honor
of offering them a glass of a national drink, 'Orange bitters,'
and propose the health of the King, the Queen, and the Princess of the Netherlands."

This curious surprise made a good impression and was
gracefully accepted. Arrived at the City Hall, they ascended
the high stoop and were received in the Burgomaster's
Chamber, by the acting Burgomaster, Mr. N. L. J. Van
Buttingha Wichers, the City Secretary, and members
of the Council. Here, the visitors being arranged in a
circle, the acting Burgomaster thus addressed them in their
native tongue:

"*Ladies and Gentlemen:* Speaking for the city of Leiden,
which I have to-day the honor of representing, I welcome
you with all possible cordiality. I deem it a great privilege
for our city, a privilege worthy of being recorded in her
annals, that your Society accords us one day out of the few
it is spending in Holland. At the same time you will not

THE PILGRIM FATHERS.

EXHIBITION OF DOCUMENTS

FROM

PUBLIC AND PRIVATE COLLECTIONS AT LEIDEN,
RELATING TO THE DUTCH SETTLEMENTS
IN NORTH-AMERICA.

AUGUST 1888.

THE PILGRIM FATHERS.

EXHIBITION OF DOCUMENTS

FROM

PUBLIC AND PRIVATE COLLECTIONS AT LEIDEN,
RELATING TO THE DUTCH SETTLEMENTS
IN NORTH-AMERICA.

AUGUST 1888.

BOEKDRUKKERIJ VAN P. W. M. TRAP, LEIDEN.

Aan het einde der zestiende eeuw had het vrijheidsbeginsel, door de hervorming in kerk en staat gewekt, reusachtige afmetingen aangenomen, en vond zoowel zijn ijverige voor- als tegenstanders. In Engeland was het clericalisme onderdrukt onder de Katholieken, maar vertoonde zich krachtig in het streven naar een hervormde Staatskerk onder de regeering van Elisabeth en later van Jacobus.

Het vijheidsbegrip in de kerk, vond in velen ijverige voorstanders. Onder de Staatskerk wilden zij onafhankelijk blijven, en als onafhankelijken, Independenten, stelden zij alles op het spel om zich die onafhankelijkheid te verzekeren. Zij moesten het opgeven. Robert Browne, een Independent, ontvlood met eenige aanhangers, en waar zouden zij zich beter vestigen dan in de Nederlanden, waar een vrijheidslievende bevolking den strijd met de grootste mogendheden van dien tijd roemrijk voerde, en binnen de muren harer steden, onder de regeering van Prins Willem van Oranje, vrijheid van Godsdienst in den meest uitgebreiden zin van het woord, huldigde.

Zij trokken van Norwich naar Middelburg in 1581, verlieten weder die plaats en trachtten in 1582 in Engeland nogmaals hun geluk te beproeven. In 1592 werd het hun te bang, zij weken naar het Nederlandsche Naarden en gingen in 1596 naar Amsterdam. Een strijd met den Amsterdamschen Smyth, deed de aanhangers van Robinson, een volgeling van Browne, naar Leiden de wijk nemen. In Amsterdam bleven de Baptisten, in Leiden kwamen de Brownisten in 1609. Onder de regeering van Prins Maurits leefden zij, en predikten hun geloof in de woning van Robinson, op het Pieterskerkplein. Sommigen meenen dat zij zich aansloten bij de Engelsche Puriteinen en Presbyterianen, doch dit is niet waarschijnlijk. De eersten hadden hunne kerk achtereenvolgens in het Catherynen gasthuis, in het Jeruzalemshof, en eindelijk in de kerk der Bagijnen, waar zij tot op het begin dezer eeuw, hun godsdienst uitoefenden. Robinson schijnt echter meer aan de Nederlandsch-Hervormden zich te hebben aangesloten. Zijn vrienden waren de Leidsche Professoren onder wien Hoornbeek Hommius en Polyander een eerste plaats bekleedden.

3

Het ging hun niet altijd even voorspoedig, zoodat zij
naar ruimer werkkring en beteren levenswelstand uitzagen.
Het plan rijpte bij Robinson om naar Amerika te vertrek-
ken, doch in 1625 stierf hij, door allen betreurd. Zijn
lijkstoet naar de Pieterskerk werd door alle professoren,
zoo men verteld, gevolgd, en Hoornbeek gaf omtrent hem
dit loffelijke getuigenis:
„Gratus nostris dum vixit fuit, et theologis Leidensibus
familiaris et honoratus".

Een jaar voor den dood van Robinson stak reeds een der-
tigtal Waalsche families, naar Amerika over, die zich voor-
namelijk aan de boorden der Hudson vestigden. Hun
leider was Jeste de Forest, een lakenverver uit Avesnes in
Henegouwen, aan wien de stichting van Nieuw Amsterdam
moet worden toegeschreven, dat kleine begin dier wereld-
stad van den grootsten vrijheidsstaat der wereld, de Vereenigde Staten.

Na Robinsons dood zijn ook de Brownisten naar Amerika
getrokken, alwaar zij zich op het eiland Manhattan, in den
mond der Hudson nederzetten.

Met ingenomenheid gaan wij na, hoe die vrijheid zich
verder ontwikkelde en nimmer zich binden liet, geen juk
werd meer geduld; Engeland moest eindelijk, evenals de
overige mogendheden, den strijd opgeven. Washingtons
beleid vestigde de republiek, die thans voor heel de Oude
wereld het toonbeeld is van ware vrije volksregeering.

De Holland Society herinnert zich dien strijd en die
zegepraal, immer dankbaar voor den oorsprong van hun
vrijer leven in Holland, en vele vrijheidsgezinden in Nederland begroeten de broeders met vreugde, die toonen, wat
men langs dezen weg in de wereld vermag te worden. Vrijheid in godsdienst, vrijheid in beginselen, vrijheid in leven
en streven op alle gebied.— Liberty above all!

Leiden, 13 Aug. 1888.

Mr. CHARLES M. DOZY, Archivaris der
gemeente Leiden.

P. DU RIEU Jr., Conservator van het Stede-
lijk Museum.

LOUIS D. PETIT, Conservator aan's Rijks
Universiteits Bibliotheek.

Dr. W. PLEYTE, Conservator aan's Rijks
Museum van Oudheden.

In the latter part of the 16th century, the ideas of liberty in Church and State, preached by the reformation, had found both zealous antagonists and protectors.

In England, where catholicisme was suppressed, clericalisme showed itself the stronger under the reign of Elisabeth and that of James, in the endeavour to obtain a reformed Church, so that the partisans of liberty, who strove with might and main to retain their independence in the Church, were forced to give up the struggle.

Robert Browne, an Independent, fled with some of his followers to the Netherlands and sought a refuge among the Dutch, then fighting gloriously under prince William of Orange, for their liberty, and securing freedom of religion to all who settled within their walls.

These Independents went from Norwich to Middelburg in 1581, left this town and returned to England in 1582, but in 1592 were obliged to fly again to Holland, this time to the town of Naarden.

In the year 1596 they settled in Amsterdam but a quarrel with the baptist minister Smyth, caused the followers of Robinson, a disciple of Browne, to go to Leiden, where Robinson lived and worked for the wellfare of his community during the reign of Prince Maurice. He preached in his own house on the Pieterskerkhof.

It is sometimes said that the Brownists joined the Puritans and Presbyterians but this is not probable. Very likely Robinson had more sympathy for the Dutch Reformed Church. The Puritans, first had a chapel in St. Catharine's hospital, afterwards in the Jeruzalem's hof and at last in the Bagijnhof, where they had their religious assemblies till the beginning of this century.

As things did not always go very well with the Independents, Robinson resolved to emigrate with his followers to America, there to seek a better fortune, but he died in 1625, regretted by every one. He was enterred in the Pieterskerk and his funeral was followed by the Professors of the Leiden University, who had all been his friends, more especially Hommins, Polyander and Hoornbeek. Hoornbeek said of him :

„Gratus nostris dum vixit fuit, et theologis Leidensibus familiaris et honoratus."

One year before his death about thirty Walloon families had already left Leyden and several of them had settled on the isle Manhattan in the mouth of the Hudson. The removal was conducted by Jesse de Forest, a Leiden dyer, who is the founder of New Amsterdam, the origin of New-York, the greatest town of the largest freestate of the world, the United States of America.

It is with warm interest that we follow the rise of this republic, during the struggle with England and its final success.

The Holland Society remembers that struggle and victory, and is thankful to Holland, the birthplace of that liberty. Therefore every Dutchman who loves liberty, cordially greets his American brothers, who prove what a people can accomplish through that principle. Freedom of religion, freedom of principles.— Liberty above all!

Bibliography.

Asher, G. M., A bibliographical and historical essay on the Dutch
books and pamphlets, relating to New-Netherland, and to the
Dutch West-India Company and to its possessions in Brazil,
Angola, etc., as also on the maps, charts etc. of New-Nether-
land, with facsimiles of the map of New Netherland, by N. L.
Visscher etc. Amsterdam 1854—67. 4°.

Catalogue of books, maps, plates on America, and of a remark-
able collection of early voyages, offered for sale by Frederik
Muller at Amsterdam. Amsterdam, 1872—75. 3 psts. 8°.
   I. Page 114—129, 336—340. New-Netherland.

1581—1582.

Engeland. — England.

Portret van Elisabeth, koningen van Engeland (1533—1603).
Gravure.
Portrait of Elisabeth, Queen of England. Engraving.

Portret van dezelfde, grav. uit de 17e eeuw.
Portrait of the same. Engraving.

Platte grond van Norwich, get.: Nordovicum. Norwich. A°.
1661. kl. 4°. Kopergr.
Plan of the city of Norwich.

Platte grond van Norwich, get.: Nordovicum. fol. Kopergravure
— Uit Bruin Civitates orbis terrarum. 1593.
Plan of the city of Norwich.

Platte grond van Norwich, get.: Nordovicum Angliae civitas. fol.
Kopergr.— Uit Bruin Civitates orbis terrarum. 1593.
*Plan of the city of Norwich, entitled Nordovicum Angliae civitas
etc.*

The North-east Prospect of Norwich (1731). obl.

A new Plan of the City of Norwich. Printed for and sold by
Sam. King Sr. London 1766. fol. engr.
With illustrations showing the most important buildings, etc.

Nederland. — The Netherlands.

Portret van Prins Willem I, (1572—1584) Grav. d. J. Suyderhoef.
Portrait of Prince William I. Engr. by J. Suyderhoef.

Portret van Prins Willem I, geschilderd door Cornelis Stooter.
Portrait of Prince William I, by Cornelis Stooter.

Bentivoglio (Guido) Relationi [di Fiandra e di Francia]. Brus-
selles 1632. 8°.

Opere, cioè le Relationi di Fiandra e di Francia, l'Historia della
guerra di Fiandra, e le Lettere scritte nel tempo delle sue nun-
tiature. Nuovam. raccolte insieme. Parigi 1645. fol.

7

H. M. Dexter, Footprints of the Pilgrims in Holland — In Sabbath at home. Vol. I. 1867.
With views on the Kloksteeg. Site of John Robinson's house and garden.

Portret van Prins Maurits. (1584—1625). Grav. d. J. Suyderhoef.
Portrait of Prince Maurice. Engr. by J. Suyderhoef.

Middelburg.

Platte grond van Middelburg, get.: Middelbvrgum, Selandiae opp. sitv, opere, et mercimoniis, florentiss. fol. Kopergr.— Uit Bruin, Civitates orbis terrarum 1593.
Plan of the city of Middelburg entitled: Middelburgium, Selandiae opp. sitv, opere et mercimoniis florentiss. fol. engraving. — Ex Bruin, Civitates orbis terrarum 1593.

Prospect van Middelburg, get.: Middelburgum. Kopergr. Uitgegeven door Fr. Schillemans te Middelburg 1619. 4 bl. fol.
Prospect of Middelburg, entitled: Middelburgium. Copperprint edited by Fr. Schillemans at Middelburg 1619. 4 sheets. fol.

Platte grond van Middelburg (zonder jaar) fol. Teekening met kleuren.
Plan of Middelburg (not dated). fol. Coloured drawing.

Platte grond van Middelburg, get.: Middelburgum. fol. Kopergr. — Uit J. Blaeu Tooneel der steden (1648).
Plan of Middelburg, entitled: Middelburgium fol. engraving.

Afbeelding van de Stad Middelburg in Zeeland. Nauwkeurig zoo de Publycke Gebouwen als alle de Particuliere Huysen Kennelijk naar 't Leven geteyckent door Cornelis Goltat. Gedruckt by Johannes Heertens. fol. Kopergr.— Uit Smallegange, Nieuwe Chronyk v. Zeeland. 1696.
Drawing of the town of Middelburg in the province of Zeeland, giving an exact picture of the public buildings and private houses by Cornelis Goltat. Printed by Johannes Meertens. fol. Engraving.— Ex Smallegange. Nieuwe Chronyk v. Zeeland. 1696.

1592—1609.

Naarden.

Platte grond getiteld: Naerden. fol. panteekening zonder jaar. Waarschijnlijk voor Blaeu's Atlas op die schaal gebracht. Nooit gegraveerd.
Plan entitled: Naerden. fol. drawn with the pen not dated. Probably brought into this scale for Blaeu's Atlas. Never engraved.

Platte grond getiteld: Naerden. 4°. Kopergr. Uit Janssonius, Tooneel d. vermaarste koop-steden.
Plan entitled: Naerden. 4°. engraving. Ex Janssonius, Tooneel d. vermaarste koopsteden.

Platte grond getiteld: Naerden. fol. Kopergr. z. jaartal.
Plan entitled Naerden. fol. engraving not dated.

Gezicht op „ Naerde "—Naarden in de 16e eeuw.—Potloodteekening zonder naam van teekenaar of jaartal.
View of the town of „ Naerde" — the town of Naarden in the 16th century. Pencildrawing, neither signed or dated.

Gezigt op de Stad Naarden. Kopergr. H. S. (Schoute) d. et f. Zonder jaar.
> *View of the town of Naarden. Engraving. H. S. (Schoute) d. et f. not dated.*

Gezicht op Naerden. J. Peeters del. G. Bouttats fec. aquaf. et exeudit Antverpia. 1672.
> *View of the town of Naerden. J. Peeters del. G. Bouttats fec. aquaf. et exeudit Antverpia. 1672.*

Amsterdam.

Plan van Amsterdam, get.: Amsterdam vertoonde zigh aldus inden Jare 1500. fol. Kopergr. zonder naam van graveur.
> *Plan of the city of Amsterdam entitled : Amsterdam as it was in the year 1500. fol. Copperprint, without the name of the engraver.*

De groote Kaart van Amsterdam in 1544, van Kornelis Antoniszoon, in 12 bladen, naar het oorspronkelijke gephotogr. en in 14 kleuren op Hollandsch papier gedrukt. Amsterdam 1885. fol. — Behoort bij J. ter Gouw, Geschiedenis van Amsterdam.
> *Kornelis Antoniszoon's Large map of Amsterdam in 1544 in 12 sheets ; photographs taken from the original and printed in 14 colours. Amst. 1885. fol. Belonging to J. ter Gouw's History of Amsterdam.*

Prospect van Amsterdam, kopergr. door Harmanus Allardus Coster en Nicolaus Johannes Visscher. A° 1611. 2 bl. fol. oblong.
> *Prospect of Amsterdam, engraved by Harmanus Allardus Coster and Nicolaus Johannes Visscher. A°. 1611. 2 sh. fol. oblong.*

J. G. de Hoop Scheffer, De Brownisten te Amsterdam gedurende den eersten tijd na hunne vestiging, in verband met het ontstaan van de Broederschap der Baptisten.— In: Versl. en Meded. d. Kon. Akademie van Wetensch. te Amsterdam. Afd. Letterk. II Rks dl X (1881) bl. 203 volg.
> *J. G. de Hoop Scheffer, The Brownists at Amsterdam during the first period after their settling in that town in connexion with the foundation of the Baptist-Brotherhood.*

1609—1625.

Leiden.

Portret van Prins Maurits, geschilderd door Cornelis Stooter.
> *Portrait of Prince Maurice, by Cornelis Stooter.*

Kaart van Holland tot aan Maas en IJssel. Teekening op perkament d. Jaques Bureau. A° 1565.
> *Map of Holland as far as the Maese and the Yssel. Drawing on parchment by Jaques Bureau. A. D. 1565.*

Kaart van het Hoogheemraadschap van Rijnland en de landen die op Rijnland uitwateren. Teekening d. Floris Balthazar en Balthazar Florissen. A°. 1610—1615.
> *Map of the Hoogheemraadschap of Rynland. Drawn by Floris Balthazar en Balthazar Florissen. a°. 1610—1615.*

Platte grond van Leiden, get.: Waarachtige Afkunterfeitinge der stad en universiteit Leiden in Holland. Copie op perkament

2

d. Jacob van Werven, 1744, naar de oorspronkelijke teekening vermoedelijk vervaardigd door Hans Liefrinck.

> *Plan of the town of Leiden, entitled: Exact picture of the Town and University of Leiden in Holland. Copy in parchment by Jacob von Werren, 1744, from the original drawing probably made by Hans Liefrinck.*

Platte grond van Leiden. Heliographische reproductie van de platte grond v. Hans Liefrinck. Uitg. d. W. Pleyte, in: Leyden vóór 300 jaren, Leiden 1874. fol.

> *Plan of Leyden. Heliographical reproduction of the plan made by Hans Liefrinck ed. by W. Pleyte, in: Leyden vóór 100 jaren en thans. Leiden 1874. fol.*

Plattegrond van Leyden, Anno 1600. Kopergr. d. P. Bastius.

> *Plan of Leyden. A. D. 1600. Engr. by P. Bastius.*

Platte grond van Leiden, get.: Lugdunum Batavorum vernaculo Leyden. Kopergr. uit Blaeu, Atlas major.

> *Plan of the town of Leiden, entitled: Lugdunum Batavorum vernaculo Leyden. From Blaeu's Atlas major.*

Prospect van Leiden: gem. „Leyden". Grav. d. C. J. Visscher (naar C. L. Rivet). Uit Blaeu, Atlas.

> *Prospect of Leiden: Entitled Leyden. Engr. by C. J. Visscher, after C. L. Rivet, Ex Blaeu's Atlas.*

G. Sumner, Memoirs of the Pilgrims at Leyden. Cambridge 1845. 8°.

> *Printed in „Collections of the Massachusets Histor. Society" Vol. IX 3d Ser.*

Gerechts Dagboeck gem. G. — Op fol. 33: Versouck van wegen 100 persoonen in Engelandt gebooren om haer residentie hier ter stede te mogen nemen, met de dispositie van die van den gerechte dato 12 febr. 1609.

> *Register of common affairs, G. — fol. 33. Request of 100 persons born in England for permission to live in this town, with a favorable disposition of the town council dated Febr. 12th. 1609.*

Portret van Jan van Hout, overl. 1609. Secretaris van de stad Leiden. Grav. d. W. Swanenburg met onderschrift van D. H(einsius).

> *Portrait of Jan van Hout † 1609. Secretary of the town of Leiden. Engr. by W. Swanenburg with a subscription by D. H(einsius).*

Kaarten van het bon Zevenhuizen (buurt waar J. Robinson heeft gewoond) met photogr. afbeeldingen van den tegenwoordigen toestand.

> *Map of the section Zevenhuizen (quarter in which J. Robinson lived) with a photographical view of its present state.*

Kaart van de Huysinge ende erve van Johan Laleyh, gelegen aen S. Pieterskerck-hoff. Teekening d. J. P. Dow, 16 January 1607.

> *Map of Johan Laleyh's house and garden; situated near the cimetary of St. Peter. Drawn by J. P. Dow. 16 January 1607.*

Caorte van Eenige Huysen ende Erven . . . . aende Westzijde vande Heeresteegh. Item langs de zuytzijde van St. Pieterskerckhof, alsook Oost en West zijde van de Commandeursteegh enz. Gedaen in Augustus des jaers 1649 door Joris Gerstecoren.

> *Map showing some houses and gardens . . . . on the Westside of the Heerestceegh. Idem on the southside of the cimetary of St. Peter and also on the East- and Westside of the Commandeursteegh etc Made in August of the year 1649 by Joris Gerstecoren.*

Gezicht op de Pieterskerk en de Kloksteeg met het Pesynshof.
Teekening in O. I. inkt.
View of the Church of St. Peter and the Kloksteeg with the Bagynhof. Drawing.

Aa, A. J. van der, Biographisch woordenboek der Nederlanden
.... voortgezet door K. J. R. van Harderwijk en Dr. G.
D. J. Schotel. 16e Deel. Haarlem. 1874. 8vo. — Bl. 378 Levens-
schets van John Robinson.
*Aa, A. J. van der, Biographical dictionary of the Netherlands.
.... continued by K. J. R. van Harderwijk and Dr. G.
D. J. Schotel. vol. 16. Haarlem 1874. 8vo. — Pag. 378
Biography of John Robinson.*

N. C. Kist, John Robinson, predikant der Leidsche Brownisten-
Gemeente, en de moederkerk der Engelsche Indepedenten en
grondlegster der Kolonie Plymouth in Noord-Amerika.— Uit
Nieuw Archief voor Kerkel. Geschied. dl VIII.
*N. C. Kist, John Robinson, minister of the Leyden Brownist-com-
munity, the mother-church of the English Independants who
occasioned the founding of the colony Plymouth in North-
America.*

Portret van Prof. N. C. Kist, overl. 1859. (schrijver van John
Robinson, pred. der Leidsche Brownisten gemeente). Lith.
d. L. Springer.
*Portrait of Prof. N. C. Kist † 1859. (Author of John Robinson,
pred. der Leidsche Brownisten gemeente). Lith. by L. Springer.*

Album Studiosorum Academiae Lugduno Batavae MDLXXV-
MDCCCLXXV. Accedunt nomina curatorum et professorum
per cadem secula. Hagae Comitum. 1875. 4°.

Quohier van 't Hoofdgeld d'anno 1622. Bon Sevenhuysen fol. 38:
In de poort van de Engelsche kerk. Jan Robbenson predicant,
enz.
*Quohier of the poll-tax A. D. 1622. — Section Serenhuysen
fol. 38. In the gate of the English Church. John Robbenson, minister.*

De Nederlandsche Spectator. 1865. Arnhem, 's Gravenhage
(1865) 4°. In n°. 35 (2 September) b. 273 een bericht
omtrent den gedenksteen in het Pesynshofje.
*Note about the memorial stone in the Pesynshofje in the Neder-
landsche Spectator 1865 Sept. 2d. N°. 35, p. 273.*

Portret van prof. Johannes Hoornbeeck, overl. 1666, schrijver van
de Summa controv. relig.; over de Brownisten. Grav. d.
Suyderhoef.
*Portrait of Prof. Johannes Hoornbeeck. † 1666, author of
the Summa controv. relig.; about the Brownists. Engr. by
Suyderhoef.*

Portret van denzelfden, grav. d. A. Santvoort.
Portrait of the same, engrav. by A. Santvoort.

Portret van prof. Festus Hommius, overl. 1642, regent van het
Staten college. Grav. uitgegeven door P. v. d. Aa.
Getuigschrift geschreven door Prof. Festus Hommius van 25
Januari 1622.
*Portrait of Prof. Festus Hommius † 1642 regent of the college of
Staten. Engraving, ed. by P. v. d. Aa.
Testimony written by Prof. Festus Hommius dated Jan. 25 1622.*

Portret van Prof. Polyander, geschilderd door ?
Portrait of Prof. Polyander, by ?

Het S. Catharina gasthuis, zo als het zig vertoonde A° 1567.
Grav. d. C. Brouwer (1783). uit v. Mieris, Beschr. v. Leiden.
*The hospital of St. Catherine, as it was A. D. 1567. Engraving
by C. Brouwer (1783), from v. Mieris Description of Leiden.*
Katharyne gasthuis. Teekening in O. I. iukt.
St. Catharine's hospital.
't St. Catharine Gasthuis. Grav. uit Rademaker, Rijnland. A°.
1736.
*Hospital of St. Catherine. Engraving from Rademaker, Rynland
A°. 1736.*
De Gasthuiskerk van binnen. (Engelsche kerk.). Teekening A°.
1787.
Interior of the Hospital chapel (English church). A°. 1787.
St. Katharyne Gasthuiskerk op de plaats te zien. Teekening
A°. 1787.
*Chapel of St. Catharine's hospital, shown in its present state.
A°. 1787.*
De gevel van het Katharyne Gasthuis op de Aalmarkt. Teeke-
ning A°. 1788.
Facade of St. Catharine's hospital on the Aalmarkt. A°. 1788.
Jeruzalemshof op de Kaiserstraat. Engelsche kerk tot 1644.
Teekening (laatst der 18e eeuw).
*Jerusalemshof in the Kaiserstreet. English church till the year
1644. Drawing from the end of the 18th century.*
Kaart van een gedeelte van het Falyde Bagijnhof achter de kerk.
Teekening d. J. P. Douw (+ 1610).
*Map of a part of the Falyde Bagynhof behind the church. Drawn
by J. P. Douw (+ 1610).*
De engelsche kerk (kerk van het Falyde Bagynhof). Teekening
d. J. J. Bylaert (18e eeuw).
*The english church (Church of the Falyde Bagynhof) drawn by
J. J. Bylaert (18th century).*
De Engelsche kerk in het Bagijnhof, van binnen. Teekening.
A°. 1787.
Interior of the English church in the Bagynhof. A. D. 1787.

Portret van Frederik Hendrik. Grav. d. J. Suyderhoef.
*Portrait of Prince Frederic Henry. Engr. by J. Suyderhof
(1625-1647).*
Portret van Prins Frederik Hendrik, geschilderd door Cornelis
Stooter.
Portrait of Prince Frederik Henry, by Cornelis Stooter.
Prospect van Delftshaven, get. De Haven der Stadt Delft,
genaemt Delfshaven. Grav. d. C. Decker.
*Prospect of Delftshaven, marked the Port of the city of Delft.
Called Delftshaven. Engr. by C. Decker.*
Afbeelding van schepen uit het begin der XVIIe eeuw. Grav.
H. Hondius, etc. (1603).
*Picture of ships in the beginning of the XVIIth century. Engr.
by H. Hondius, etc. 1603.*

Portret van Prins Willem II. Grav. d. Corn. Visscher, naar
G. van Hondthorst.
> *Portrait of Prince William II. Engr. by Corn. Vischer, copied
> from G. von Houdthorst.*

Portret van Maria van Engeland. Grav. d. Corn. Visscher, naar
G. van Hondthorst.
> *Portrait of Mary of England (Wife of William II) Engr. by
> Corn. Visscher, copied from G. von Houdthorst.*

Portret van Prins Willem III (Stadhouder, Koning v. Engeland.
Zwarte kunst d. J. Smith.
> *Portrait of Prince William III (Stadtholder, King of England)
> by J. Smith.*

Governour Bradford's Letter Book. — To our beloved friends Mr.
William Bradford, Mr. Isaac Allerton, Mr. Eduard Winslow, and
the rest, whom they think fit to acquaint therewith (1624). — In :
Collections of the Massachusetts Historical Society for 1799.
Vol. III p. 27 s. q.

1624-1690.

Amerika.

Aveniae, vulgo Auesnes, insigne Hannoniae Opp: ad hostiles pro-
pulsandos conatus, munitiss. fol. Kopergr.
> *Plan of Avesnes, the birthplace of Jesse de Forest.*

Prospect of Avesnes. 4°. Engraving.

Gerechtsdagboeck van publicke zaken A. in dato 27 Augustus
1622 (vergunning aan Jesse de Forest om Waalsche Kolonis-
ten aan te werven).
> *Register of State affairs A. fol. 123 August 1622 (authorisation
> given to Jesse de Forest for enrolling walloon Colonists dated
> Aug. 27, 1622.*

Gerechtsdagboeck in dato 4 Januari 1624 (vergunning aan Gerard
de Forest om zijn broeder Jesse „laatstelijk naar West-Indie
vertrokken" als verver in coleuren te vervangen).
> *Register of common affairs L. fol. 52 (permission granted to
> Gerard de Forest to take the dyer's place of his brother
> Jesse „gone lately to the West-Indies" dated Jan. 4, 1624.*

Laet, Joa. de. Nieuwe Wereldt ofte Beschrijvinghe van West-
Indien enz. Met kaerten. Leyden, Is. Elzevier. 1625. fol.
> *Laet, Joa. de, The New world or description of the West-Indies,
> etc. With maps. Leyden. Is. Elzevier. 1625. fol.*

Laet, Joa. de, Beschrijvinghe van West-Indien. IIe druck, ver-
meerdert, met caerten, beelden enz. Leyden by de Elzeviers.
1630. fol.
> *Laet, Joa. de, Description of the West-Indies. IId edition,
> augmented with maps, illustrations, etc. Leyden, Elzevier.
> 1630. fol.*

Documents relative to the Colonial History of the State of New-
York: procured in Holland, England and France, by John
Romeyn Brodhead. Ed. by E. B. O'Callaghan. Vol. I, II. Holland Documents 1603-1678. Albany 1856-58. 2 vol. 4°. w. portr.
and map.

Vryheden by de Vergad. van de Negenthiene van de Geoctr.
West-Indische Comp. vergunt aen allen den ghenen, die

eenighe Colonien in Nieu-Nederlaudt sullen planten. . . . .
Amsterdam voor Mr. Jz. Brandt . . . 163°. 4°.
  *Privileges granted to all settlers in New Netherland, by the
  Assembly of Nineteen of the authorized West India Com-
  pany. Amsterdam for Mr. Js. Brandt . . . . 1630. 4°.*
Vertoogh van Nieu-Neder-land, weghens de gheleghentheydt,
  vruchtbaerheydt en soberen staet desselfs. (Door Adr. van
  der Donck c. s.) 's Gravenhage 1650. 4°.
  *Account of New-Netherland, its situation, its fertility the miserable
  state there (by Adr. van der Donck c. s.) The Hague 1650. 4°.*
Breeden-Raedt aen de Vereenichde Nederlandsche Provintien
  Gelreland, Holland, Zeeland, Wtrecht, Vriesland, Over-Yssel,
  Groeningen. Gemaeckt ende gestelt uyt diverse ware en
  waerachtige memorien. Door J. A. G. W. C. Antwerpen,
  F. van Duynen . . . . 1649.
  *Homely Advice to the United Netherland Provinces, Gelreland,
  Holland, Zeeland, Utrecht, Vriesland, Over Yssel, Groningen,
  made of and composed from diverse true and faithful documents.
  By J A. G. W C. Antwerp F. van Duynen . . . 1649. 4°.*
Vertoogh van Nieu Nederland, and Breeden Raedt aende
  Vereenichde Nederlandsche Provintiën. — Two rare tracts,
  printed in 1649-50, relating to the administration of affairs
  in New Netherland. Translated from the Dutch by H. C.
  Murphy. W. map. New York. 1854. 4°.
Remonstrance of New Netherland, and the occurences there.
  Adressed to the States general of the United Netherlands,
  on the 28th July, 1649, with Secretary van Tienhoven's answer.
  Translated from a copy of the original Dutch Ms. by E. B.
  O'Callaghan. Albany, 1856. 4°
Beschrijvinghe van Virginia, Nieuw Nederlandt, Nieuw Engelandt,
  met d'eylanden Bermudes. Berbados en S. Christoffel. M. fig.
  Amsterdam J. Hartgers. 1651. 4°.
  *Description of Virginia, New Netherland, New England, and
  the islands of Bermudes, Barbadoes, and St. Christoffel.
  With illustrations, Amsterdam, J. Hartgers. 1651. 4°.*
Donck, Adr. van der, Beschrijvinge van Nieuw-Nederlant (gelijck
  het tegenwoordigh in staet is) enz. Den IIen druck. Met kaertje.
  Amsteldam. 1656. 4°.
  *Donck, Adr. van der, Description of New-Netherland (in its pres-
  ent state) etc. 2d edition, with Map, Amsteldam, 1656. 4°.*
't Verheerlickte Nederland door d'Herstelde Zee vaart ; klaerlijck
  voorgestelt, ontdeckt en aengewesen door manier van 't samen-
  sprekinge. . Waar inne sy luyden . . . . malkander voor-
  houden: 1. Den slechten en soberen toestant in Koophandel
  enz. . . . 2. Aenwijsende door wat middelen dit is te herstellen.
  . . . . 3. Hoë en op wat manier dese middelen moesten aange-
  vangen ende uytgevoert worden . . . . Gedruckt A°. 1659. 4°.
  *Netherland glorified by the restauration of commerce : clearly rep-
  resented, discovered and shown by manner of a dialogue. . . .
  In which those persons represent to each other : 1. The deplorable
  and meagre state of commerce, etc. 2. showing by what means
  this is to be restored. . . . 3. How and in what manner these
  means must be began and carried out. . . . Printed 1659. 4°.*
Otto Keyens kurtzer Entwurff von Nen-Niederland und Guajana.
  Einander entgegen gesetzt Umb den Unterscheid zwischen
  warmen und kalten Landen herausz zu bringen und zu weisen
  welche von beyden am füglichsten zu bewohnen am behende-

steu au zu bauen und den besten Nutzen geben mögen. Denen Patronen so da Colonien an zu legen gesonnen als auch denen Personen und Familien die ihr Vaterland zu vergessen sich bey dergleichen Bevölckerung nach fremden Küsten und Reichen gebrauchen laszen wollen. Aus dem Holländischen ins Hochteutsche versetzt durch T. R. C. S. C. S. Leipzig. Im Ritzschischen Buchladen. 1672. 4°.

Otto Keyen's short sketch of New-Netherland and Guyana compared together to obtain the difference between warm and cold countries and to show which of the two is the most pleasant to live in, the most capable of culture and can give the most profit to those patrons who think of establishing colonies there, as also for those persons and families who to forget their country, wish to find a similar in foreign lands and regions. Translated from Dutch into German by T. R. C. S. C. S. Leipzig, Ritzschischen Buchladen, 1672. 4°.

Kort Verhael van Nieuw-Nederlants Gelegentheit, Deughden, Natuerlijke Voorrechten, en bijzondere bequaemheidt ter bevolkingh: Mitsgaders eenige Requesten, Vertoogen, Deductien, enz. ten dien einden door eenige Liefhebbers ten verscheide tijden omtrent 't laetst van 't Jaer 1661. gepresenteert aen de . . . . Burgemeesteren dezer Stede, of der zelver . . . . Gecommitteerde, enz . . . Gedrukt in 't Jaer 1662. 4°.

Short Account of New Netherland's situation, virtues, natural privileges and peculiar fitness for population. Together with some requests, representations, deductions, etc. presented for that purpose by some amateurs at different times about the end of that year 1661, to the . . . Burgomasters of this city or to their deputies, etc. . . Printed in the year 1662.

Moulton, J. W., History of the State of New York. Part II (Novum Belgium). New York, 1826. 8°.

Alphen, D. F. van, Diss. hist. pol. inaug. de Novo Belgio colonia quondam nostratium. Lugd. Bat. 1838. 8°.

Young, Alex., Chronicles of the pilgrim fathers of the colony of Plymouth from 1602 to 1625. Now first collected from original records and contemporary printed documents and illustrated with notes. Boston 1841. 8°. W. engr.

Koenen, H. J., Pavonia. Eene bijdrage tot de kennis der voormalige Nederlandsche Koloniën.— In Bijdr. v. vaderl. geschied. V (1847).

Koenen, H. J., Pavonia. Contribution to the history of the former Dutch colonies.—In Bijdr. v. vaderl. geschied. V.—The colony Pavonia, in New Netherland, was founded by Mich. Panw in 1628.

Rees, O. van, Geschiedenis der Nederlandsche Volkplantingen in Noord-Amerika, beschouwd uit het oogpunt der koloniale politiek. Drie voorlezingen Tiel, 1855. 8°.

Rees, O. van, History of the dutch colonies in North America, with a view to colonial politics. Three lectures, Tiel, 1855. 8°.

Watts de Peyster, J., The Dutch at the North Pole and the Dutch in Maine. New York, 1857. 8°.

Bartlett, W. H., De Pelgrim-vaders of Puriteinen, stichters van Nieuw-Engeland. Naar 't Engelsch, met aanteekeningen en bijlagen door E. B. Swalue. Met een pl. Leiden 1859. 8°.

Bartlett, W. A. The Pilgrim fathers or Puritans, founders of New-England. From the English with notes and documents by E. B. Swalue, with pl. Leiden 1859. 8°.

Baird, Ch. W., Histoire des réfugiés Huguenots en Amerique. Traduit de l'anglais par MM. N. E. Meyer et de Richemond. Toulouse 1886. 8°.

Knickerbocker, [ps. of Wash. Irving.] A history of New-York from the beginning of the world to the end of the Dutch dynasty. New-York 1809. 2 vol. 8°.

Riker, J., Harlem (city of New York) its origin and early annals, with illustr. and maps. New York. 1881. 8°.

Conditien die door de Heeren Burgemeesteren der Stadt Amstelredam, volgens 't gemaeckte Accoordt met de West-Indische Comp ... gepresenteert werden aen alle de gene, die als Coloniers na Nieuw-Nederlandt willen vertrecken, etc. Amsterdam, J. Banning .... 1656. 4°.

> *Conditions which were offered by the Burgomasters of Amsterdam, to all starting as colonists for New Netherland, in accordance with the agreement made with the West India Company. Amsterdam J. Banning 1656. 4°.*

Octroy, van de ... Staten Generael, aeng. de Colonie op de Wilde Kust van America. Onder het beleyt van den Ridder Balthazar Gerbier Baron Douvily. Gedruckt in 't Jaer o. H. 1659. 8°.

> *Patent by the States General regarding the colony of the Wild Coast of America. Under the conduct of Chevalier Balthazar Gerbier Baron Douvily. Printed A. D. 1609. 4°.*

Kort en klaer ontwerp, dienende tot een onderling Accoort, om den arbeyd, onrust en moeijelijckheyt, van Alderley-handwercxluyden te verlichten door een onderlinge Compagnie ofte Volckplanting (onder de protectie vande. ... Staten Generael... en bysonder onder het guustig gesag van de Achtb. Magistraten der Stad Amstelredam) aen de Zuytrevier in Nieu-Neder-land op te rechten. ... t'Samen gestelt door Pieter Cornelisz Plockhoy van Zierck-zee .... Amsterdam, Otto Barentsz. Smient. Anno 1662. 4°.

> *A short and concise plan, intended as a mutual agreement for lessening the labour and difficulty of all kinds of artissans, by a common company or colony (under the protection of the States General. ... and specially under the favourable authority of the Worthshipful Magistracy of the city of Amsterdam) to be founded on the South River in New Netherland ; Composed by Pieter Cornelisz Plockhoyen of Zierikzee. Amsterdam, Otto Barendz. Smient. Anno 1662. 4°.*

Remonstrantie, Van de Bewinthebberen der Nederl. West-Indische Compagnie, aende d'Heeren Staten Generael over verscheydene specien van Tyrannye, ende gewelt, door de Engelsche in Nieuw-Nederlant, aen de Onderdanen van haer Hoogh. Mog. verrecht, en hoe sy reparatie, ende Justitie versoecken. Schidam .... P. Sanders. 1663. pl°.

> *Remonstrance of the Governors of the Dutch West-Indian Company to the States General, on several instances of tyranny and violence, committed by the English in New Netherland on the subjects of their H. M.; and how they beg for reparation and justice. Schidam P. Sanders. ... 1663. pl°.*

Naeder Klaghend Vertoogh aende ... Staten Generael, wegens de Bewindhebberen vande ... West-Iudische Comp., ter sake vande onwettelijcke, ende grouwelijcke proceduren der Engelsche in Nieu-Nederlant, met versoeck van hulp enz ... Beneffens een Clagh-brief aen de ... Staten van de Koopluyden te

Nantes in Vranckrijck, over . . . 't heffen vande vijftigh stuy-
vers per vat, etc. . . Nae de Copije, Anno 1664. 8°.
*Further address of complaint to the . . . States General ; on the
part of the Governors of the . . . W. I. Comp. respecting the
unlawful and scandalous proceedings of the English in New
Netherland with a petition for help etc. . . Together with a lam-
entation to the States from the Merchants of Nantes in France
on the levying of fifty pence a vat etc. From the copy A. D.
1664. 8°.*

Verdere Aenteyckeninge of Duplyque op seeckere Replyque van
den Heer George Downing, Extr. Envoyé van den Con. van
Groot Brittagne, jegens de Remarques van de Gedeputeerden
van de . . . . Staten Generael . . . . Ingestelt op des selfs inge-
diende Memorie van den 30 Dec. 1664. 's Gravenhage, Hillebrant
van Wouw . . . 1666. 4°.

Verdere Aenteyekeninge of Duplyque op seeckere Replyque van
den Heer George Downing, Extr. Envoyé van den Con. van
Groot Brittagne, jegens de Remarques van de Gedeputeerden
van de . . . . Staten Generaal . . . . Ingestelt op des selfs inge-
diende Memorie van den 30 Dec. 1664. Nae de Copie van
Hellebrandt (sic) van Wouw enz. 1666. 4°.
*Further remarks or duplique to a certain replique of Mr. G. Down-
ing, extra Envoyé from the King of Gr. Brittain, against the
remarks of the Deputies of the States-General on his memorial
presented the 20th of Dec. 1664. The Hague. Hill. v. Wouw
1666. 4°.*

Sommiere-Aenteyckeninge ende Deductie ingestelt bij de Gedeput.
van de . . . . Staten Generael . . . . op de lestingediende Memorie van den Heere G. Downing Extr. Envoyé van den Coningh
van Gr. Britt. (9 Febr.) . . . . In 's Gravenhage, in de Maent
Febr. 1665. 4°.
*Summary remarks and deductions made up by the Deputies of the
States General on the last memorial presented by Mr. G. Downing, extra Envoyé from the King of Gr. Brittain. 9 Febr. . . . .
The Hague . . . Febr. 1665. 4°.*

Remarques succinctes et Deduction faites par les Deputés des . . . .
Estats Goueraux . . . . sur le dernier Memoire du S. G. Douning
(9 Febr.) . . . . A la Haye, au Mois de Feurier 1665. 4°.

O'Callaghan, E. B., The register of New Netherland, 1626 to 1674.
Albany, 1865. 8°.

Bodel Nijenhuis, J. T., Jonas Michaëlius, Eerste Predikant der
Nederduitsche Hervormde gemeente op Manhattans of Nieuw-
Amsterdam, het later New-York, in Noord-Amerika.— Uit
Kerkhist. Archief I.
*Bodel Nijenhuis, J. T., Jonas Michaëlius, first Minister of the
dutch Reformed Congregation at New-Amsterdam. — From
Kerkhist. Archief I.
First publication of a very interesting letter of J. Michaëlius,
written from New-Amsterdam in 1628 and giving an account of
his arrival and his first adventures in his new home.*

Murphy, H. C., Jakob Steendam.— Noch vaster.— A memoir of the
first poet in New-Netherland, with his poems descriptive of the
Colony. Hague 1861. 8°.
With portrait of J. Steendam.

Steendam. J. J. Den Distelvink. Amsterdam 1649—50. 3 vol.
in 1 4°.
The Thistle-Finch.— Very rare collection of the poems of the First

3

18

Poet of New-Netherland. Steendam was minister of the Protestant Church in New-Amsterdam and afterwards governor of the Orphan-house at Batavia.

Year Book of the Holland Society of New-York 1886—87. By the Secretary (Geo. W. van Siclen). New-York 1887. W. pl. 4°.

Maaltijd van het Hollandsch Genootschap van New-York. Den 8en van Louwmaand 1886 . . in het Hotel Brunswick. M. portr. (New-York 1886). gr. 8°.
First Annual Dinner of the Holland Society of New-York. At the Brunswick Hotel on the 8th of January 1886. With portrait (New-York 1886). 8°. maj.

Map annexed to the memorial presented to the States-General of the United Provinces, on the 18th of August 1616 by Gerrit Jacobsz. Witsen, cum sociis, Directors of New Netherland; Copied in fac-simile from the original in the national Archives at the Hague . . . by E. Spanier. fol Chromolith.

Map of New Netherland According to the Charters granted by the States General, on the 11th October, 1614, and 3d Juni 1621. To illustrate Brodhead's History of the State of New York.
Penteekening van J. C. Wendel naar het oorspronkelijke uit Brodhead's Hist. of the State of N. Y. 1863.
Pendrawing made by J. C. Wendel from the original in Brodheads Hist. of the State of N. Y.

Kaart get.: Nova Anglia, Novum Belgium et Virginia. (Met karton get.: Bermuda majori mole expressa). fol. Kopergr.— Uit J. de Laet, Nieuwe wereldt. 2e druk 1630.
Map entitled: Nova Anglia, Novum Belgium et Virginia. fol. engraving ex J. de Laet, New World. 2d edit. 1630.

Novi Belgii Novaeque Angliae nec non partis Virginiae Tabula multus in locis emendata per Nicolaum Visscher. Kopergr.— Met gezicht op „Nieuw Amsterdam op 't Eyland Manhattans.
Engraving. With a view of „New Amsterdam on the Island Manhattans."

Kaart get.: Nova Belgica sive Nieuw Nederlandt. Kopergr. door E. Nieuwenhoff. Met gezicht op Nieuw Amsterdam op 't Eylant Manhattans.— Uit v. d. Donck Beschr. v. Nieuw Nederlandt. 2e druk 1657.
Map entitled: Nova Belgica sive Nieuw Nederlandt. Engraved by E. Nieuwenhoff. With a view of New Amsterdam on the Island of Manhattans.— Ex e. d. Donck Description of New Netherland. 2d edition. 1656.

Totius Neobelgii nova et accuratissimi tabula. Typis Joachim Ottens Amstelodami.— Met gezicht op „Nieuw-Amsterdam „onlangs Nieuw jorek genaamt, ende hernomen bij de Neder- „landers op den 24 Aug. 1673 eindelijk aan de Engelse weder afgestaan." Met allegorisch randwerk waarschijnlijk gegraveerd door Rom. de Hooghe.
Totius Neobelgii nova et accuratissima tabula. fol. engr. Typis Joachim Ottens Amstelodami.— With View of „New Amsterdam „formerly called New York and retaken by the Dutch Aug. 24th „1673. finally again surrendered to the English" With an allegorical border probably engraved by Rom. de Hooghe.

Nova Belgica et Anglia Nova. Amstelodami Apud G. Valk et P. Schenk. Kopergr. gekleurd.
Coloured engraving.

Nova Anglia, Novvm Belgivm et Virginia. Amstelodami. Johannes Janssonius Excudit. Kopergr. gekleurd.
Coloured engraving.

Belgii Novi, Angliae Novae, et partis Virginiae Novissima Delincatio. Prostant Amstelaedami apud Petrum Schenk et Gerardum Valk. (c. 1164—1674), fol. Kopergr. gekleurd.
fol. Coloured engraving.

Novi Belgii quod nunc Novi Jorck vocatur, Novae Angliae & Partis Virginiae accuratissima et novissima delineatio. fol. Kopergr.— Uit Ogilby, America 1671.
fol. engraving. ex Ogilby, America 1671.

Batavorum Coloniae, Occident: Indis Septentrionalis Americae implantatae. Kopergr. door P. Schenck (1690 à 1710) gekleurd. Met gezicht op Nieuw Amsterdam.
Engraved by P. Schenck (1690—1710), coloured. With a view of New Amsterdam.

Recens edita totius Novi Belgii, in America Septentrionalis siti, delineatio cura et sumtibus Tob. Conr. Lotteri. Sac. Caes. Maj. Geographi August. Vind. fol. Kopergr. gekl.— Met gezicht op : Neu Jorck sive Neu Amsterdam.
With a view of : Neu Jorck sive Neu Amsterdam.

A new Map of Virginia, Mary-Land and the Improved Parts of Pennsylvani & New-Jersey. Sold by Christopher Browne . . . London. fol.
Coloured engraving.

Kaart van Nieuw-Nederland, naar de kaarten van A. Roggeveen, A. Montanus en van de Vereenigde Staten van America door A. Arrow Smith, gevolgd door J. P. Bourgé. fol. Kopergr. J. P. Bourgé del. J. C. Bendorp sculp.
J. P. Bourgé's Map of New-Netherland from the maps by A. Roggeveen and A. Montanus and from A. Arrow Smith's map of the. U. S. of A. fol. engraving J. P. Bourgé del. J. C. Bendorp sculp.

Gezicht op Nieuw Amsterdam get.: Novum Amsterodamum. Kopergr.— Uit A. Montanus Beschr. v. Amerika 1670 (de vroegst afgebeelde toestand) — In Ogilby America 1671 komt hetzelfde prentje voor.
View of New Amsterdam entitled : Novum Amsterodamum. Engraving ex A. Montanus Beschr. v. Amerika 1670.—The oldest map known.—In Ogilby's America 1671 we find the same map.

Gezicht op Nieuw Amsterdam get.: Nieu Amsterdam, een stedeken in Noord Amerikaes Nieu Hollant, op het eilant Mankattan (sic).: namaels Nieu jork genaemt, toen het geraekte in 't gebiet der Engelschen.— Amstelodamum recens, postea Anglis illud possidentibus dictum Eboraeum novum, Hollandiae novae, id est Americae Mexicanae sive Septentrionalis oppidulum. Pet. Schenk. Amsteld. Kopergr.— Uit P. Schenk, Hecatompolis etc. 1702.
Prospect of New Amsterdam entitled : New Amsterdam, a small town in North America's New Holland, on the isle of Mankattan (sic), called New Jork after having been taken possession of by the English.—Amstelodamum recens, postea Anglis illud possidentibus dictum Eboracum Novum, Hollandiae novae, id est Americae Mexicanae sive septentrionalis oppidulum. Pet. Schenk. Amstelod.—Engraving ex P. Schenk. Hecatompolis etc. 1702.

JESSE DE FOREST,

FOUNDER OF NEW AMSTERDAM.

Jesse De Forest was born, probably between 1570 and 1580, at Avesnes, in Hainault, from Jean De Forest and Anne Maillard. His family evidently occupied a rather high social position; lack of documents renders it impossible to trace back its history till a questionable connection with the Sires De Forest, who had their castle near Le Chateau en Cambresis. But in the beginning of the XVIth century members of it were aldermen and jures of Avesnes and one of them married the daughter of the bailiff of the town. The parents of Jesse left Avesnes to escape religious persecution or from some other motive; they arrived at Leyden from Bergen op Zoom in 1603, but remained there only for a year and a half. In the last of 1604 they settled at Amsterdam. Their son Gerard returned to Leyden in 1605 and lived in that place as a dyer till his death in 1654.

Jesse did not accompany his parents to Holland. In 1601 he married, at Sedan, Marie du Clou; he is called in records of that time either a merchant or a dyer. In December, 1608, he was still living near Sedan; in February, 1615, one of his children was baptised at Leyden. Here he made his schemes of emigration, which he tried to realize in 1621. In July of that year he applied to the ambassador of England at the Hague, Sir Dudley Carleton; in the name of 56 Walloon families at Leyden, who wished to go to Virginia, and asked the permission and the assistance of the king of England. Dr. Baird in his history of the Huguenot refugees in America gives the address in extenso, with the names of the subscribers. The English government was very willing to permit the settlement in Virginia, but refused to give any assistance, and thus rendered the project impracticable. In 1622 Jesse sent a petition to the States General of the United Provinces; he speaks in it for himself and asks to be allowed to enroll Walloon families for emigration to the West Indies, as America was commonly called in that time. The permission was granted, a ship was equipped, and in March, 1623, the "New Netherland" left Holland with thirty Walloon families aboard. In May the mouth of the river Hudson was reached and the Dutch flag hoisted on the Isle of Manhattan. A Dutch sailor had passed a winter there and sometimes Dutch vessels had taken in fresh water. But the permanent occupation of the emplacement of New York dates from the arrival of the "New Netherland." In May, 1623, New Amsterdam was founded by one division of the colonists whilst another went on further and built the fort Orange, the origin of the present Albany.

The names of these pioneers are not known, but there is no doubt that Jesse De Forest was one of them, nay, occupied a first place amongst them. It was he who had written the address to England, and who was their advocate before the ambassador; he had organized the whole expedition as we see from his petition to the States; he was the leader as matter of course. Yet there has been discussion about his going to Manhattan. After his departure, his brother Gerard asked the burgomasters of Leyden the authorization to replace as a dyer his brother Jesse, lately gone to the West Indies. The authorization was given the 4th of January, 1624. This fact has been a source of confusion. The 21st and 22d of December, 1623, a naval expedition had sailed from Holland to Brazil in order to conquer this country. Mr. Riker in his History of Harlem (City of New York), 1881, thinks that the word *lately* must mean the expedition that started in December rather than that of March, eight months past. Mr. Baird in his above named work is not convinced by this reasoning, but has no other argument than the improbability of Jesse's not going with the colonists he had enrolled himself.

Luckily there is no doubt at all. The mistake is this, that only the date of the authorization is noticed; the petition was sent for advice to the guild the 21st of December; the word *lately* was written before that date, and so before the Brazilian expedition. There had been at that moment no other voyage to the West Indies *lately* than that of the "New Netherland" and we may be sure that Jesse De Forest belonged to it. If so, the fact that he prepared and organized the Walloon colonization of 1623 gives him a right to be called the founder of New Amsterdam.

Ch. M. DOZY.

think me conceited when I add that we had not expected it otherwise. Now that you have come from over the ocean in order to visit the land of your ancestors, you could not pass Leiden unnoticed. You are no strangers here, although you see our town for the first time in your lives. You all know Leiden and are familiar with the place it occupies in the history of the Netherlands.

" Our annual celebration of the Third of October has been one of the moving causes which awakened your interest in this part of the country and decided you to honor it with your visit. The glory of our University, dating from the time when your ancestors lived in this country, is dear to you as well as to every Hollander. But this is not all. The town you esteem as a seat of learning, and because of the courage of its citizens, is also a sacred spot for every inhabitant of your present fatherland.

" The Pilgrim Fathers enjoyed our hospitality and John Robinson's grave is situated within our city limits. That, therefore, which you represent in your persons, is closely related to this ancient town ; that is to say, New Netherlands and New England remember the soil which you still respect even when you do not regret its possession, while we do not wish to be behind you in admiration for the new empire.

" Ladies and Gentlemen : We appreciate your presence in our midst higher still because we felt that we could rely upon your coming here. Your time is precious, and I shall not rob you of much of it by a long speech. Allow me to say this, only, that from the bottom of my heart comes the wish that among the recollections you will carry homeward with you, the reminiscence of this day, spent in Leiden, may occupy a not unworthy place."

While the wine of honor was being served, Mr. Geo. W. Van Siclen was the spokesman of all in thanking for the cordial reception met with from the government of a city where many of their forefathers had resided or had found a shelter and refuge ; a city also world renowned and well known to them for its scientific eminence. Mr. Van Siclen thereupon introduced the Rev. Dr. J. H. Suydam, who delivered an oration.

In the mean time the crowd in front of the Stadhuis had dispersed, also the band, which was replaced by the playing of the chimes. The American brethren, all wearing an

11

orange badge and " geuzenpenning," viewed with interest
some of the other rooms in the City Hall, and then went in
groups to the historical Burg, which excited general interest
for its appearance, the recollections surrounding it, and the
fine view to be had of the town and its vicinity. Escorted
by their guides a walk was taken through the city, the
visitors being divided in sections, especially along the
Nieuwstraat, Hooglandsche, Kerkgracht, Haarlemmer-
straat and Mare. Meeting again in the Lakenhal, the
exhibition awaited them of everything relating to the
ancestors of our present guests. Dr. W. Pleyte, Conservator of the Municipal Museum, greeted them on the piazza
in a speech, which has been printed in the preface of the
catalogue of the collection, of which booklet charming
ladies presented a copy to each of the guests with a pretty
souvenir of their visit to Leiden, in the shape of a little map
representing Leiden in 1888, and New Amsterdam shortly
after its foundation. Thereupon they went to the next house,
where this collection was exhibited, and many a word of
praise was bestowed upon Dr. W. Pleyte the projector of it.
It is indeed a collection well worthy the examination of historians and others. It embraces objects from 300 years
back and ends with a photograph of Mr. Geo. W. Van Siclen,
the leader of our present visitors. The histories of past and
present are here combined.

The next step was to the famous Leiden University,
where the Senate Chamber and its splendid chimney, with
numerous coats of arms, and the portrait gallery of celebrated professors, who shed glory upon the University,
transformed the interest into admiration. Tired as the
visitors were, they were loath to leave this solemn, sacred
spot, so rich in reminiscences. The large auditorium also
attracted much attention. About the time, half-past one, that
the foreigners were due at the Van der Werff Park a large
crowd had collected there around the monument, the steps
of which were several times ascended; not only Van der
Werff's statue itself but also the representations on the
pedestal relating to the siege and relief of Leiden were carefully inspected. Long they tarried here, in small groups,
and it was long after the hour set for the déjeuner when
all were assembled in the Maison Wijtenburg. In the large
hall, in the midst of cheerful conversation, seated at small
tables, and under the sounds of the music of the infantry

regiment, commencing with the American national air, and continuing with "Piet Hein," the menu was discussed, which read:

BOUILLON.

SMALL PATTIES.

"HUTSPOT."

ROAST BEEF SANDWICHES.

HERRING AND WHITEBREAD.

DESSERT.

First, Mr. Brouwer had, in a few words, wished them a good appetite, whereupon Mr. Van Sielen quoted, in Dutch, the old saying: "Eet wat gaer is, drink wat klaer is, spreech wat waer is," after which, amid cheers, the déjeuner began. During the repast Mr. Brouwer spoke again, this time in Dutch:

"*Ladies and Gentlemen*," he said, "I feel the need of saying a few words in the name of the Third of October Association. I might commence with the words of Uriah Heep, one of Charles Dickens's creations, and say 'I am so very humble.' Yes, Leiden is a 'very humble' city. It is no Amsterdam or Rotterdam, and when these large cities precede us in a splendid reception to our trans-Atlantic brethren and sisters, Leiden takes a back seat in all humility. But when it comes to keeping alive the recollection of the glorious deeds of the forefathers; to strengthening the ties of fraternity; to showing that we feel that we are one in origin, one in principles, one in purpose; to proving how dear we hold our brethren and sisters, when it comes to that, Leiden does not intend to be behind. Then we do our very best, then we practise the old motto, 'In union there is strength,' and we plant a young shoot, saying to ourselves, 'At last the shoot becomes a tree.'

"With that conviction our forefathers waged the war against despotism and slavery of conscience, and they held their own till they knew themselves safe in the shade of that tree. The tree of liberty has blossomed anew. Has not your great historian, Motley, pointed out that the rebellion of the North American colonies against England found its prototype in our revolt against Spain? And the mother has not forgotten her offspring. Although the vast ocean separated her from her children, her example was an admonition to hold aloft the banner of freedom. Your sprout too became a tree, which excites our admiration, as the United States of North America. But as true children you, sons and daughters of the North American Republic, have not forgotten your mother. You have had the feeling of brothers and sisters of one family, and by means of the foundation of The Holland Society you have revived the feeling of consanguinity. You have been attracted towards the land of your fathers, and you have joined our Leiden Third of October Association, which wishes to keep green the memory of our great ancestors. Accept our thanks for these proofs of fraternal feeling. Ladies and gentlemen, I wish to drink to The Holland Society of New-York, the shoot which will become a tree; to the American Republic, the shoot which has become a tree; to the love for political and religious liberty, the tree that never withers but always produces new shoots, which become trees in their turn.

"Ladies and gentlemen.
"The Holland Society of New-York.
"The great American Republic.
"Liberty above all.
" 'A thing of beauty is a joy forever.' "

These words were cheered to the echo, and the toast drank in foaming beakers.

Mr. Van Sielen drank to the growth of the Third of October Association, which now regaled her guests with hutspot, which, he was forced to confess, tasted excellently. Leiden knows how to treat her guests, Leiden, the source of liberty.

The time had now come to continue the trip, fortified and refreshed. The last visit was to the club "Musis Sacrum," the entrance of which bore the legend "Homage to our American brethren"; the garden and hall were ornamented with Dutch, Orange, and American flags and pennants, which floated in the strong breeze. The members of "Musis," and their ladies, were present in large numbers. The staff of the National Guard had again offered its band of music to the Third of October Association Committee. On the veranda seats had been reserved for the guests.

While the American national air was being played they took their seats and the champagne was served.

Shortly afterwards Mr. J. J. van Masijk Huyser Van Reenen greeted the friends from the far West with a triple welcome to this spot devoted to social intercourse within the walls of Leiden, which occupies, as does the whole country, such glorious pages in history. No matter what differences exist in religious and political matters, when it comes to receiving strangers, all are united, especially when it concerns guests on whose breasts Orange is seen and in whose hearts love for Orange is felt. Mutual friendship is there; it is now fortified by a cordial glass and a heartfelt handshake. The speaker hoped that the American brethren might carry with them the pleasantest of recollections of their brief stay, as to the old Dutch hospitality. That this would be the case was evident from the cheers evoked by this speech, whereupon one of the members of the Leiden Corps of Students, Chevalier A. Roëll, in the name also of a few friends and as a token of their respect for the Hollando-Americans, offered to one of the lady guests a small silken American flag, with satin orange ribbons, mounted on a bamboo stick with ivory knob.

This courtesy caused an explosion; the guests commenced to sing a song composed on the way over; the cordial affectionate feeling increased; the music was accompanied when playing the national airs and the Io vivat, till the hour of departing came, only too soon, for the visit had only been brief.

The gentlemen and ladies, the latter with a fresh supply of bouquets which had been offered them on arriving, again entered the carriages which were to take them to the station. On the way the guests were again treated at the Minerva Club, this time to pure gin (or "oude klare"). The idea for this treat, and for that of the morning, originated with Chevalier Rudolph Six.

This delay came near causing them to be too late, and before all had alighted, the 4:37 train, which was to carry them back to Amsterdam, had arrived. Notwithstanding the large crowd and the great excitement, the measures taken by Mr. de Bruyn, the stationmaster, and by the police, insured the most perfect order. With many handshakings and words of thanks the train was reached. All great praise was given the committee of the Third of October Association for the splendid manner in which it had fulfilled its task.

When the train commenced to move, the departing guests, upon the initiative of Mr. Van Sielen, raised the cries: "Long live Leiden University!" "Long live the Third of October Association!" in Dutch, which, of course, was loudly applauded and caused great enthusisam among those on the platform.

MARKEN AND HOORN.

ON Tuesday, August 14, we were the guests of the City of Amsterdam for an excursion to the island of Marken and the old City of Hoorn. The steamer "William III." had been prepared for us, and on board, ready to receive us, were the burgomaster, some of the aldermen, the committee, and the high sheriff of Amsterdam, Count Westenberg, with many ladies of their families. The start was made in good time from the De Ruyter Kade, and the day was beautiful. As we left the harbor, the weeping tower, so beautifully described by De Amicis, was pointed out to us. We soon passed through the locks separating the harbor from the Zuider Zee, and after a sail of about two hours we arrived at the entrance of the harbor of Marken. Here we were obliged to take two smaller boats as our steamer was of too deep a draught to enter the harbor. As we approached the entrance nothing was to be seen but a long row of high piles; turning the point, however, and entering the little haven we dis-covered all the children of the island gathered at the end of the dock to give us a song of welcome. We quickly disembarked and were received by the burgo-master. We made a tour of inspection of the quaint

houses, the little church, and the old museum, and
were impressed by the quaintness and simplicity of
everything on the island. We seemed to have been
suddenly taken back some two hundred years or
more to the primitive days. Those of our party who
spoke the Dutch of the Mohawk and the Hudson,
here found a tongue like their own. The costumes
of the women and children were most picturesque,
and impressed us greatly. As nearly as the historian
can describe this costume, it is as follows: A cap
fitting closely around the head and inclosing all the
hair, except a curl on each side, is a distinctive feature. The body of the dress is a red and white
striped cotton waist, over this an embroidered
sleeveless bodice, while around the body is bound a
broad cotton belt. The petticoats are thick and
always number two, sometimes of different colors,
with an apron tied behind with double tapes. The
stockings are woolen, and all wear klompes. All the
women have yellow hair and blue eyes. The young
children up to the age of seven are dressed alike, except that the boys, to distinguish their sex, have a
little circular disk sewed at the apex of the cap.
After the boy is seven years old, he is dressed in a
jacket and knee-breeches of most enormous amplitude. The men wear the same costume as the older
boys, except that their hats are old-fashioned beavers
of a type that was probably worn 300 years ago. The
few men we saw were of an advanced age, as the
active male population of the island go off fishing on
Monday morning, not returning until Saturday night.
The houses are built on piers and arranged in rows;
little paths, raised high above the meadows, connect
the various groups of houses, as these meadows in

the wet season are covered with water. The houses
are small, some of them two stories in height, and
are most quaintly arranged and decorated with treasures in pottery and furniture which have come down
through many generations. The old women brought
out from their lockers their embroidered bodices, the
heirlooms of many years, and showed them with
great pride. Our pictoriographer made several successful pictures which are among the most interesting
of the expedition, but more than one mother refused
to have her child's picture taken, fearing that some
harm might come to it from the deadly instrument. The inhabitants received us with wonder, and
some of them were heard to exclaim, "Why, they are
white!" We visited these points of interest under
the guidance of the burgomaster, Mr. De Groot.
Many of the party thoroughly enjoyed the scrambles
by the children for the small coin thrown in the air;
the children, finding it an occasion of equal pleasure,
seemed loath to have us leave.

In due time we embarked on the tugs and were
transferred to our steamer. On our way to Hoorn a
bountiful luncheon was spread upon the deck of the
steamer, which was thoroughly enjoyed by all. Songs
and toasts prolonged the repast until Hoorn was in
sight. As we approached the city we could see an
enormous crowd filling the piers, and heard the band
of the National Guard playing our American national
airs. All Hoorn was covered with flags. We landed
at the water gate, and preceded by the band and by
the chief of police, Heer Terpstra, marched in procession through the enthusiastic crowd to the Town
Hall. Here Baron K. W. Van Dedem, the burgomaster, gave us a most excellent address of welcome

SOUVENIR

AANGEBODEN

den leden van de „HOLLAND SOCIETY" van New York,

bij hun bezoek te HOORN.

op DINSDAG 14 AUGUSTUS 1888,

door de Vereeniging „SAPPHO" te Hoorn.

Het Nederlandsche Volkslied.

Wien Neêrlandsch bloed in de aders vloeit,
  Van vreemde smetten vrij,
Wiens hart voer land en koning gloeit,
  Verheff' den zang als wij:
Hij stell' met ons, vereend van zin,
  Met onbeklemde borst,
Het godgevallig feestlied in
  Voor vaderland en vorst.

Bescherm, o God! bewaak den grond,
  Waarop onze adem gaat;
De plek, waar onze wieg op stond,
  Waar eens ons graf op staat.
Wij smeeken van uw vaderhand,
  Met diep geroerde borst,
Behoud voor 't lieve vaderland,
  Voor vaderland en vorst.

Dring' luid, van uit ons feestgedruisch,
  Die bee uw hemel in:
Bewaar den vorst, bewaar zijn huis
  En ons, zijn huisgezin.
Doe nog ons laatst, ons jongst gezang,
  Dien eigen wensch gestaad.
Bewaar, o God! den koning lang
  En 't lieve vaderland.

H. TOLLENS.   Muziek van J. W. WILMS.

DRUK VAN P. GEERTS, HOORN.

in English. He is a distinguished looking man, a member of the Upper House, and created a most favorable impression on all the visitors. In his address he gave a brief sketch of Hoorn's greatness in past centuries, and of the part the city took in the history of Holland. He acknowledged that the city of Hoorn of the present day was no longer the prominent city of which that history speaks, but it was far from being a "dead city," as some well-known author had wrongly termed it. He drew the attention of the guests to the many curiosities the city was able to show at the present time, and assured them that in hospitality Hoorn was never behind any other city in the Netherlands, so that nothing would be spared to make this brief visit as pleasant as possible.

Mr. Van Siclen, in a few well-chosen words, returned thanks in the name of the guests for the kind reception accorded them. A fine luncheon was served. The principal civic authorities were present. The glee club of the Sappho Society then sang some beautiful songs; the delightful singing of this Society can only be compared to that of the Mendelssohn Glee Club of New-York City; three couplets of the Dutch national hymn were also sung, and were in printed form presented to the visitors as a memento of the occasion. The Baron then presented to the Society an old jewel to be preserved in its archives, and this was received in behalf of the Society by the youngest visitor. We were afterwards taken to the West Frisian Museum, in the building formerly occupied by the old tribunals, and inspected the many curiosities and antiquities preserved there. Some of the party then took carriages, and went off under the

12

guidance of Mr. Van Akerlaken, member of the First Chamber, and Mr. A. Keurenaer, engineer of the "Water State," to inspect the elaborate system of dykes, while the rest of us took a walk through the principal streets, being particularly attracted by the houses whose fronts were adorned with stone-work representing a naval battle. These were erected in memory of the defeat of Bossu. We also were greatly interested in the Kermiss then in full vigor in the streets of the city; we inspected the booths and were much pleased with the puffejes and waffles. We went through the old cow gate, and through the grounds laid out on the site of the old walls, enjoying the beautiful evening and the fine views over the waters of this inland sea. At 6.30 we took a special train to return to Amsterdam. On our way we passed through Zaandam with its 400 windmills. In passing over the North Holland canal we were amazed to see a large ocean steamer apparently making her way through the fields. We were told she was just arriving from the East Indies, and on her way to Amsterdam. We arrived at our destination about 7.30. In the evening we attended, by special invitation, a concert at the De Hereeniging Club. We found a large building with spacious grounds around it, and here was a band stand occupied by an orchestra which gave us a most enjoyable programme, which is here inserted:

SOCIETEIT "DE HEREENIGING."

DINSDAG, 14 AUGUSTUS, 1888.

CONCERT DOOR DE ORKEST-VEREENIGING.

Kapelmeester, de Heer J. F. WEDEMEIJER.

PROGRAMMA.

In den tuin.

1e DEEL.

1. Jubiläums Marsch . . . . J. NESVADBA.
2. Ouverture, "Athalia" . . . . F. MENDELSSOHN.
3. Largo aus der Grosse Sonate, No. 7, L. VAN BEETHOVEN.
4. Fantaisie sur l'Opera "Le Cheval de Bronze" F. AUBER.

2e DEEL.

5. Ouverture, "Manschaft an Bord" . . . F. VON SUPPE.
6. Fantaisie sur l'Opera "Le Barbier de Seville" G. ROSSINI.
7. "Tausend und eine Nacht," Walzer . . . . J. STRAUSS.
8. Fantaisie aus der Operette "Der Bettelstudent"
MILLÖCKER.

In de Zaal.

1e DEEL.

1. Feest Marsch . . . . J. STRAUSS.
2. Ouverture, "Die Fingals Höhle" . . F. MENDELSSOHN.
3. Reverie, "Adagio" . . . . H. VIEUXTEMPS.
4. Potpourri sur des Airs Suisses . . . . . G. SCHRÖDER.

2e DEEL.

5. Ouverture, "Martha" . . . . F. VON FLOTOW.
6. Norturne pour Flute, Violin, et Cor . . . . F. DOPPLER.
7. "Wo die Citronen blüh'n," Walzer . . . . J. STRAUSS.
8. Fantaisie sur l'Opera "L'Étoile du Nord"
G. MEIJERBEER.

Aanvang 8 uur.

In these grounds the members with their families enjoy the music in the evening air and light refreshments are served, an example which seems worthy of imitation by American clubs.

DELFT AND THE HAGUE.

EARLY in the morning of Wednesday, the 15th August, we gathered at the station, being joined by our fellow-member, Senator C. P. Vedder of New-York, and his friend Senator Geo. Z. Irwin, and at 8.20 took the train for Delft. The ride was a short one, and we were soon at this historic place, great in its memorials of the past. Here we were met by the Hon. Levyssohn Norman, who most kindly guided us in person. We first viewed the statue of Hugo Grotius, the most distinguished of Dutch scholars, which was erected here to commemorate the fact that Delft was his birthplace. We then proceeded to the Nieuwe Kerk and gazed upon the magnificent monument erected in 1621 to the memory of William of Orange. The historian will not try to describe this most elaborate and beautiful piece of work, the finest of its kind in Holland, nor will he attempt to portray the emotions excited in the breasts of all the party as they looked upon the last resting place of the greatest man of his time, and one who alone with Washington deserves the warmest love and reverence of all lovers of liberty and humanity.

From the Nieuwe Kerk we proceeded to the Oude Kerk and saw the monuments of two of the great Dutch admirals; that of Old Tromp, who hoisted the broom to his masthead to show that he had swept

THE HOLLAND SOCIETY

OF

New-York.

A VISIT TO DELFT AND 'S-GRAVENHAGE

ON

Wednesday the 15th of August 1888.

D E L F T.

The Statue of HUGO GROTIUS.

The New Church. The tomb of WILLIAM THE SILENT.

The Old Church. The tombs of the admirals MAARTEN HARPERTSZOON TROMP AND PIET HEIN.

The Prinsenhof, residence of WILLIAM THE SILENT. The staircase on which he was shot the 10th of July, 1584.

Gemeenlandshuis of Delfland (front.)

Per steamtram via

RIJSWIJK (Peace of 1697)

TO

'S-GRAVENHAGE.

Statue of SPINOZA.

The Great Market place. Prinsengracht. The Townhall (16th century. Front) Gevangenpoort (old State-prison.) The DE WITTS.

Het Buitenhof (The outer Court.) The statue of King WILLIAM II.

Het Binnenhof (The inner Court.) The study of JAN DE WITT. The Spring in honor of Count WILLIAM II, Roman king, founder of 's-Gravenhage.

The Lower House.

The Grand Hall (front.)

OLDENBARNEVELD.

The Trèves Hall.

Het Plein. Statue of WILLIAM THE SILENT. The Houses of Amsterdam and Rotterdam (front). The Department of Justice. The new Pottery of 's-Gravenhage, ,, Rozenburg."

Het Mauritshuis. (Picture-gallery). REMBRANDT'S Anatomical Lesson. PAUL POTTER'S Steer.

Korte Vijverberg. The Municipal Museum. Lange Vijverberg. Kneuterdijk. Voorhout. Tournooiveld.

Luncheon.

The Theatre (front).

Het Voorhout. The Royal Library.

Het Noordeinde. The King's Palace (front.) Equestrian statue of WILLIAM THE SILENT.

De Zeestraat. The Panorama of Scheveningen by H. W. MESDAG ESQ. Reception by the painter himself.

De Laan van Meerdervoort. The studio and picture-gallery of H. W. MESDAG ESQ.

The Monument of 1813.

The Royal Bazar.

The Old Road to Scheveningen.

The house of the painter Mr. C. BISSCHOP (inside, style of the 16th century).

Scheveningen.

The New Road.

The Wood.

Het Huis ten Bosch (The Palace in the wood). Built in the middle of the 17th century by AMALIA VAN SOLMS, widow of Prince FREDERIC HENRY. The famous Orange Hall.

At 7 o'clock:

DINNER in the Bellevue Hôtel, Bezuidenhout.

In the evening:

CONCERT of the Philharmonic Society of Berlin at the Kurhaus (Scheveningen, steamtram).

CONCERT of the Royal Military Band of the „ Regiment Grenadiers and Jagers " at the Pavilion in the wood of the New or Literary Club. Introduction required.

Printed by MOUTON & Co. — The Hague.

the Channel, and that of Piet Hein, who captured the
Silver Fleet, an exploit even now commemorated in
the songs of our Society. We noticed with interest
the beautiful monument of a daughter of Philip Van
Marnix. From the church we went to the Prinsenhof, the residence of William the Silent, now con-
verted into a barrack. Here we looked upon the
stairway where, on the 10th July, 1584, the assassin
fired the fatal bullets, the marks of which still remain
upon the wall. From these somewhat sad memorials
of one of the greatest tragedies of Dutch history, we
turned with something of relief to the lighter pleasures of the Capitol. We embarked upon a steam
tram, gaily decorated with flags and bunting in honor
of the occasion, and were welcomed by the committee
from The Hague. Among the gentlemen who thus
received us were His Excellency Minister Roosevelt,
the Hon. H. D. Levyssohn Norman, Member of the
Second Chamber of the States General, Deputy of
Rotterdam, late Member of the Indian Council at
Batavia ; Count O. van Limburg Stirum ; Baron
van Heeckerentot Waliën; Hon. A. A. Vorsterman
van Oyen; the celebrated painter Israels ; Jonkheer
Teding van Berkout; Count van Hogendorp, and
others. On our way we passed through the station of Ryswyk where was concluded, in 1697, the
celebrated peace between England, France, Holland, Germany, and Spain. We arrived at The
Hague in due season and entered barouches for
a long drive through the principal parts of the city.
It would be difficult to note the many points of
interest which we visited, or to tell of the many
things we saw. Passing the statue of Spinoza we
drove through the great market-place and arrived at

the Town Hall, a most picturesque building of the
XVIth century. Thence we went to the old city
prison and viewed with interest the remarkable collection of the old instruments of torture, and realized
as never before the vivid descriptions of the terrors
of the Inquisition, and of the Spanish treatment of
the unfortunate Netherlanders. From thence to the
Buitenhof (the outer court) to the statue of King
William II.; thence to the Binnenhof (the inner
court), and were admitted as a special favor to the
study of Jan de Witt; then with a hurried view of
the old Hall of the Knights we passed to the Cham-
bers of the States General. We greatly admired the
beautiful Treves saloon with its elegant decorations.
From thence we went to the Maurits Huis, erected by
Prince John Maurice of Nassau, but now containing
the famous picture gallery of The Hague. Here of
course we saw the two world-famous pictures, the
Rembrandt "Lesson in Anatomy" and Paul Potter's
"Bull"; we also reveled in the beautiful examples of
Jan Steen, Gerard Dou, Adrian van Ostade, Adrian
van de Velde, and the other famous Dutch painters.
Thence we drove to the beautiful mansion of Levyssohn Norman, the deputy and representative of Rotterdam. The house is a square one, delightfully situated
near the park, and filled with objects of taste and
beauty. The entire arrangement and effect struck us
as very similar to the handsomest houses of our own
country. Here we were received by the deputy and
his charming wife, Madame Israels, and a few other
ladies and gentlemen. We partook of a bountiful
luncheon, served exquisitely, and among the courses
were several dishes prepared for their national origin
and significance. Among them we had the waffles of

Holland, which are almost identical with the waffles of America, though somewhat smaller and sweeter. We noted here a custom which seems universal in Holland, and which is yet characteristic of that country; at all private houses after meals the ladies are offered cologne at the conclusion of the feast. After a few moments spent in social intercourse, we again entered our carriages and were driven through many of the beautiful streets of the city to the Cyclorama of Scheveningen, where we were received by H. W. Mesdag, the distinguished artist, who showed us in person this the largest of his many beautiful works. Here we spent a very pleasant half hour, and from there went to his residence. In this beautiful mansion we were received by the artist and his artist-wife with extreme cordiality, and were amazed at the magnificence of the house, filled to overflowing with works of art and beauty. The entire third story is taken up by the studio, and here he has gathered some of the best specimens of the great modern painters, which with his own works constitute an enviable collection. In the rear of the house are spacious gardens, beautifully arranged, and altogether the visit was a most charming one. From thence we drove through the park, and on our way passed the imposing national monument built to commemorate the restoration of Dutch independence in 1813. One part of this monument had a particular interest to us from the fact that one of the three leaders of the rising of November, 1813, whose statues are grouped on the monument, was the grandfather of one of the party who acted as our hosts for this day, the Count van Limburg Stirum. We paused for a few moments to visit a bazaar filled with every possible object to

attract the tourist, and then stopped at the house
of Mr. C. Bisschop, another of the distinguished
artists of whom Holland has every right to be proud.
We were received by the courtly and kind old gentleman and his charming wife with cordiality, and
made welcome to the house. This was one of the
most unique pleasures we enjoyed in Holland. The
house is a reproduction of the style of the XVIth
century, and is furnished completely with articles of
that time. Here were quaint furniture, rare books
(a beautiful old edition of Kats in the place of honor),
exquisite tapestry, everything to attract and please
the antiquarian and artist, and we lingered long over
its many beauties. Our time had passed so rapidly
that we found evening was approaching and we
could only drive hurriedly through the beauties of
Scheveningen, and scarcely caught more than a
glance of this most noted of the seashore resorts of
Europe, and the most beautiful summer resort in
Holland. Returning by the new road we drove
through the celebrated wood where for hundreds of
years the Counts of Holland pursued their game in
its recesses. We at length came to the beautiful
House in the Wood, a royal villa built in the mid
dle of the XVIIth century by Amalia van Solms, the
widow of Prince Frederick Henry. The historian
again cannot attempt to describe the beauties of this
place, the favorite retreat of the Kings of Holland,
and can only say that each room is perfect in itself,
illustrating either some particular country, or some
particular epoch, representing gifts to the House of
Orange from most of the potentates of the world.
We saw the famous Orange Hall, filled with paintings by artists of the school of Rubens. The walls

THE HOLLAND SOCIETY OF NEW YORK

EENDRAGHT MAECKT MACHT GEEN ZORG VOOR MORGEN

13 Août — 1888.

MENU

Printanier ——— Potages ——— à la Royale.

1º Service.

Saumon S.ce Hollandaise et
Génévoise.
Filet de Bœuf à la Bohémiennes
Estomacs de Volaille à la financière.
Cotelettes de Mouton à la Maréchal aux petits Pois.
Riz de Veau à la St Aout.
Mayonnaise de filets de Soles.

2º Service.

Salade ——— Poulardes roties ——— Salade.
Compôte ——— Canetons ——— Compôte.

Entremots

Fonds d'artichauds à l'Espagnole.
Haricots verts à l'Anglaise.
Turban d'Ananas.
Charlotte glacée.
Pièces Montées.

Dessert.

HÔTEL DE BELLEVUE - LA HAYE

C.J. van Velsen, Propʳ

are about fifty feet in height, and rich in color. As
a special favor we were shown the private apartments of the Queen, and the historian took great
pleasure in recalling to the matron in charge the
fact that two years before he had obtained from her
the same privilege by an exhibition of his certificate
of membership in The Holland Society and a pathetic
appeal to her patriotism. Thence, as the sun was
sinking, we returned to our hotel, the Bellevue, and
there in the evening invited to dine with us the committee who had entertained us during the day, and
the distinguished artists who had so graciously shown
us their hospitality. The dinner was somewhat informal in character, although several speeches were
made. The most apparent hit of the evening was
made by Deputy Levyssohn Norman, when he claimed
that the word "Yankee" came from the Dutch, its
derivation being "Jantje Man," Jantje meaning kind.
After dinner we were invited to a concert, at the
pavilion in the wood belonging to the New or Literary Club, by the superb Royal Military Band of the
regiment of Grenadiers and Jagers. Most of the
members accepted the invitation, and the party were
given the distinguished courtesy of having the American national hymn played by the orchestra as the
party entered the house, the audience standing while
they did so, this being an honor of the most distinguished kind and generally reserved for royalty alone.
Some few of us with some of our hosts afterwards
proceeded to the spacious club-house of the Litteraire
Societeit on the Plein, where we spent a rather late
and social hour in conversation and interchange of
sentiment. Towards the close of the session we were
rather astonished to see one of our worthy dominies

13

enter. Our good friend only served, however, to
enliven our discourse and to show that he was determined to see all the best of Holland in a spirit that
could well be emulated by many of his cloth.

Brielle, Dordrecht, and Rotterdam.

EARLY in the morning of Thursday, August 16,
we left The Hague by rail for Rotterdam, arriving
at the latter place about 9.30, where we were met
by the Rotterdam reception committee, Mr. J. V.
Wierdsma, Jhr. Otto Rewehlin, and Mr. Hendrik P.
N. Muller, Hzn, "het uitvoerend comitté," and taken
to the North Island, and embarked on the steamer
"Merwede." This was kindly offered for the occasion
by Mr. Smit, one of the leading firm of shipbuilders,
who are the grandchildren of the original founder of
the business. The steamer was a fine one and the sail
down the Maas very interesting. We were accompanied by the band of the Chasseurs, who added much
to the pleasure of the occasion. Everywhere all the
vessels we passed saluted us, and our small cannon
gave notice of our coming to every point. Our first
landing was at the old town of Brielle, a place that
bears the same relation to the great struggle for Dutch
independence that the little village of Lexington does
to the American Revolution; for here it was that the
water-beggars, by a sudden descent, captured the
town, April 1, 1572, and afforded a nucleus for the
first armed resistance to the Spaniards. The city is
now small and of but little pretense to activity or
commerce, and it is chiefly interesting for its part in
the glorious history of the past. As we approached

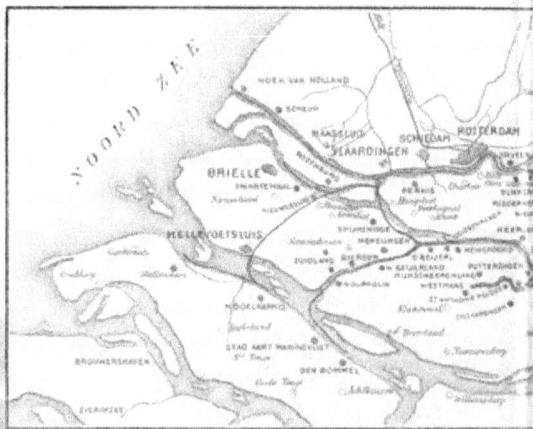

RIVER EXC

offered to

Holland Society

on **THURSDAY** AUGUS

from Rotterdam to Brielle, Dordrec

SALON-STEAMER

Messᴿˢ. Fop S

EERGAM

HEUKELUM SPEREN

ZALT BOMMEL

GUDERICHEM

POEDEROUEK   AALST

VEEN

ARKBURG   HCERMESTONT

HEUSDEN

RIVER EXCURSION.

offered to the

Holland Society of New-York

on THURSDAY AUGUST 16th 1888

from Rotterdam to Brielle, Dordrecht and back to Rotterdam.

SALON-STEAMER "MERWEDE I."

Mess.rs Fop Smit & Co.

the dock at the end of a long causeway built of earth, and with a roadway lined on both sides with trees, we found almost the entire population of the place awaiting us. Before we landed, copies of the "Week Blad," the newspaper of the place, containing a special welcome to our Society were placed in our hands. This is so quaint, and at the same time so hearty in its welcome, that it is here reproduced:

TO THE MEMBERS OF THE HOLLAND SOCIETY OF NEW-YORK.

The old City of Brielle, pride on the honnour to may receive in her walls the noble descendants of the Dutch farmers, who settled theirselves two hundred and fifty years ago in the far country of North America, brings them the most gracefull wellcome.

In accord to the sublime truth of the proverb of the city-weapon "Libertatis Primitiæ," she feels allways a sympathetical attraction to the citizens of a free land and still too more if there consists a not forgotten relation of blood between them and herself.

Which the greatest reverence she turns her eyes to the land of Washington, Lincoln, Eddison, Parker, Motley, and Sheridan and remembers herself thankfull the excellent services, proved by this noble democratical people to the sake of humanity and science, mercatury and industry, egality, freedom, and fraternity.

She prays also the members of The Holland Society to agree the assertainment of this high affection and to beheld the remembrance of their old fatherland and the city of Brielle, when they would be returned to their good and free land.

As we landed and formed in procession the crowd accompanied us on our way. The delight of the children in the music could well be appreciated by us when we were informed that all the children there

under the age of twelve years had never before heard
a band. At first we were objects of wondering interest, and the remarks of the bystanders were sometimes amusing, as when one of them was heard to
exclaim after looking upon the party, "Why, they
don't wear feathers!" But soon the curiosity of the
younger female portion gave way to a warmer feeling,
and in a short time every member of the party who
was under fifty years of age, and who was not accompanied by a lady, was surrounded by at least four
blushing, chattering, demonstrative damsels, who did
their best to entertain us with flattering remarks in
various tongues, and who accompanied us to every
point we went. When shut out by the police they
waited at the gate until we reappeared, and then took
up the line of march as before. We first went to the
old church of St Catharina and hastily inspected the
tombs and ornaments; then to the Merula Orphan
House, erected in the year 1553 by Angelus Merula,
a martyr of the reformation in 1557. This was
founded as an orphan asylum for the children of
sailors and is still maintained for the same purpose.
The orphans wear the quaint costume originally designed by the founder. Here we had a touching instance of the care and thought bestowed everywhere
upon our welcome. When we had all gathered
within the small hall of the institution, the orphans,
some twenty in number, were arranged around the
melodeon, and under the guidance of their venerable director sang the Star Spangled Banner in English, ending with one verse of the Dutch national
hymn. From there we went to the general orphan
asylum called the Geuzengesticht. This is of modern
construction and is for the orphans of the entire

DIPLOMA

VOOR

de "Holland Society" te New-York,

ALS EERELID

der Vereeniging tot Opvoeding en Verzorging van Weezen of Nalatenen in het

Nationaal Weezengesticht "Wilhelmus van Nassauw" te Brielle,

op 1 April 1872 wezen als een Gedenksof aan de verlossing uit de handen der Spanjaarden, door van het liefdadige Volk en het op indien onderhouden door het liefdadige Volk.

UITGEREIKT

bij gelegenheid van het door de leden van de Stichting gebracht bezoek.

Brielle, 16 Augustus 1895.

Namens Bestuurderen,

ARTICLE 1 (abbreviated).

It is the aim of the Association to provide for Sailors' Orphans, and for other helpless ones, so far as means and circumstances allow it.

ARTICLE 2 (abbreviated).

The Association is in favor of all education given in the Asylum being solely and exclusively founded upon the Reformed principles.

DIPLOMA

FOR

THE HOLLAND SOCIETY OF NEW-YORK

AS

HONORARY MEMBER

of the Association for the Receiving of and Providing for Orphans and Helpless Ones in the

NATIONAL GEUZEN ASYLUM "WILHELMUS VAN NASSAUER" AT BRIELLE.

Erected on April 1, 1872, as a Monument to the deliverance out of the hands of the Spaniards. A gift *from* the Benevolent Nation, and sustained till now *by* the Benevolent Nation.

AWARDED

on the occasion of the visit paid to the Asylum by the Members.

(W.S.) J. VERMEULEN.

President of the Board of Regents

BRIELLE, August 16, 1888.

community. Here the children sang for us an original
ode of welcome prepared for the occasion, which is
here inserted:

*Welkomstgroet aan onze Amerikaansche Stamverwanten, Leden
der "Holland Society," Bij hun bezoek aan het genzenge-
stight. "Wilhelmus van Nassauen" te Brielle.*

Hun welmeenend toegezongen door de in die Stichting
verpleegd wordende Weezen en arme Verlatenen.

(Melodie: "Wilhelmuus van Nassauen.")

Weest welkom, Stamgenooten
 Van't Volk, dat door Gods hand
Zoo ruim is beweldadigd:
 Het volk van Nederland.
Weest welkom in het Weeshuis,
 Dat mag ten teeken staan
Van's Heeren zoo doorluchte
 En groote wonderdaân.

Weest welkom, roepen w'allen
 Uit éénen mond U toe;
Dat God Zijn vriendlijk aanschijn
 Voor U steeds lichten doe,
Dat boven wensch en bede
 't U en de Uwen gâ;
En G' onzer moogt gedenken
 Ook in Amerika.

Ons: arme ouderloozen
 En kindren, aan den dijk
Verlaten eenmaal staande,
 Verhoogd dus uit het slijk.
Ons, voor wie God de Heere
 Een plaats hier heft bereid,
Alwaar we moeten leven
 Van de liefdadigheid.

Brielle, 16 Augustus, 1888.   P. J. B.

Here one of our party found a very sweet-looking
orphan of the same name as his own, and the little

girl was made happy by a large sized gold coin with which to remember her namesake from America. Time was passing and we were compelled to form our line and proceed to the steamer. We were accompanied on our way by our escort of damsels, and although sorry to part from them were forced to bid them farewell at the gang-plank of the steamer.

After we left Brielle, we proceeded up the south branch of the Maas to Dordrecht. Between Brielle and Dordrecht an elegant luncheon was served in the saloon of the steamer. The menu cards were beautifully gotten up, and each one contained in colors a figure from one of the striking paintings of Franz Hals. The menu is here inserted to give some slight idea of the good things which we had in Holland.

HOLLAND SOCIETY OF NEW-YORK.

TWEEDE ONTBIJT. ROTTERDAM, 16 AUGUSTUS, 1888.

Vleeschnat.	*Wijnen.*
Geroerde Eieren met Truffels.	Oude Marsala.
	Bleeke Sherry.
Gebakken Tong met Colbert Saus.	St. Julien.
	Champagne Mumm Extra Dry.
Gesneden Ossenhaas met geroosterd Brood.	Champagne Louis Roederer.
Gebraden Hoenders.	
Gestoofde Vruchten.	
Sla met Ei.	
Maarschalkpodding.	
Vruchten.	
Nagerecht.	

We were pleased to recognize in the attendants the stewards from the steamer "Amsterdam," and it seemed like old times to be greeted by their familiar voices, and to receive their cheerful services. In due time we reached Dordrecht, about 3.30 in the afternoon. On the dock carriages were waiting and we took a rapid drive around the city. Here, as everywhere else, the entire populace turned out to do us honor, and the streets were gaily decorated. We drove to the Groote Kerk, an immense Gothic edifice of the XIVth century. Here we admired the brass screen, the marble pulpit, and the fine old oaken carved work of the choir stalls, the most important work of the kind in Holland. We were shown with pride the gold and silver communion service. In the church we were welcomed by Mr. H. Hoyer in behalf of the people of Dordrecht.

He welcomed the visitors most heartily, and expressed regret, in the name of the people of Dordrecht, that the shortness of their visit to that city would not enable him to show them more of the attractions of the place; but, remembering the words of the American poet, Longfellow, that our life must consist of deeds, it was truly a fact that the American visitors made use of every minute at their disposal to take personal notice of and to observe everything of interest they met with on their way.

Het Nieuws van den Dag, of Saturday, August 18, 1888, quoted as follows:

Referring to the great and general kindness shown to the tourists on their trip, and which was in smaller localities more remarkable even than in the great capital, Amsterdam, the *Nieuwe Rotterdamsche Courant* remarks as follows: "Here again, [at Dordrecht], many people were in the streets, and the visitors while driving past were freely saluted by the waving of hats, hands, and handkerchiefs. The masses were entirely conscious of

what was meant by this train of open carriages, filled
with tourists. Somehow it had penetrated the minds of
the multitude that from far over the sea strange men and
women had come to visit the land of their forefathers. That
these strangers all, without exception, wore orange badges
did the rest. That wearing of orange caught the popular
fancy. It caused many hands, rough as well as gloved ones,
to touch the hats. Our people are generally not so quick
at saluting people in open carriages."

When we left Dordrecht it was raining, the only
shower we had during our stay in Holland. This
did not last long, and we soon had an opportunity to
view on both sides of the river the enormous ship-
building establishments, lining both banks for miles,
and we were impressed with their extent. We were
told by Mr. Smit that the preceding year they had
built quite a number of small iron vessels for England, and that the entire commercial navy of Holland
was being rapidly changed from wood to iron.

We reached Rotterdam about six in the evening,
and drove in open carriages along the famous Boompjes, and through many of the fine streets to the Zoölogical Gardens. Although our time was so short,
we were convinced of the commercial importance of
Rotterdam, and of the wealth and taste of its citizens
as shown in their houses and gardens. The Zoo,
although not so large nor so important a collection
as the one at Amsterdam, is still of much interest.
The large building in the gardens is a fine edifice.
Here in the reception-room we were presented to the
burgomaster and other dignitaries, and shortly after
were escorted to the dining-room, a large room beautifully decorated. Here the most elaborate banquet
given us while in Holland was served. A fine
orchestra hidden behind a bank of flowers played

between the courses, and the entertainment was in every way a delightful one. The menu is here presented :

MAALTIJD

TER EERE DER HOLLAND SOCIETY OF NEW-YORK.

ROTTERDAM, 16 AUGUSTUS, 1888.

Spijslijst.	*Wijnen.*
Koninginnesoep.	Bleeke Sherry.
Gehakt Kippenvleesch in Korst.	Sauternes Wijn.
	Chateau de Cantemerle, 1877.
Zalm met Hollandsche Saus.	Marquis de Terme Margaux, 1878.
Ossenhaas met Groenten.	
Kalfslappen, Pompadourstijl.	Bourgogne Chambertin.
	Rudesheimer Berg, 1857.
Kippenpastei, Toulousestijl.	Champagne Mumm Extra Dry.
Kalfszwezerik.	
Artisjokken met Saus.	Champagne Louis Roederer.
Gebraden Snippen.	
Gestoofde Vruchten.	
Versche Kreeft.	
Sla.	
Maria Theresia Podding.	
Ijs.	
Vruchten.	
Nagerecht.	

One striking feature of the repast was the fish course. When the time had arrived, the head waiter entered bearing on uplifted arms an enormous platter whereon lay in royal splendor a forty-pound Dutch salmon, beautifully decorated. This was carried in a sort of triumphant procession up and down the length of the tables, and then served, to the delight of the guests. There was one departure from the

14

usual course of procedure, made necessary by the
fact that we were to take a special train at 11, and it
was feared that time would not allow proper attention being given to the toasts. Hence the first toast
was introduced after the first course, and this was
followed until the end of the dinner. The historian
cannot attempt to give more than a summary of
some of the principal speeches.

The Burgomaster was the first one who held up his
glass as a toast to the welfare of His Majesty the
King of the Netherlands, coupled with the President
of the United States. He was followed by a toast
from Mr. J. Visser, Vice-Consul of the United States,
who spoke as follows:

When claiming the honor to answer the honorable
burgomeester, I do so in my official quality as vice-
consul of the United States, and must in the first
place thank the honorable speaker for his toast in
favor of the President of the United States. I am
only sorry that this task I fulfil in consequence of
the United States minister, Mr. Roosevelt, being
absent, which absence his Excellency has been compelled to by personal matters, and which he very
much regrets as well as no doubt we all do, but
nevertheless, ladies and gentlemen, his Excellency
authorized me and requested me, in answering the
kind words of the burgomeester of Rotterdam, to add
in name of his Excellency a frank expression of the
strong friendliness of feeling which exists in the
United States towards the Netherlands.

His Excellency wished to have declared that there
are still residing in America many persons of Dutch
descent, especially is this the case in the neighborhood of New-York, who cherish the memory and
traditions of their ancestors with warmth and sincere
appreciation.

His Excellency further states that it is due to these citizens, a portion of whom are here on a visit to the land of their ancestors, that America has throughout its length and breadth come of late to a proper understanding of the great obligations it owes to Holland. The late Governor Seymour, one of the most distinguished of public citizens, published a pamphlet showing that without the sturdy honesty of the Dutch character and its fairness of treatment of the Indian tribes the American Republic would never have existed. This Governor Seymour also, in another production, traced the roots of much of the American laws to Dutch origin. The American people, his Excellency declares, recognize in free schools and free worship an outcropping of the teachings of Holland. It was one of the eminent American writers who first gave to the English language a true history of the glories and greatness of the fatherland. No words, his Excellency says, could exaggerate the sincere respect and hearty good-will which exist in America towards the country which its great-grandchildren are now revisiting with feelings akin to reverence, and his Excellency is sure all will join him in the confident hope that these kindly relations will never be disturbed.

Ladies and gentlemen, I have transmitted this as it has been given me to understand by his Excellency, Mr. Roosevelt, and, in finishing, I personally do not hesitate to invite you all to drink with me the continuance of the friendly feelings between the United States and the Netherlands, and that this may be more and more strengthened by the peaceful development of commercial enterprise in both countries.

Mr. J. V. Wierdsma, Director of the Netherlands-American Steam Navigation Company, responded to the toast by paying warm homage to Mr. Roosevelt, in whose person he recognized one of the most worthy bearers of a Netherlands name in foreign lands, also one of the noble founders of The Holland Society, and a man whose talent and amiable character give evidence of his special fitness for representing America in Holland. The applause with which these words were received proved that the American guests quite agreed with the speaker.

Mr. Martin Mees, a member of the reception committee, Vice-President of the Chamber of Commerce, and President of the Board of Directors of the Netherlands-American Steam Navigation Company, then addressed them, as follows:

Honorable Gentlemen:

I should like, in my double capacity, to express our satisfaction that the honorable members of The Holland Society did us the pleasure of visiting Rotterdam. It is extremely gratifying to observe that the descendants of our fellow-countrymen, who left our country two centuries ago, wished to see Holland. The honorable members of The Holland Society will have observed that we are somewhat proud of our history. When your ancestors left this country Holland was at her culminating point; she was foremost in trade and commerce, compared with other countries. We remember with pride the time when, after an unsuccessful attempt to find a new way to India, daring and clever men like Moucheron and others induced the East India Company to send Captain Hudson with the vessel *Half Moon* to explore the land that was discovered in the West Indies; when, after the discovery of the way round the Cape of Good Hope, private merchants brought together capital, and did, with great risks, send out vessels to trade with the nations in East India. Of course a small country like Holland could not long retain the command of the sea. It is, moreover, a recognized fact that riches work frequently enervation;

and the members of The Holland Society, when passing by the fine old houses on the Kaizersgracht and Heerengracht at Amsterdam, will have seen the proof of the enormous profits made by our ancestors. But those fellow-countrymen who did emigrate at that time to New Amsterdam did prove that the energy of the Dutchman revives at any favorable opportunity. We are accustomed to call the United States the *New World*, and a new world it is, with its fertile soil, containing within its boundaries all climates, producing almost everything that man can desire. Planted in *that* soil the Dutch tree did grow in a way that astonished the whole civilized world. But in the best soil a sick tree cannot grow. What your countrymen, Members of The Holland Society, did achieve, not only in commerce and manufacturing, but also in science and art, is the best proof of the excellent moral and intellectual qualities you possess. We are very much obliged for your giving us the opportunity to make your acquaintance, and to show you our country.

An old rhyme, attributed to George Canning, says:

In matters of commerce, the fault of the Dutch
Is giving too little and asking too much.

I trust that you will not have got this impression by your visit here. We wish you prosperity in your families; we hope and trust that the United States will thrive well. Allow me to end with the wishes of your poet Longfellow:

Sail on, O Union, strong and great! * * *
Our hearts, our hopes, are all with thee.

This was followed by a short address from Mr. Van Siclen, especially devoted to thanking the committee for the hospitality the members of The Holland Society had received in the Fatherland. It was true that the descendants of Holland residing in America had lost the use of the mother tongue, but the love for the Motherland remained in the home where their ancestors founded the New Netherlands. The kindness bestowed upon them in that Motherland would certainly be welcome to the many who bear Dutch names, and who are to be found in nearly every city and village of the United States — Dutch names which are honored everywhere. He had observed to his great satisfaction the increasing welfare of Rotterdam; and the growth of the city and her commerce at this moment impressed him so deeply, that he felt that the interest taken in this progress should be expressed by a more eloquent speaker than himself — the Rev. Dr. Elmendorf.

The very eloquent little speech of Dr. Elmendorf was as follows :'

Mr. Burgomaster, Ladies and Gentlemen:

Our most worthy and esteemed Secretary, Van Sielen, with tender appreciation of the deeper meaning of things,— which to common natures seem commonplace,— again and again in conversation has characterized the excursion of The Holland Society of New-York to Holland as a poem.

A poem it truly is, and like many other great poems it is being lived before it is written.

The things, the accurate descriptions of which, by and by, will seem to others extravagant creations of a too excited fancy, are literally entering into the daily experience of us all.

Whatever may have been the cause or character of the *inception* of this excursion, when it came to its birth it was found to be vital with the best inspirations of filial reverence and affection. All constituting our company only need to tread the localities, and look upon the mementoes of those sublime events which should make real to our apprehension what has been so familiar to our knowledge, in order to make our souls susceptible to their full historic power.

So the heroic elements of our poem were assured. We are to know and feel, henceforth, as we never have before, the transcendent meaning of those marvelous demonstrations of patriotism, piety, and philanthropy, which made Holland preëminently the parent and the perpetual exemplifier of these divine principles.

But whence should come the touch which would reach and stir to its depths our poetic sensibility, and cause a stream of pure and true and ennobling emotion to break forth and flow with increasing volume ?

The answer came in the look, the words, the grasp of the first greeting of our brethren here ! And every hour since, not only an exhaustless generosity, but a masterly ingenuity of hospitality, has taxed itself to the utmost to emphasize that welcome and make our enjoyment perfect.

You all know the words and their authority : " As in water face answers to face, so the heart of man to man."

An old writer has said : "If you would make me weep, you must first weep yourself." You, indeed, have not wept, brethren of Holland, nor have you made us weep. But you have so illustrated the principle and truth stated, that we find *our* love and longing in the revelations and as the reflections of *your own*. So we know the meaning of the poem you have evoked, and while we cannot translate it into spoken words, the beauty and sweetness of its rhythm shall go singing on in our hearts while they have life enough left to throb. And if you would know just how this feels, you must come to America, and let us kindle a new and noble joy for you, as you have kindled ours by the glow of genuine fraternal affection.

Mr. Burgomaster and brethren, let me offer my closing sentiment in words as fervent to-night as they are familiar:

> God bless your native land,
> Firm may she ever stand,
>   Thro' storm and night;
> When the wild tempests rave,
> Ruler of wind and wave,
> Do thou this country save,
>   By thy great might.

He was followed by Mr. Hendr. P. N. Müller, Hzn., who proposed a toast in honor of the ladies. In his remarks he said: It was one of the characteristics of the Netherlanders as well as of the Americans — which the latter have perhaps inherited from their Dutch forefathers — that they have so great a regard for the fair sex. He alluded to the fact that it was very likely that the Netherlands would in the course of time be governed by a member of the weaker sex, the beautiful child of the king, and the pride and love of the whole nation. He alluded also to the friendship which had increased more and more between the sons and the descendants of Dutch blood, just as the Boers in South Africa, who plucked the British lion by the beard, are now on terms of friendship with the Fatherland. He closed his speech by remarking that, considering women govern the world, he found it a pleasant duty to drink to the health of the ladies present. The Rev. Dr. Suydam added another toast here, and drank to the health of Princess Wilhelmina, the daughter of the lawful monarch of this grand little country. Mr. Van Siclen here read a telegram just received, as follows:

PRINCESS WILHELMINA.

VISIT

of the

Holland Society of New-York

to Rotterdam

in August 1888.

Offered

to the Visitors

by the

Committee.

ROTTERDAM — HOLLAND.

Lat. 51° 55′ N. — Longt. 4° 30′ E.

DISTANCE FROM SEA 18 Eng. Miles.

POPULATION nearly 200,000.

TRADE.

Import. GRAIN, COALS, ORES, MANUFACTURES AND MACHINERIES OF ALL KINDS. SUGAR, COFFEE, TOBACCO, RICE, PETROLEUM, COTTON, RAGS, GUANO, AFRICAN PRODUCES, ETC.

Export. MANUFACTURED GOODS, SUGAR, GIN, CATTLE, SHEEP, PIGS, HORSES, PROVISIONS, FRUIT, VEGETABLES, CHEESE, BUTTER, ETC.

Rotterdam is one of the cheapest and certainly the most important port on the continent, through its connection with the Rhine; the river Maas being the only direct river-communication from the Rhine to the North Sea.

PORTCHARGES ROTTERDAM: Harbourdues $1\frac{6}{10}$ d. (about 3 Am. Cents) per ton. No Tonnage or Light-dues; Sea- and River-Pilotage moderate.

Of the total navigation of the Netherlands no less than three-fifths pass through the port of Rotterdam. Since the construction of the New-Waterway, vessels of the largest size are able to reach *Rotterdam* quietly and safely; ships drawing 21 feet coming up at any time, and those drawing 24 to 26 feet, at high water.

A few years ago it took two or three days to reach *Rotterdam* from Sea, now it is done **within two hours.**

Improvements are being steadily carried out, in the direction of increasing facilities for shipping, with the result that the Trade of the port has more than doubled within the past ten years.

Rotterdam is surrounded and traversed by three RAILROADS: the Staatsspoorweg, the Rhinespoorweg and the Hollandsche Spoorweg, having sheds and all the required facilities and implements for transhipping goods direct on and from the Railway-trucks.

There are several floating dry docks with large capacities; patent-slips for vessels up to 1200 tons; a Coaltip, different powerful steam- and hydraulic Cranes.

Coming up thro' the New-Waterway to *Rotterdam* there are on the Portside: *Maassluis, Vlaardingen*, an important fishing centre, and *Schiedam* which has a large grain-trade and about 400 Distilleries.

Some 25 years ago the only quay-room for large sea-going vessels was the Boompjes, about 800 meters long (2650 feet). Trade improved and our Town-authorities being persuaded of the necessity to provide more quay-room, did what was required, and for the moment the quay-room on both sides of

the river is already 18,550 meters (31,830 feet). The Town-Community being convinced that still more is required, is constantly proceeding making more quay-room. Besides this, the river is properly provided with a great number of Mooring-buoys, to enable ships and steamers to tranship their cargoes direct in Lighters and Rhine crafts. Since the commencement of the new cut at *Maassluis* for the direct New-Waterway up to *Rotterdam*, our Government already laid out for it 27½ millions of Guilders, equal to 11 millions of Dollars. The improvement of this entrance is still going on.

To meet the demand of the trade, expected by this New-Waterway, our Town-Community did spend for improvements of harbours, moorings, quay-room and other works already 13 millions of Guilders, say fully 5 millions of Dollars.

To show that this money is spent with success, the following Tables are taken from the original reports, viz.:

	Number of Sea-going Vessels entered at Rotterdam.	Tonnage.
1850	1,940	346,186
1860	2,449	592,978
1870	2,973	1,026,348
1880	3,456	1,681,650
1887	4,153	2,488,284

	Number of vessels entered at Rotterdam from the interior of Holland and from the Rhine.	Tonnage.
1878	62,071	1,276,064
1887	90,363	2,167,019

Of the sea-going Vessels, entered at Rotterdam in 1887, the percentages according to the tonnage is as follows:

from England . . . . 40,^{59}%
    "   Spain . . . . 14,^{04} "
    "   Russia   . . . . 15,^{38} "
    "   United States of North America 8,^{43} "
    "   other countries   . . . . . 21,^{56} "
                                        _____
                                        100%

The percentage from the United States increased from 5,^{26} in 1883 to 8,^{43} in 1887.

The Imports from the seaside consist chiefly of the following Goods:

Goods.	Tons.	Percentages of the total.
GRAIN	1,036,603	34,^{75}
ORES	681,851	23
METALS . . .	180,116	6
OIL	147,556	5
SUNDRIES . . .	937,603	31,^{25}
	2,983,729	100

The Exports to *England* are principally agricultural products of *Holland*, Butter, Cheese, etc. and Gin.

To *Germany* the exports are almost entirely transit Goods, as Grain, Ore, etc.

As the trade is still increasing (the tonnage entered in the first half year 1888, was about 10% above that of the corresponding months of 1887), the Community has again commenced the extension of harbours on a large scale.

HOMBURG, Aug. 16, 1888.

Van Sielen, Holland Society, Rotterdam :

Very sorry I could not be with you, but the Greater Holland is well represented.

DEPEW.

The last toast was proposed by the Burgomaster to The Holland Society, which he said had not, according to their motto, grown into a single tree, but rather into a forest; which toast was responded to by Hon. L. L. Van Allen, one of the members of The Holland Society, for the continued welfare of Rotterdam.

The hour for breaking up too soon arrived and the party made their way to the train and were safely carried to Amsterdam.

While seated by the Burgomaster at this dinner the Secretary received a telegram from the Committee of Utrecht, whose telegrams and letters had been for three days following the Society about, inviting the Society to a public reception, drive through the city, and luncheon at Utrecht on the following day, Friday. It was now impossible to accept, as the invitation of Alkmaar had already been accepted; but the Society will never cease to regret the fatality which prevented those letters and telegrams reaching it in time ; though sent to Amsterdam and The Hague, the Society was so on the move that each one came just after the Society had left, and thus was prevented what would have undoubtedly proved one of the most hospitable, interesting, and soul-stirring receptions of the trip. It is most to be regretted, too, that the labor and pains and preparation of the Utrecht Committee should thus have all been turned into disappointment.

15

In Rotterdam we were presented by the committee with a daintily gotten-up little book descriptive of the place, specially prepared for our benefit, and containing a convenient map of the city. This little volume can properly be here inserted to show the wonderful development of the commercial interests of this important city.

ALKMAAR.

ON the morning of Friday, August 17, we were joined by our fellow-member, Warner Van Norden, and his son, and made our last trip as an organized body. At nine in the morning we took a steamer on the North Holland Canal for a visit to Alkmaar and the agricultural districts of Holland, under the auspices of the Alkmaar Division of The Holland Society of Agriculture, in pursuance of the following invitation :

ALKMAAR, August, 1888.

To Mr. GEO. W. VAN SICLEN,
    President of The Holland Society, Amsterdam.

Dear Sir : Regretting very much your being prevented to receive me, I take the liberty of writing to propose to you and the members of The Holland Society to reserve one day for a visit to the town of Alkmaar and its neighborhood.

If possible, we should prefer to have the honor of your visit on a Friday, that being the day of the cheese market (the principal in Holland).

The Committee of the Agricultural Society of Alkmaar would be delighted if you would allow them to be your host, and propose the following plan :

A special steamer will be ready for you at Amsterdam at 8 or 9 o'clock in the morning, and will bring you along the River Zaan past Zaandam and the Zaan villages, and arrive,

after a passage of about two hours, at Alkmaar. There we
will visit the market, the town hall, and the cathedral, after
which we are to visit a North Holland farm and take
luncheon at the place of Mr. Van Forrest, one of the members of our committee, at Heiloo, and make a drive through
the picturesque environs, visiting the villages of Egmond
and Bergen.

You will then be back at Alkmaar in time to take the
train of five o'clock for Amsterdam.

Hoping that our proposition may be accepted, and expecting, if possible, an early answer, to make the necessary
arrangements,

Most respectfully yours,

H. F. DE WILDT,
Burgomeester of Heiloo, near Alkmaar,
President of the Agricultural Society, District of Alkmaar.

This was a very interesting excursion, and showed
us a section of the country differing in many respects
from any we had visited, and illustrating one source,
the agricultural, of the many industries which make
Holland rich and prosperous. The trip on the canal
was full of incidents, and the pictoriographer was
successful in obtaining many striking pictures of the
country, the windmills, the locks, and other objects
of interest. Shortly after leaving Amsterdam our
attention was attracted on the bow of the steamer by
quite a crowd of rather strange looking men clad in
some peculiar costume, and all of them with packs of
agricultural instruments on their backs. On inquiry
we learned that these men were German farm laborers,
who found it more profitable to pay their expenses
down the Rhine from Germany to Holland to do the
harvesting for the Dutch farmers, and then return to
Germany, than to stay at home and receive the small
wages of their own country. This was quite an instructive object-lesson as to the prosperity of the

agricultural regions of Holland. When we reached Alkmaar, a pleasing city of about 15,000 inhabitants, the committee of the Agricultural Society at Alkmaar, viz.: Mr. H. F. de Wildt, Burgomaster of Heiloo, President, Mr. H. Siebert Coster, of Alkmaar, Secretary, S. Kramer, Burgomaster of Koedijk, and K. Oly of Schermeer, members, escorted us to the Town Hall where we were received by the civil authorities. The Burgomaster, Mr. A. Maclaine Pout, welcomed us in a brief but very hearty address. This it may be remarked was the only official address made to us, while in Holland, that was not delivered in English, a fact which speaks much for the general high education of the official class. We enjoyed our Burgomaster's speech, however, from the evident kindliness and sincerity of his welcome, and from the opportunity it afforded us of hearing the national language in its best state. Mr. Van Sielen replied in French, and then at his request Mr. Sheldon T. Vielé made a further response to this address of the Burgomaster, expressing our pleasure at receiving so hearty a welcome so far away from home. Mr. Vielé was selected for this purpose because he lived the farthest West in our own country of all the excursionists, thus bringing together, as Alkmaar was the farthest North of any point we reached in Holland, representatives of the two extremes of America and Holland. After the address the wine of honor was passed, and we then made a visit to the museum of the city. Here we were much interested in many of the antiquities. We were particularly pleased to see the original letter written by the authorities to Father William, in 1573, informing him that the Spaniards had beleaguered

the town, and asking him for assistance. This letter
was on parchment, long and very narrow; when
written it was wrapped around part of the hollow of
a stick, and inserted in a long leaping pole. The
following is a translation of it:

We are greatly surprised that your Grace does not send us
any relief according to your Grace's promise, or send us a
messenger in daytime, as it was easier for you to send one
in to us than for us to send one out; and therefore, unless
you relieve us as soon as possible, either by troops or by
piercing the dykes, we shall be obliged to surrender the
town to the enemy, and if this comes to pass we protest
before God and the world that it is not our fault, or due
to our unfaithfulness, but the fault of your Grace; reason
wherefore we first admonish you to relieve us immediately,
because we have no powder to resist half an attack; if this
messenger has arrived let the galley or ship float a flag on
the top of the mast when he comes, and let the flag be taken
down when he goes back; when we are going to be re-
lieved by soldiers show the sign 4 at the top of the mast of
the galley or ship, and if you want to relieve us by water
show 2 fours at the top of the mast of the galley or ship,
and if there is no relief for us let the galley or ship fire two
shots, and if you intend to save us and these good citizens
send us ships and boats between the buoy and the houses
at Bokkelen, and give us a sign in daytime when those
ships are going to come at night by showing two flags at
the stem of the galley or ship; do this speedily.

May the Lord protect you. If there is no relief send as
many boats and ships as your Grace may think is right
in our behalf. We had not expected that your Grace
would have left us so long without relief or succor, as you
had promised us quite differently.

JACOB CABELIAU.
WILHELM VAN ZONENBERCH.
JACQUES HENNEBERT.
JAN SPIEGEL.
DIRCK DUNEL.
FLORIS VAN TEYLINGEN.
CLAES HERENSZ.

A carpenter took this and at the peril of his life swam the moat, passed the lines of the Spaniards, and made his way across the country, leaping ditches and canals by aid of the pole, and finally reaching his destination in safety. The inhabitants of the little city bravely held out, and after a long siege Father William finally succeeded in coming to their rescue. This city and Leyden claim the proud honor of being the only two cities, formally invested by the Spaniards during those terrible years, that succeeded in driving off the enemy. We saw a very curious picture of the siege, also many cloth seals, and official stamps of the old time; and the picture of Aphan, who once upon a time sailed away with a fleet on a voyage of exploration into unknown waters, and was gone so many years that he and his companions were given up for lost, but who finally, to the surprise and gratitude of all the city, sailed into port again with all his ships. We also saw some relics of the Romans, showing that this remarkable people had reached these regions and left evidences of their wonderful civilization and power. The Secretary of the City Council of Alkmaar, Mr. J. Nuhout van der Veen, presented the visitors, in the name of the committee of the museum, with some coins made in 1573 for paying off the troops, photographs representing some buildings of the city, a portrait of the Burgomaster Van Teylingen, a book on the siege of Alkmaar, written by the late Mr. Hofdyke, and several other articles of value.

We were also presented by Mr. Twisk of the Agricultural Society with a number of the bulbs of a new tulip called by him the "Abraham Lincoln." These were distributed among the members and

WEIGH HOUSE, ALKMAAR.

now bloom in many gardens of America, recalling a pleasant incident of our trip to the North of
Holland.

We then visited the cheese market, which is held
in the small square in front of the weighing house,
erected in 1582. The neighboring streets were filled
with quaint and curious wagons and chariots, of
which the pictoriographer obtained several good pictures. As this was Friday, the weekly cheese market
was in full operation, and the place was thronged
with the peasantry of the province of North Holland,
who had come together to sell their produce to the
dealers. The square was divided into little lanes, all
of them filled with piles of the familiar yellow and
red cheeses which are seen all over the world.

There are in the weigh-house four sets of scales,
each attended by its own crew. There is a lively
competition between the sets to accomplish the
greatest amount of work, and their movements are
correspondingly lively. Two men bear between them
a sort of hand-bier, which they rapidly load with
cheeses from the piles in the market, and carry to
the weigh-house, where they are weighed and returned. The scales are of the old-fashioned kind,
and for every 500 pounds of cheese placed on one
side of the scale, they place 500 pounds of iron on
the other. In honor of our visit the men were attired
in their best clothes and looked picturesquely in their
bright colored costumes, of which the coat, hose, and
peculiar stiff varnished straw hat are of a color distinguishing each crew. We visited the principal
church of the place, the Church of St. Laurence,
which has some interesting features. Here a concert
was given on the fine organ for our benefit, and we

heard the "Priest's March," from Athalie, followed
by "Yankee Doodle."

From here we were driven to Heiloo, a short distance from Alkmaar, and received at "Nyenburg," the
residence of Jhr. P. van Foreest, the president of the
Society. This is a beautiful old house, very picturesquely situated in the midst of a fine old grove, with
vistas cut through the trees affording many fine views.
It was a fine representative of the best type of Dutch
farms, but very different from any ideas of ours as-
sociated with a farm-house. The house was commodious and handsomely furnished, and situated upon
ground formerly owned by the Egmont family, so
illustrious in the annals of Holland, and from whom
the present family have descended. On the walls
were pictures of two brothers, from one of whom the
Chevalier van Foreest claims descent; one was the
physician of William of Orange, and the other the
Burgomaster of Alkmaar at the time of the siege.
We were received by the Chevalier and his agreeable
wife and attractive children. Besides Mrs. van
Foreest there were also present, to greet and entertain us, Mrs. de Wildt, Miss J. van Foreest, Miss J.
Momma, Mr. G. Kalff, Mr. Th. A. Sannes, Mr. D.
Bosman, Mr. H. Momma, and Mr. H. Cohen Stuart.
Here, in the agricultural regions of the northern
part of Holland, we found this entire family, parents
and children, all speaking most excellent English, and
none of the family, with the exception of the father,
having ever been out of their own country. We partook of a luncheon embracing many appetizing delica-
cies peculiar to the country, after which we viewed
the barns of the establishment, and were impressed
by their enormous size, wonderful neatness (the pro-

verbial neatness of the Dutch certainly being in no way overestimated), and methodical arrangement. The cattle are quartered at one end of the barn, and the successive stages of the manufacture of cheese go on until the cheeses are stored at the other end ready for shipment. We were also introduced to the massive black and white bull of the farm, a winner of many prizes, and a magnificent animal.

After this interesting inspection we took a long drive to Egmond-binnen, to the scanty ruins of the castle of Egmond. This was our best opportunity for a glimpse of some of the most characteristic scenery of Holland. The roads were excellent, through fields covered with herbage on which innumerable cattle were grazing. As we approached the sea the dunes were before us, mounds and hillocks of sand tossed up by the waves and winds, beyond them the dark waters of the North Sea, and above all the cold gray sky. After a drive of several miles, stopping at the ruins of a fine church, which was sacked and burned by the French, we returned to Alkmaar and took the train at 5 p. m. for Amsterdam, feeling that this had been one of our most instructive days, and one which gave us a higher idea of the solid agricultural foundation upon which much of the commercial prosperity of Holland depends.

On arriving at Amsterdam we partook of a rather hasty dinner, paid our bills, gathered together our effects, and turned our faces homeward. There were no parting ceremonies, as the time was short, and all the members of the expedition were thoroughly tired out by their nine days' pleasure. Our little party, who formed the advance-guard of the return trip, just twelve in number, took their seats in the train about

16

nine in the evening, feeling loath to leave the scenes
of so much pleasure, but our faces were turned homeward and in talking over what we had seen the time
passed pleasantly until we reached Rotterdam about
eleven. We got out of the cars and found the station
dim and almost deserted; we were looking around for
our trunks, when a gendarme with two or three of
the railway porters suddenly appeared and practically
put the party under arrest. With the little Dutch at
our command we soon found that the desired victim
was that one of the party who had the least knowledge of the Holland tongue. We could not imagine
of what crime he had been guilty, until it finally
transpired that on purchasing his tickets in Amsterdam, the ticket-seller had given him about a dollar too
much in change. This had been promptly reported by
telegraph and the direful result was before us in the
person of the military gentleman who was now de-
manding satisfaction. Our innocent fellow-traveler
held out a handful of coin, told him to help himself
to what he wanted or take it all, if he would only let
him go; this was finally accomplished, and an inter-
national episode was thus happily averted. The next
morning we spent a couple of hours in a hasty survey
of the shops of Rotterdam and promptly at twelve
o'clock found ourselves again on board the good ship
" Amsterdam," homeward bound.

Here ends the chronicle of the first part of the expedition. It was only nine days in all, but it gave
us experiences and pleasures that will ever remain
in our memories. The expedition was begun as a
sort of sentimental journey to their common Fatherland beyond the sea by a party of strangers united

by a shadowy claim of kinship. We hoped for a few
privileges beyond those enjoyed by the passing
traveler; but, on reaching Holland, the whole nation,
responding to the sentiment which prompted our journey, received us with open arms.

Of Holland and its people too much cannot be
said in praise. Thrift, prosperity, and commercial
activity are everywhere apparent. A noticeable indication of this prosperity was the fact that of the
many children we saw, both in the cities and the
country districts, all were comfortably clad and none
were barefooted. When the children are thus cared
for, all is well with the nation.

A FRISIAN BABY.

NARRATIVE OF THE VISIT OF
THE HOLLAND SOCIETY OF NEW-YORK
TO THE NETHERLANDS.

♦

PART II.

By Rev. J. Howard Suydam, D. D.

APPOINTED BY THE SOCIETY HISTORIAN COADJUTOR TO
SHELDON VIELE, ESQ.

N the 19th of August the larger part of The Holland Society returned to America. A company consisting of four members remained, and determined to visit the surrounding provinces. All official engagements were canceled. Due notice was given to the municipalities and societies which had extended invitations to visit them that they would travel in a private capacity. This announcement did not accomplish its object. These gentlemen were still regarded as representing the Society; the same lavish hospitality was tendered them that had been bestowed upon the whole company. To express this so as to lead to its full appre-

17   125

ciation by those at home is the main object of this part of our narrative.

This company consisted of the following gentlemen, viz.: John H. Voorhees of Washington, D. C., Menzo Van Voorhis of Rochester, N. Y., Frank Hasbrouck of Poughkeepsie, N. Y., and the Rev. Dr. J. Howard Suydam of Jersey City, N. J.

LEEUWARDEN.

ON Monday, August 20, we journeyed by rail to Leeuwarden in the province of Friesland. Our course lay along the southern and eastern shores of the Zuider Zee, some distance inland, and through the considerable cities of Amersfoort, Zwolle, Meppel, and Heerenveen. For a few miles the country was fertile, and the crop of vegetables seemed very abundant. For the first time in our travels orchards were seen; the trees presenting a fair display of apples, pears, and plums. Soon, however, we came to a desert of sand dunes. These continued for a long distance, followed for many miles by drowned lands. When the grazing country reappeared, it was like the coast southward of Haarlem, dotted with numbers of spotted black and white cattle, which the natives say are erroneously called "the Holstein." A marked feature in this region is the magnificent breed of horses; they are of a coal black color, with wide frontals, arched necks, and broad tails, which sweep the ground; and their motion is with a high, proud step. This was remarked even of those driven before the plow.

At the station at Leeuwarden, the delegation was met by Mr. Battaent, conservator of the Museum, who accompanied them to the Hotel Doelen. Here they were greeted by Burgomaster Lycklama, Justice Boerles, and Professor Bruggencate. These gentlemen spoke the English language fluently. Mr. Bruggencate is professor of English literature in the gymnasium.

A visit to the Town Hall was followed by a long delay in the Museum, in which the authorities and citizens generally take a deep interest. It is rich in local antiquities, including the bones of extinct animals, skulls of a powerful pre-historic race of men, excellent classifications of coins, and many evidences of the Roman occupancy of the territory. A stone with a Latin inscription, and containing the name of the reigning Roman Emperor and also of the commanding military officer, had been exhumed and deposited here only two weeks before.

The company were afterwards driven over brick paved roads several miles into the country to visit an ancient institution for the care of respectable aged women. The burgomaster was *ex-officio* the president of the corporation, and he manifested special pride in its management. It occupied a castle and an ancient convent, which, together with an ample endowment, was the gift of Baron Pepta, who died in the year 1711. The treasury has an income of 10,000 florins a year. Each person is furnished with a room, and two florins a week. A peculiar rule enjoined by the terms of the will, requires that each inmate in turn shall polish a certain piece of furniture once a year. The founder was a bachelor.

A banquet at the residence of the burgomaster, which was formerly owned and occupied by the family of the Stadtholder, concluded the day. It would not be proper to publish a detailed description of the elegant appointments. The report in a local journal of the following day — a copy of which has been deposited in the archives of our Society — indicates the hearty enjoyment of the whole company.

The cordial welcome, in excellent English, extended by the burgomaster, in his toast "To The Holland Society of New-York," was happily responded to by Mr. Frank Hasbrouck.

An interesting incident at this banquet was the first introduction of a new brand of cigars, named and marked "The Holland Society of New-York."

The following representative gentlemen were invited to meet us: viz., A. Du Parc, member of the Town Council; P. A. Bergsma, LL. D., secretary of the town; P. Lycklama à Nycholt, burgomaster; B. J. Lycklama à Nycholt, son of the burgomaster, and a student at law at Leiden; W. B. S. Boerles, LL. D., vice-president of the court of law, and librarian of the Frisian Society; J. U. Z. A. Corbelyn Battaerd, keeper of the prints, coins, etc., of the Frisian Society, and K. ten Bruggencate, professor of the English and German language at the Municipal College.

As mementoes of the visit our Society was presented with the following volumes, viz., a copy of "Kunst en Kunst Geschiedenis van Bolsvard"; "A Catalogue of the Museum of Leeuwarden"; Holland's "Silver feast," a historical eulogy, by Samuel Richard van Campen; Vol. I. of the "Dutch in the Arctic Sea," by the same author; also three current copies of the "Leeuwarden Courant," containing reports of the visit of the delegation.

MR. P. LYCKLAMA Λ' NYEHOLT.
SUB-MASTER OF LEUWARDEN

MR. D. ALMA.
BURGOMASTER OF SNEEK

Among the many pleasant recollections of our visit to Holland none will stand out more vividly than this reception at Leeuwarden.

GRONINGEN.

IN response to an invitation received by the Secretary on Tuesday, August 21, we visited the city of Groningen in the province of the same name.

Groningen lies due east of Leeuwarden, at a distance of about three hours travel. The country traversed is a dry upland; the field crops were large, orchards were numerous, and among the staple products were chicory and a poor quality of tobacco.

The city of Groningen, like all the others in the Netherlands, is intersected by numerous canals, in which were a large number of vessels of various kinds, including ocean steamers. Everywhere there were indications of considerable commercial activity. It was noticeable, however, that, different from other formerly walled cities which we had visited, the streets and squares were wider.

The ancient walls had been leveled and the unused canals filled up, so that the places they once occupied now furnished excellent boulevards for driving. The principal church edifice dated from the XVIth century, the ante-Reformation period. It is chiefly remarkable for its tower of unusual massiveness, and also for the chancel or choir, which is much higher than the other parts of the building.

Mr. Boeke, of the mercantile firm of Huydekoper & Boeke, had been deputed by the burgomaster to be his substitute as host for the occasion, important official business having prevented his presence.

Mr. Boeke is connected by marriage with the Huydekoper's of Pennsylvania, one of whom was a distinguished general in our army and postmaster of the city of Philadelphia during President Arthur's administration. Mr. Boeke's business as a dealer in agricultural implements had brought him into constant correspondence with Americans, so that he spoke our language with perfect ease.

After a pedestrian tour through the city, we visited a school for girls, the first we had entered, because our journey was made during the summer vacation. It had been reopened on the day previous.

It was a primary school for the training of children up to twelve years of age. With the youngest the teaching was after the mode of Froebel's Kindergarten. All were taught from the blackboard, the larger scholars having text-books in their hands.

The teachers, all of whom were familiar with the English language, indicated a thorough qualification for their work. The normal schools in the Netherlands have the reputation of being unexcelled. The salaries of the teachers range from $300 to $800 a year. The cost of board and lodging for a single person is $250 a year.

The children were scrupulously clean and neatly dressed, without any attempt at display. The blonde complexion, with flaxen or brown hair and brown and blue eyes, were particularly remarkable. The few with dark eyes and hair were unmistakably of Hebrew extraction. Here was the evidence of a purer Germanic people than any we had as yet observed.

Another peculiarity also learned from these inhabitants of the extreme North was that, while with difficulty they understand the language of their own countrymen living in the Southern provinces, they hold ready communication with the people of Scotland.

Subsequent investigation led to the discovery that the first inhabitants of this region of which there is any historical record were Celts.

The head ornaments of the ladies of Groningen are of the same pattern as those in Friesland; although many wear silver-gilt instead of pure gold. A house servant may often be found wearing a golden helmet of the value of $300. They are heirlooms, and their owners cannot be induced to part with them, any sooner than with the carved chests which contain the wedding trousseau.

In the Museum at Leeuwarden, the evolution of the peculiar head-gear of the Holland ladies is shown by a series of examples, beginning with a narrow metal band used to keep the hair out of the eyes.

Much has been said by American travelers about the beauty of the ladies in the Northern Netherlands; our judgment confirms this report. The women are remarkable for their clear complexions, good form, and fine eyes; their features are not always harmonious, but their faces are full of expression.

Mr. Boeke led the company to the Exchange, where our presence, with the orange-colored badges conspicuously displayed, caused considerable pleasant diversion. The traffic here in rape-seed and Russian rye was to us a novelty.

After luncheon the party was driven about the environs of the city. We here availed ourselves of an opportunity to explore a veritable farm-house.

Everything of a movable character pertaining to a farm was under one roof. The building appeared

to be about 200 by 150 feet in dimensions. The
arrangement, although not so pleasant as the homes
on our American farms, is nevertheless not as disa-
greeable as it would seem. In the extreme end is
the private apartment; next to it is the pig-sty;
then, on either side, come the stalls for the cattle and
the horses. When the weather demands that they
shall be brought beneath shelter, the pigs are washed,
the cows are curried and blanketed, and their tails
are suspended to a wire. The flooring of the sty and
stable is made of brick and slightly inclined; and
they are as thoroughly scrubbed as a floor in a house.
Next to the cattle is the department for vehicles and
farm implements; then follows the threshing machine and churn, both driven by horse power. The
next apartment is the store-house for the fuel, which
consists of peat holding a great amount of woody fiber.
Then comes the dairy, containing large vats of milk,
both from the sheep and the cows. After these,
follow the kitchen, the sitting-room, and the parlor
in succession. In none of these rooms is there an
indication of a sleeping place; yet, in each of them
are beds behind the papered walls. Sometimes they
are placed one above another, like the berths in
a ship. On the parlor table the fine china ware —
hereditary treasures — is conspicuously displayed.

As an item of interest not only of health, but
of economy (and to which Victor Hugo directs
special attention), we learn that the night-soil of
Groningen is daily collected from the convenient
earth-closets and sold to the farmers. The revenue
from this source amounts to one florin annually for
every inhabitant of the city, including men, women,
and children.

In the cattle-market here we witnessed the ancient custom of "striking hands." It is worthy of a picture. At each offer and at each bid the buyer and seller, looking intently into each other's eyes, strike hands with great earnestness. As the bargain approaches a conclusion the vigor increases, and at its close the parties shake hands and retire to the inn.

Mr. Boeke informed us that for a short time the mowing machine was used in Holland, but now it was entirely discarded, because in harvest time large numbers of industrious and frugal Germans are accustomed to cross the line and perform the work. This is done so thoroughly and cheaply that the machines are not deemed necessary.

After expressing our grateful appreciation of the attentions received, and desiring our compliments to be presented to the burgomaster, we returned to Leeuwarden, arriving at 10 o'clock in the evening. We were met at the station by the hospitable Burgomaster Lycklama, and Professor Bruggencate, who accompanied us to our hotel and entertained us in delightful good-fellowship.

SNEEK.

A VISIT to the city of Sneek was not contemplated when the quartette delegation of The Holland Society left Amsterdam on their northern tour. The inducements presented by their attentive hosts at Leeuwarden, however, were too powerful to overcome. When they consented to go, the burgomaster telegraphed the burgomaster of Sneek and the president of the yacht-club at what hour they might be expected. They were well repaid. The experience

18

was unique. The day was the first of the two consecutive holidays of the year.

Sneck has no drives, theater, or opera, hence the recreations of the people are entirely upon the water. Their yacht-races are famous; boats are entered for the contest from the different provinces of the Netherlands, and from Belgium, England, and Scotland. The prizes awarded are not of great intrinsic value, but, like the laurel crown in the Olympic games, they confer distinguished honor. The people come for many miles from the surrounding country to participate in the festivities. It is a favorite time for the reunion of old and young. Business is suspended, and everything is surrendered to witness the great yacht contests.

We were accompanied by Professor Bruggencate, who acted as interpreter.

The whole population of the city seemed to be gathered at the station. We were met by the "Direction" of the "Yacht Association," accompanied by an unusually excellent band of music. Our barouches were escorted through the dense crowd to a public hall, where an address of welcome was delivered by Mr. Clignetts, to which Mr. Voorhees of Washington, D. C., made a happy reply.

The burgomaster, who had been detained by a marriage, arrived later, and read from a paper another welcome on behalf of the Municipality in the following words:

"It may be allowed to me to speak some words to our American, no! to our old Dutch visitors.

"More than 250 years ago your ancestors had left this, our country here, and have taken part in the earliest American settlements. Two centuries and a

half! It is a long time. And the Atlantic Ocean is
a great sea, but neither the distance of place nor
the length of time did forget you, the worthy
descendants of our common fathers, that the same old
Dutch blood, untainted, free and strong, flows in
your and our veins and hearts. You have been
coming here to visit the old native country. Old
Holland and Old Friesland agree to your noble feeling, and are happy to welcome the American-Hol-
landers, our brethren from the other side of the
world.

"I propose, my countrymen, to drink their health.'

Dr. Suydam made an appropriate response.

It may not be out of place here to remark that the
personnel of the burgomasters, everywhere, is distinguished. They are appointed by the king, and some
of them are members of the National Parliament.
They are gentlemen of high character and of superior
culture. In order to maintain the dignity of their
position, they must have an income independent of
the stipend of their office. All marriages are performed by them or by their deputies.

The burgomaster of Sneek (Mr. Alma, uncle to
the celebrated artist Alma Tadema), is no exception to this rule. He stands six feet four inches
in height, is well proportioned, and dressed in excellent taste; he appeared like a typical New-York
gentleman.

The open space in front of the hall was crowded
with people, who greeted the company with vocifer-
ous cheers upon their entrance and departure.

Sneek is an old city, and was once encircled by a
wall and also by water. It now contains twenty
thousand inhabitants, and, like many others in Holland, does not appear to maintain any special indus-

try. As in Hoorn, Middleberg, and Arnhem, there is a very large number of people here who are living upon the capital accumulated in former years.

There still remains of the old wall, the beautiful water-gate, in perfect condition, a photograph of which is kindly forwarded to the Society by Miss Ten Ocner of Bellingwolde, Groningen.

We were received on a steamer conveying the "Direction." Another one preceded us, occupied by the band of music, and one followed us which contained a squad of men who, we were amused to see, were armed with old-fashioned muskets, loaded at the muzzle by powder-horn and ramrod; these were to furnish the salutes for the occasion.

In this order we proceeded through the canals to the large fresh-water inland sea called "Snecker-Zee." Here we landed upon an island so low that it seemed as if a very slight breeze would entirely submerge it. Many vessels had already arrived, others followed in rapid succession, and made fast to the little island and to each other until they formed a compact mass. The most of them were the blunt-bowed, oiled, and sloop-rigged boats, which are chiefly used for traffic on the Rhine and other inland waters. They have no center-board, but a wing arrangement on either side serves the same purpose. The speed those skilled sailors could get from such unpromising craft was indeed remarkable. It was reported that there were about five hundred vessels in sight on the sea.

The day was perfect. The people in festive mood, the peasantry in their picturesque attire, the unceasing music, and the happy laughter of the multitude, constituted an ideal holiday. The foreign visitors

ZEILVEREENIGING SNEEK.

2. A. J. PIJTTERSEN, President.

3. J. TER HORST, Gen. Treasurer.

4. J. HESSELINK, Secretary.

1. W. HUBERT, Ass't Sec'y

divided the honors of the day with the competitive yachtsmen. We deemed it a high compliment that the vessels from England, Scotland, and Belgium, as well as those of the Netherlands, displayed the American colors. The musicians not knowing our national airs, substituted "God Save the Queen," which was gracefully acknowledged. The leader (Mr. Graefe) apologized, and to atone for this omission, kindly offered to compose a march for the "Holland Society," and if we would forward him a copy, to interweave the air of the "Star Spangled Banner."

In accordance with this request a copy was sent to his address in the care of Burgomaster Alma. But before he received it, and while engaged in the composition of the march, Mr. Graefe was stricken with apoplexy and died. A musical journal has been sent to our Society containing his portrait and a sketch of his life. He was evidently a man of genius, and a composer of unusual merit; it was a pleasure for the Americans to transmit a contribution toward the erection of a monument to his memory.

The visiting yachts vied with each other in their attentions to the Americans, who were obliged to pass from vessel to vessel to enjoy their hospitality.

The race was conducted in admirable order. Six classes of vessels were entered. The prescribed course required to make a circuit three times around the island. As they drew near, their sails bellying to the breeze, the sailors prone on their backs, with features fixed and eyes aflame, restraining, relaxing, and guiding their craft as a racer his steeds, the interest of the thousands of spectators became intense. The whole, together with the anchored vessels, bedecked with all the bunting at their command, presented a scene worthy to be preserved on canvas. How much we regretted then, as on other occasions, the absence of our photographer!

It is sufficient to say that the hospitality here was of the same generous character as in other places. The banquet was spread on the deck of the large steamer which conveyed the "Direction." The English-speaking ladies, with the gracious manners of the best society, placed their guests at their ease. There was a dance on a little green island, which trembled beneath the hundreds of feet keeping time to the music. The company was also entertained by the provincial Frisian dance, which is a lively combination of the Virginia reel and the quadrille.

Our return to the city began as the sun was near his setting. The three steamers had in tow the six victorious yachts. The whole fleet followed. The sea seemed crowded with craft. As we passed through the canals the decks of the steamers were on a level with the dykes; these were thronged with good-natured men, women, and children, who sang responsive songs to those on deck.

The music of "Neerlandsch-Bloed" inspired the whole multitude, and they rolled out the chorus "For Prince and Fatherland" with fine effect.

The whole scene of the procession of vessels, the incessant music, the salutes from the musketeers, the people singing in chorus their familiar songs, and, as we neared the wharf, the chimes of the church bells ringing out a welcome, as witnessed in the deepening twilight, produced a picturesque impression which can never be effaced.

It is a pleasure to report that not a single intoxicated or disorderly person marred the harmony of that holiday license.

In a large hall we witnessed the award of the prizes. An address was delivered by Mr. Pyttersen, the president of the Yacht Association, a large part of which was devoted to a eulogy of America and a welcome to The Holland Society of New-York. Mr. Frank Hasbrouck ascended the platform, and made the happiest of his many speeches. It was interpreted by Professor Bruggencate, and at its close the vast audience rose and applauded.

The train was in waiting; we were obliged to take a hurried departure. As we passed through the hall the people rose *en masse* and cheered with great vigor.

At Leeuwarden we were again met by the burgomaster, who accompanied us to our hotel. On the following morning he, with others, escorted us to the station, and bade us a hearty farewell. Here we were joined by our fellow-member, Mr. Warner Van Norden, and his son, of New-York.

ARNHEM.

OUR narrative is not to be regarded as a guidebook: its main purpose is to note incidents by the way which shall best indicate the spirit of the people in their reception of the members representing The Holland Society of New-York. The enthusiasm manifested in all the cities previously visited did not abate, but rather increased as we continued our journey.

The route to Arnhem was, in part, the same as
that by which we had traveled northward, through
many miles of watery waste, of dreary heather-covered
peat-fields, and of rolling sand-dunes. At Meppel,
near which was the hive of the Voorhuises, the
ground was slightly elevated, fertile, and well
wooded by arboriculture. The wilderness soon reappeared and continued until we approached Voorst;
here it was a great relief to look upon an undulating
landscape, where orchards abounded, and where
forest trees, the result of cultivation, were more
numerous. The roads were perfect; indeed they are
unsurpassed all through the Netherlands. Occasion-
ally in this region a herd of red-spotted cattle appeared, indicating a mixture of breeds.

The country presented the same character as far as
Deventer and Arnhem.

Arnhem, with its environs, is the most beautiful
city in Holland. This is largely due to the contrast with the monotonous level of other parts of the
country. It is located on the main branch of the
Rhine.

An association, which, with commendable frank-
ness, bears the title of "The Society Wishing to
Attract Visitors to Arnhem," sent a committee to
receive us at the station. We were driven to the
hotel Bellevue to breakfast, where the elegance
of appointments and the urbanity and heartiness of
the hosts showed the high appreciation in which
they held The Holland Society of New-York.

The location of the table was opposite wide-open
doors, overlooking a beautiful lawn which sloped
down to the river, and across which, beyond the
intervening miles of low-land, one could see the

Morch Portrait of Washington.

spires and distant hills of Germany. The delicate cut glass, the trailing vines, and dishes embossed in flowers, evinced great refinement of taste.

Here, we are happy to record an incident which is of great interest to every American patriot. It is best told in the accompanying reprint of an article published in the February number of the "Magazine of American History":

"THE DE VRIES PORTRAIT OF WASHINGTON."

A RECENT DISCOVERY IN HOLLAND.

The visit of The Holland Society of New-York to the Netherlands in August, 1888, will ever be a memorable event, both to the hosts and to their favored guests. The official and civic receptions, the excursions and banquets, and enthusiastic welcome of the multitude which crowded the thoroughfares and the housetops, the music, addresses, and original songs, the lavish display of flags and bunting, the cathedral bells ringing out the national airs of America, all made an impression which seems like a dream. It was a continuous ovation of ten days, and more befitting royalty than a company of simple citizens of a republic. It was the home sentiment greeting the members of the family after an absence of 250 years.

The company then disbanded. Some returned by the same steamer which carried them over, while others departed for London, Paris, and the Rhine. Their visit had been limited to the provinces of North and South Holland.

A few members of the Society determined to devote two weeks more in travel through the other prov-

10

ERRATUM.— For "*Utrecht* portrait" read "*Arnhem* portrait of Washington."

inces. They were everywhere received with the same hearty demonstrations. It continued to be a royal progress to Leeuwarden, Sneek, Groningen, Utrecht, and Middelburg. But nowhere was the hospitality more pronounced than at Arnhem on the Rhine, in the province of Guelderland.

The company of gentlemen who here received them bore the peculiar title of "The Society Wishing to Attract Visitors to Arnhem." The midday breakfast at the Hotel Bellevue, arranged according to the characteristic taste of the cultured Hollander, appealed to the poetic sentiment. The table on the veranda commanded a view down the lawn sloping to the Rhine, across which, and beyond the intervening meadows, were visible the spires of the churches in the villages lying among the German hills. Afterward, in response to an invitation, they were driven to the residence of Mr. Peter de Vries, Sr.

It was what Americans would call an old-fashioned house. It bore the appearance of wealth, indicative of comfort rather than of ostentation. The interior arrangements, the furniture, and decorations were similar to those of the old Knickerbocker homes of New-York. This, together with the manner of the reception accorded by the family and invited friends, immediately placed the visitors at their ease.

Their attention was at once arrested by a portrait of our Washington, standing upon an easel, and decorated with Dutch and American flags. Their surprise was greatly increased when Mr. de Vries read from a carefully prepared manuscript a history of the portrait, a part of which I have the privilege to present:

He said: "Under every government which our fatherland has had the love of liberty has manifested itself; it was only modified in its expression in accordance with the circumstances under which the people live. The proper and natural consequences were, that the principles proclaimed more than one hundred years ago in America, in the founding of an independent nationality, met with sympathy and support in the Netherlands, not only from their political leaders, but also from men who were not invested with public office. Hence they did not hesitate to extend their commercial enterprises to those countries which were in need of help and capital. This was the principal cause why my great-grandfather, over one hundred years ago, dared to take the initiative, according to his ability and influence, to support the Americans in their struggle for liberty against the odds of England. Actuated by such a spirit, Claas Taan, living at Zaandam and carrying on business under the firm name of 'Claas Taan & Sons,' sent a portion of his commercial fleet, at that time consisting of eighteen vessels of the largest tonnage, to America. He was successful in running the English blockade and carrying provisions into Baltimore. This deed was afterwards remembered by the Americans, and my great-grandfather, Mr. Claas Taan, received, in 1793, a present from America in commemoration of this service (pointing to the portrait of Washington), and his descendants cherish it as an evidence how an independent nation values the voluntary services of a foreign friend in adversity. This, gentlemen, is a contribution to the history of America's War for Independence."

Mr. de Vries then stated that the portrait was presented by Washington himself to Claas Taan, accompanied with an autograph letter.

Here was discovered an original portrait of Washington, and connected with an event in our War of Revolution of which the Americans were totally ignorant.

The writer of this article made reply to Mr. de Vries's address, in which he expressed the delight of the visitors, and promised, upon his return to America, to investigate the genuineness of the portrait, and to verify, if possible, the historical incident. He began his researches as soon as possible, which were attended with no little difficulty. He received the names Pau and Pauk, as transcribed from the canvas; but, as these could not be found in the catalogue of artists, he requested a photographic copy of the portrait. Mr. de Vries replied that he had never permitted a reproduction of the portrait in any form; still he complied with the request, and, after ten copies were taken (two of which were sent to the writer), the plate was purposely broken. The photograph very distinctly presented the artist's name — *C. Polk*, 1793.

It now became interesting to identify the painter. The writer at first proceeded to compare the photograph with the reproduction of known original portraits of Washington, but could not find its counterpart; nor could he find the name *Polk* in any one of the conventional lists of contemporary portrait painters. After a long research the following brief sentence was discovered in Tuckerman's "Book of Artists": "More than one portrait of Washington bears the name of Polke, who passed a year or two in America. One of these belonged to the estate of Arthur Lee, and was sent to Washington during the civil war, but was returned by the government at its close."

A letter was addressed to Governor Lee of Virginia, describing Mr. de Vries's picture, and inquiring if it corresponded with the one in the possession of his family. The governor referred it to Mr. Poindexter, State librarian, who directed attention to a description of the Lee portrait in Johnston's "Original Portraits of Washington," of which the following is a summarized extract:

It is proper to record here three portraits which legitimately come in a list of Peale's works. They are attributed to Charles Peale Polk, a young Virginian, who was a relative, namesake, and pupil of Peale's; and it was said that

Polk painted only the figures, while his master painted the heads. The likeness obtained in the portraits is a close rendering of the Washington head, according to the Houdon standard. One of these portraits was painted for Arthur Lee, Commissioner to France, being sent to him while abroad. It is a three-quarter picture of Washington in Continental uniform, with three stars in the epaulets. His hand, holding a chapeau, rests on the hilt of his sword. Princeton, with the college buildings, furnishes the background. A remark in the letter accompanying the transmission indicates that there were two pictures of this kind. The second picture identified is called kit-cat, and is marked Cs. Polk, and is now in the possession of the Historical Society of Pennsylvania. The third is in the Corcoran Gallery at Washington.

The extract from Tuckerman implies that the artist was a foreigner, or that he resided abroad, and it gives his name as *Polke*. There can be no doubt but that he is the same person alluded to in Johnston, since both speak of a portrait for Arthur Lee, although the latter says that this picture bears the name Chs. Peale Polk, while the one in Philadelphia has it *Cs. Polk*, but does not state in what form it stands on the picture in the Corcoran gallery.

Mr. de Vries's picture bears the name *C. Polk*.

If the other data should be found to be satisfactory, this confusion of names and place of residence would prove to be no serious objection to the claim of the De Vries portrait as an original. Favorable results from the investigation of the historic event, on account of which the portrait was presented by President Washington to Mr. Claas Taan, are necessary to corroborate the above testimony. This subject is at present engaging the interested attention of the Maryland Historical Society. Mr. Browne, librarian of the Johns Hopkins University, writes that " there is no doubt but that Baltimore was virtually blockaded by the English cruisers, and the distress of the inhabitants arose from the want of such things as could only be procured from Europe, and not from the need of food, since they had the whole South and West from which to draw supplies."

In the family of Mr. de Vries it was always understood that an autograph letter of Washington's accompanied the gift of the portrait to their ancestor, and that this, together with other important documents, was lost at the time Napoleon's army took possession of the Netherlands. It is positively known that Mr. Claas Taan was a property-holder in or near Baltimore. Twenty thousand gulden were paid to Mr. de Vries's family as proceeds of the sale of some portion of this estate, many years after the close of the Revolutionary War. A record of this transaction should be easily ascertained.

Does a diary of Washington cover the year 1793?

Has the family of Mr. Polk, or of Peale, the artist, any letters referring to this interesting transaction?

Is there authority for the statement, made by a lecturer (Mrs. van Helden) on "Art in Holland," that the Hollanders loaned the American Congress fourteen million dollars in aid of our Revolution?* If this be true let us cite it with this act of Claas Taan, whenever we refer with gratitude to Kosciusko, Pulaski, Von Steuben, and Lafayette.

On the 4th of July, 1876, Mr. de Vries prepared a

---

* In reply to an inquiry the writer received the following:

No. 413 Locust Street,
Philadelphia, Pa., March 6, 1889.

Rev. J. Howard Suydam, D. D., New-York City.

Rev. and Dear Sir: Some time ago you asked of my wife the authority for her statement in a public lecture, "that a large loan was made by Holland to the American People during the War of the Revolution." She was not able at the time to collect for you any definite proofs. These proofs, after a long and tedious search, it is now my pleasure to present to you.

The fact known to every student of history in Holland, but (premeditatedly or inadvertently?) omitted by American historians, is officially banquet in honor of the centennial of the Declaration of American Independence, to which Mr. James Birney and the Consul-General of the United States for Holland were invited. This portrait of Washington, appropriately draped with the American colors, was placed in the position of honor at the table; and under this inspiration the appreciative host and his friends expected to grow eloquent in their eulogium of the republic which Washington so greatly aided to establish, but unexpected family circumstances compelled its abandonment.

Investigation thus far leads to high probability that this is an uncatalogued original portrait of Washington. The writer submits this cumulative evidence: First, it has been in Mr. de Vries's family from the year 1793, the year in which it was painted. Second, it bears the name of an artist known to have painted original portraits of Washington. Third, one portrait painted by him is not accounted for. Fourth, it bears evidence of having been painted at the alleged time, in the canvas, the frame, and the artist's name. Fifth, the memorable service rendered our country by Claas Taan has ever been cherished with pride by his descendants.

In the opinion of the writer, investigation will confirm the claim of the "*De Vries Portrait*" of Washington as original; at the same time it will do tardy honor to a deserving friend of America, whom history seems to have forgotten.

stated in the report of the Tenth Census (1880), where in vol. vii, pp. 396–401, the twelve Holland Loans, aggregating 32,500,000 florins, or 13,000,000 dollars, are specified. On some of these loans no interest was paid for several years (see among others "Diplomatic Correspondence," vol. xii, p. 494), which unpaid interest added to the principal make up the $14,000,000 alluded to by my wife in her lecture on "Holland, its People, and its Art." The last instalment of these loans, amounting to 600,000 florins or $240,000, was paid off in the year 1809.

It will interest you to know that the old banking firm of Willinck at Amsterdam, with which most of the said loans were negotiated, is still extant. I am, Rev. and Dear Sir,

Very truly yours,

ADRIAN VAN HELDEN.

After this pleasant reception, the American visitors were driven to the hospital for invalid and superannuated East Indian soldiers. An English-speaking guide was placed at their disposal, who explained the various objects of interest.

Everything here suggested the colonial possessions of the Netherlands, which were far more extensive in former years than now. Holland was a formidable rival of England when she held New Amsterdam, a large portion of Brazil, and islands in the West Indies. Even now, she is the second colonial power in Europe and holds under her sway the islands of Java, Sumatra, a large portion of Borneo, territory in the Trans-Vaal, and Dutch Guiana. The demands of these dependencies furnish an explanation of the comparatively little intercourse between Holland and the United States.

This hospital building was a gift from the present king. It was at one time the residence of the Prince de Chambord. Its ample endowment and complete appointments are not only suggestive of Holland's great though diminished territory, but are also proof of the tender concern of the Government for her veteran soldiery.

The Castle of Rosendaal, in the environs of Arnhem, is of great interest to the traveler. It dates back to the VIIIth Century, and is still surrounded by a moat across which are the romantic ruins on an ancient Italian garden.

Its owner and occupant is the Baron Pallandt, who kindly extended to us an invitation to visit him. He gave us a cordial greeting, and personally conducted us through the ancient building and explained the special objects of interest.

This was once the residence of the Duke of Guelder; whose remarkable statues we had already seen in the old cathedral in the city. One of these, cut in marble, is in a recumbent posture; and the other, in bronze, mounted high against a pillar and sitting in a chair, is clad in the chain armor which he wore in life.

We were led through tortuous passages and up and down winding stairways, until we descended into a dungeon four by eight feet in dimensions. It was almost entirely dark, and contained only a narrow wooden bench. In this dungeon this same Duke of Guelder had kept his brother imprisoned for three long years! What reflections were aroused at the thought of those feudal days, of the cruel suffering below in contrast with the revelings in the spacious halls above!

The walls of this castle are fifteen feet in thickness. The love for the antique had induced the present baron, at great expense, to preserve and collect a most valuable museum.

As a memento of our visit he presented The Holland Society of New-York with an ancient drinking-cup, found some years ago in the moat.

Upon examining the badge of our Society, he said, to our surprise, that he possessed an original in gold. We afterwards found another in the museum at Middelburg.

The record of our visit to Arnhem would not be complete if we should fail to mention the great wine-house of the Messieurs Hasselink, with which is connected an interesting private museum.

This building was once a part of the old Court of Guelder. It was subsequently called the "Alva
20

Hall," because that infamous duke once resided here. As the house deals exclusively in **Spanish and Portuguese wines**, so the museum contains only curiosities **gathered from those countries.**

We were hospitably entertained with a unique luncheon amid these quaint surroundings.

At Arnhem is a school called "Velperplein," where boys are taught mechanical trades. As in Leeuwarden **we found an** old ladies' home dating from **1711, so** here we discovered the original Cooper Institute and the Williamson Free School for Mechanical Arts.

After a drive over the hills and through the clean, cultivated forests, we returned to the city and partook of a princely banquet.

Witty and patriotic speeches **were made by our** hosts. Mr. Menzo van **Voorhis made reply in behalf** of the guests. **Among** other things he said : **"That** the spontaneous expressions of welcome everywhere received by the representatives of **The Holland Society** had filled them with wonder and gratitude; **that they had been taken to the homes and hearts of the people, as if they were near** kindred returned **after a long absence; and that** he regarded this **hearty demonstration as conveying** a meaning not limited to our Society, but as having special reference to the great country which they represented."

Although the day had **been so crowded with matters of interest, and the** time had extended far into the evening, there was still more in **reserve for us.** It had been thoughtfully prearranged by the **Society** representing Arnhem, that we should attend one of **their famous** garden concerts, under **the most favorable auspices.** Carriages were provided, and we were rapidly driven to a music garden in the suburbs and distant about two miles.

When we arrived, we found an immense amphi-theater, rising gradually from a little lake, in which were seated thousands of people listening to the music from the band in a pavilion across the water. As soon as the Americans appeared under the escort of their hosts, the programme was changed, and one of our national airs was rendered; while the whole vast assembly arose in complimentary acknow-ledgment.

It was remarkable to a degree, and should be spec-ially emphasized, that the bands of music in every place visited took special pains to honor our country by performing our national airs.

Our pleasure here was enhanced by the beauty of the scene. The torches shining through the forest trees, the gaily dressed company, the little lake be-neath, with a flock of white swans swimming to and fro in the reflected lights, added romance to the music.

Our coaches had been dismissed. It was deter-mined to return to the city by tramway. A gentle-man, passing in his private carriage, recognized us by our badges, as we stood beneath the street lamps. Leaving his family at his villa, near at hand, he quickly returned and kindly placed his coach and servants at our service. We were then driven to the principal club-house of the city, where the hospital-ities of the day were concluded. The names of those of our hosts which we are able to decipher from their peculiar chirography are as follows: Mr. J. Everts B. Hzn; W. F. Hasselink, vice-consul de España; Mr. A. C. von Daalen; K. D. Punt, First Lieutenant der Rydende Artillerie; M. A. Sipman of the "Arn-hem Courant." They have since forwarded to our Society a beautiful copy of a "Guide for Arnhem and its Environs" containing their autographs. They were promptly at the station the next morning, and bade their guests a God-speed. Two issues of the "Arnhem Courant" devoted considerable space to the visit of the Americans.

UTRECHT.

IT was a cause of sincere regret to the members of The Holland Society that, through a misunderstanding, they were unable to visit Utrecht at the time fixed by the city authorities. It was intended to extend to them a welcome as hearty as those received in other places. We were told that the Burgomaster and Council had assembled in the Town Hall, that the music was in position, that the carriages were in readiness for the guests, that the banquet had been ordered, that the line of procession was gorgeous with flags, that all business was practically suspended, and that the people had gathered in the streets. It was nearly noonday when the intelligence was received that we had gone to Alkmaar.

If there was a momentary feeling that due regard was not paid to their generous intentions, the explanation entirely exonerated the management of the Society from neglect, indifference, or the least want of courtesy.

The four gentlemen who up to this time had represented the Society in Leeuwarden, Sneek, Groningen, and Arnhem, were reënforced at Utrecht, by the arrival of the Secretary and the Messrs. Van Norden from Amsterdam.

Here we were the special guests of Mr. de Wilde, a leading notary of the city. He was brother-in-law to the late celebrated Professor Van Osterzee, whose services the General Synod of the Reformed Church in America sought to secure as a theological teacher in the seminary at New Brunswick.

We were conducted to the principal points of interest in this ancient city, which abounds in historic associations. The great church, the art galleries, the museum, and the University received our earnest attention. The Hall of the Seven Provinces deserves separate mention. There was enough here to inspire the most sluggish nature with enthusiasm. In this room was formed the Union of the Provinces, which was never broken until after nearly three generations the people of Holland succeeded in casting off the galling yoke of Spain. It is confidently asserted that here was found the germ and the model of our own United States of America!

The luncheon at the residence of Mr. de Wilde, in company with his interesting family, including representatives of the Army and Navy, is photographed on the memory, and furnishes one of the most pleasing pictures in the retrospect of our visit to the Netherlands.

A drive through the surburban villages for miles in the shade of overarching elms, with swift horses on a perfect road, terminated at the settlement of a peculiar people who were called "Heerenhutters." These form a community very closely resembling the Shakers in America. The peculiar head-dress of the women indicates their state,— whether single, married, or widowed. There is also a distinctive dress which proclaims a woman as unmarried, and not to be sought after! The wife is selected for a man by an official committee.

The day in Utrecht closed by a visit to the most famous establishment of silver-work in Holland; Mr. C. J. Begeer is proprietor. We watched with interest the busy operatives, as they were casting, cutting, ornamenting, and polishing the magnificent set of many massive pieces of silver, to be presented by King William to his daughter, the princess, on her approaching birthday.

We were surprised and delighted also to receive for each lady and gentleman visiting Holland, a beautiful bronze medal, which had been designed and engraved as a special memento of the event, by this establishment.

MIDDELBURG.

THE Secretary departed for Amsterdam, to return to America on the following day. At the same time, the other members of the Society, now six in number, took the train going in the opposite direction, for Middelburg. This is the principal city of Zeeland the southernmost province of the Netherlands.

We arrived here a day sooner than was expected. By some means, however, it became known, and the Secretary of the city immediately called and made arrangements for our visit. The American flag, loaned by the American consul, Mr. Smidt, of Flushing, was raised over the hotel, where we were the subjects of much curiosity.

Middelburg once contained a population of 70,000, but it has now diminished to 16,000 inhabitants. Of these, but 1600 are Romanists; nearly all the others are members of the Reformed Dutch Church. As in the other cities throughout Holland, the churches here are Collegiate. The ministers alternate their preaching services; but each pastor has his peculiar parish work.

As in Hoorn, Leeuwarden, and other cities of the Netherlands, so at Middelburg, there are many who live in dignified retirement, upon the income of capital secured by former generations. The buildings being too numerous for the reduced numbers of the population, many of them have been demolished, so as to furnish ample space for the beautiful gardens which abound in the city. Here Jacob Cats, one of Holland's greatest poets, had his home from 1603 to 1623, as indicated upon the tablet on his dwelling.

The municipal museum here has a peculiar interest. Mr. G. N. de Stoppelaar, one of our generous hosts, has at his own expense erected a beautiful building, and arranged it for the interesting collection of antiquities and curiosities, already very large, and rapidly increasing. The elegant volume published for private circulation, a copy of which was presented to The Holland Society, is at once a proof of his artistic and literary taste, as well as an indication of the wealth of the museum, of which he is the liberal patron.

Here we found an original gold "Beggar's badge," like the one owned by Baron Palandt van Rosendaal, and also one in silver. Both contain the same device; the one in gold is the size of that now worn by the members of our Holland Society; while the one in silver is much larger. Neither of them have the cups or the flagon attached.

In this museum, also, is the original trumpet, through which De Ruyter thundered his commands to his ever-victorious fleet. And still more suggestive was the sight of the first telescope, invented by Jansen. The Americans had found so many "first things" during their journey, that they were led to ask whether everything in the scientific world did not originate in Holland ?

We partook of a midday breakfast at the club-house, where the Rev. Dr. Zynen, a leading clergy-man of the city, who adds to his clerical duties the office of President of the Zeelandian Society of Sciences, read the following address :

" *Gentlemen :* In our city of Middelburg have we the honor to bid welcome to some members of The Holland Society of New York. This is but a small town, not to compare with towns in America or elsewhere.

"Wherefore we are glad that Middelburg has so great signification in the eyes of the travelers that they found it worthy to pay a visit to this place. Therefore will I propose to drink to the health and the farther good journey of the travelers to the Fatherland from great America."

After visiting other prominent objects of interest in the city, and notably the Town Hall, which is the most beautiful of its kind in Holland, and which furnished the model for the one at Antwerp, the company were then driven to Flushing, where they were the guests of Mr. R. P. Smidt, the American consul. Mr. Smidt had caused a new American flag to be made, which was raised over his residence for the first time in honor of our visit.

Consul Smidt possesses a private museum of great value and rare beauty. We here visited the Pilot Club-House; and saw the magnificent statue of the great naval commander De Ruyter: Flushing was his birthplace, and they cherish his memory with pride.

At the banquet in the evening at the Hotel Doelen, there were present the following gentlemen: Deputy Burgomaster F. Ermerrius, J. W. de Raad, secretary of the city; W. Polman Kruseman; M. Fokker; Dr. J. C. de Man; Dr. J. P. Perdennis van Berlekom; Henry Tak; G. N. de Stoppelaar; J. A. Frederiks; the Rev. Dr. Sibmacher Zynen; R. P. Smidt, American consul at Flushing.

The company was soon *en rapport*. All the Hollanders spoke the English language. The "Middelburg Courant" of the date, as well as the menu, in honor of our Society were printed on orange colored paper. The enterprise of the proprietor was displayed in publishing the day's proceedings and furnishing a copy to each guest while at dinner in the early evening. A proper acknowledgment of this courtesy was signed by all present and forwarded to the editor. The Deputy Burgomaster made a speech of welcome, in which he expressed his regret that "Volapuk" had not become general. He, however, did not need it on this occasion.

21

John H. Voorhees, Esq., of Washington, made the following reply :

"I thank you, gentlemen, most heartily in the name of The Holland Society, for the courtesies extended to us both on this and other occasions during our visit to our and your fatherland. Our visit has been full of surprises — most delightful surprises.

"We were not unfamiliar with your history. Our Motley has recalled and painted in lively and enduring colors the record of that marvelous struggle for civil and religious liberty in which the grand figure of William the Silent stands out in bold relief, and which recalls two other grand figures, those of Washington and Lincoln, a trio inseparably connected in the history of the great battle for human rights.

"We knew, too, something of the no less marvelous and ceaseless battle which you as a people have maintained against the powers of the sea, driving back old ocean, saying, 'Thus far and no further,' erecting Titanic battlements to resist his assaults, redeeming from his grasp whole provinces, and clothing his oozy bed with fertile fields of waving grain.

"We knew, too, something of the creations of your painters, whose canvas glows with the light of genius, whether depicting sacred and classic story or domestic life; but our conceptions were of an ideal and dreamy character until we trod your streets and gazed upon your public buildings and edifices, every stone of which is eloquent with memories of scenes enacted in the olden time, and consecrated by the blood of your martyrs to freedom.

"But one thing we did not know; it is the charm of your home life, the lessons of the hearth and the family altar, and when you took us by the hand we felt a warmer glow in our veins; when you introduced us to your firesides we felt the secret of the influence of Dutch civilization and colonization. It is the education of the home, the Bible in the house, the mother teaching the deference to age and parental authority.

"There is a stream in the ocean which is warmer than the surrounding waters. It rises in the sunny regions of the South. It melts the iceberg in its course, and the winds which sweep over it impart new life and beauty and a more vigorous vegetation to every land which feels their balmy influence. There is also a stream in the ocean of humanity. It is warmer and more life-giving than surrounding nationalities. It rises in our and your fatherland and motherland. It is warmed by the domestic virtues of your homes. It is purified and invigorated by the traditions of your history and the proud memories of your ancestry, by the perseverance and integrity of your character. This stream broke upon the New World, and a new Amsterdam rose to greet her mother, and from the principles then and there planted have sprung a free school, and a free press, and a free pulpit, and a free ballot, and the tree of knowledge, whose leaves are for the healing of the nations. We rejoice to meet our kin beyond the sea, and to feel, as we do feel, that blood is thicker than water; and that we have a common inheritance with you in the glory, the traditions, and the history of Holland.

"Gentlemen, it is the influence of Holland upon civilization that is her proudest glory. The fame of

her painters and jurists and statesmen, and the
learning of Leyden, will live when the triumphs of
Van Tromp and De Ruyter are forgotten.

> "Though from thy unsceptered hands shall pass away
> The pomp and vast dominion of the sea,
> Still shalt thou reign; nor shall the loss of these
> Enroll thee with earth's dead sovereignties,
> Not these thine empire, but the human soul,
> And they thy kings, thy nobles, who control
> In that dread realm where bends no servile knee.

"Let me give you, gentlemen,

"The mothers and daughters of Holland."

A toast was also given "To the Princess" by one
of the gentlemen of Middelburg, at the latter end of
the feast. The consul, who is a native Hollander,
was asked if this was in accord with recognized eti-
quette. "Oh, yes," he replied, "in Holland — ours is
a free country." A photograph of the princess was
presented to each one of the guests.

On Sunday we attended church where the services
are conducted in the English language. They are held
in an ancient building which was in use when the
people were Roman Catholics, and previous to the
Protestant Reformation. It is Collegiate, with the
church at Flushing.

These churches were established and fostered by
Queen Elizabeth for her troops, when aiding the
Hollanders in the war against Spain. They were of
peculiar interest to some of our company, since Dr.
Archibald Laidlie was called from his pastorate over
them to be the first English-speaking preacher in the

Reformed Protestant Dutch Church in New-York.
The building erected for him stood until quite recently on the corner of William and Fulton streets.
At the close of the service, the organist performed
several American national airs in an admirable
manner. The minister and members of the con-
sistory also recognized our visit by ordering a
record of the incident to be placed upon the official
minutes.

The day was warm, and the atmosphere dreamy as
that at Sorrento. After writing letters to those
across the sea, with thoughts still dwelling upon
them, we strolled through the clean, quiet streets,
and when beneath its shadow, the sweet chimes of
the bells in the tower of the great church broke
forth into the strain of "Home, Sweet Home,"
our emotions, already stirred, were, as may be
supposed, greatly intensified.

ANTWERP.

IT was reasonable to conclude that our visits were
now ended, since we had reached the southern limit
of the Kingdom of the Netherlands. Imagine our
surprise when we were informed that a dispatch had
been received by our Secretary, Mr. Van Siclen, in
Amsterdam from The Holland Society of Antwerp,
inviting us to be their guests. The dispatch was
followed by a special messenger, who traced us to
Middelburg, and thence to Flushing, and finally
found us at a seaside hotel in the suburbs. He
urged us so earnestly to visit Antwerp that we
changed the plans already formed and consented.

Mr. Bisdom, the president of The Holland Society of Antwerp, called upon us at the hotel, immediately upon our arrival in that city.

Here we were joined by Mr. Peyton Miller, a fellow-member of our Society, from Albany. The Rev. Dr. Isaac S. Hartley, a prominent clergyman, and pastor of the Reformed Church of Utica, N. Y., was invited to be our guest. He courteously accepted, and shared with us the honors and hospitalities tendered.

Under the escort of President Bisdom, we first visited the pleasant rooms of their Society. Quite a company of gentlemen had gathered there to receive us. Behind a screen of plants a band of music extended a welcome with the air of the "Star-Spangled Banner." In his address, the president alluded in happy terms to our Society, and to our blood relationship. He expressed their appreciation of the constitution of the Government of the United States, and referred to the growth and prosperity of our country in terms which indicated unusual intelligence in these matters. Mr. Warner Van Norden made reply as follows:

" *Mr. President of The Holland Society, and Friends:*

" It is with profound pleasure that we stand here to-day as representatives of The Holland Society of my native city of New-York, and tender greeting from the metropolis of America to this great commercial city on the continent of Europe.

"The very existence of our prosperous city is a monument to the wisdom and foresight of our ancestors and yours. And the civil and religious liberty it now enjoys, the broad commercial and patriotic spirit of its people, and its reputation for integrity and fair dealing, are an inheritance from our Dutch forefathers.

" One of our own poets has said that a man's education begins a hundred years before he is born. We rejoice in our birthright as Americans, but we realize that our education was begun not on the western continent, but on the shores of Holland, and in a time of war and persecution ; it was begun in a time of trial and suffering, and through these of victory. We delight this afternoon in claiming the privileges of kinship. We speak a different language, but we are of the same blood as yourselves. You dwell in the fatherland ; we inhabit a greater Holland beyond the sea. We bear different names, but we are one in ancestry, one in aspirations, one in that blood and catholic spirit which has ever been a characteristic of the Hollander, and which is combining all nations in those works of practical benefit to the race in which the Netherlands and the United States stand foremost.

> "Thicker than water in one rill
> Through centuries of story,
> Our Saxon blood has flowed, and still
> We share with you its good and ill,
> Its shadow and its glory !

" We thank you for this cordial reception, a continuation of the generous hospitality which has greeted us everywhere in the Netherlands. We rejoice in your prosperity, and in reciprocating your kindly good wishes, we utter no exaggeration when we say that love and admiration for the Netherlands

and its noble people fill the warmest corner in the
American heart."

After refreshments we made a rapid drive through
the city, when we took a special steamer for an excursion on the Scheldt River. Mr. Van Maanen, the
president of the steamboat company, accompanied
us; it was the same company which had furnished
the one for our Society at Rotterdam. The arrangements were on the liberal scale for the six, as they
were for the fifty members of the Society, who visited
Brielle and Dordrecht. A full band of music attended us; two American flags floated from the
masts, and a table was spread with the usual variety
of viands. We passed the shipping, and the admirable wharves of the city, and then steamed up the
river to the town of Brooklyn, and thence to Hoboken. These familiar names recalled our homes
across the sea. Upon our return to the city we were
greeted by scores of American flags, which during
our brief absence had been run up the rigging of the
ships and the staffs on the public buildings.

Of course, we visited the famous cathederal, and
enjoyed a view of the magnificent works of art there
exhibited, including the "Elevation" and "Descent"
from the Cross, and the "Ascension," by Rubens.
We also availed ourselves of a favored opportunity
to visit the gallery so rich in the chief works of the
old masters, and the triennial exhibition of modern
art, under the intelligent escort of the well-known
artist, Mr. E. W. Boks.

The following account of our visit as published in
an Antwerp journal, and translated by Mr. Ittman, of
Brussels, will be of more interest than the monotone
of our own narrative:

THE HOLLAND SOCIETY AT ANTWERP.

As we have already communicated, the members of The
Holland Society of New-York were received by the Hol-
landsche Club at 1 o'clock. The foreign visitors were, viz.:
Messrs. Van Norden and son, the bankers; the Rev. J.
Howard Suydam, and the Rev. Isaac S. Hartley of N. Y.;
John H. Voorhees, lawyer at Washington, and Peyton
Miller, from Albany. These gentlemen with the exception
of Mr. Hartley descended by the masculine branch from
Dutchmen who in 1613 built the town of New Amsterdam,
now known as New-York. Mr. Hartley's Dutch descent
was on his mother's side, whose name was Wiltsie. None
of these gentlemen know the Dutch language. But, though
having been estranged from the native tongue of their ancient cousins, their hearts still beat warmly for the olden
country. One may, speaking as a reporter of a newspaper,
be wearied with after-dinner speeches and allocutions of
welcome; however, we must sincerely confess that we could
not hear these descendants of our ancient compatriots
praise heartily the olden country without feeling a real
emotion,— that olden country, we say,— the glory of which
they exalted, proud of being the sons of a race that produced the heroes of the Flemish community, and of the war
against Spain,— the race excelling in trade, industry, and
art at Antwerp and in the Netherlands.

The excursion on the Scheldt terminated well. Mr. Van
Maanan would by all means convey his guests stream upwards till Hoboken. One knows that one of the suburbs of
New-York bears the same name, probably imported over
the ocean.

After dinner in the "Rocher de Cancale," at which assisted
the American gentlemen, some members of the Hollandsche
Club, and some citizens of Antwerp, the party rode to the
Palace of Industry, where they arrived amidst a concert,
and where they were received by the American and Dutch
national hymns, and welcomed by the directors of the Society
and the enthusiasm of the people. This morning at eleven
o'clock there was a reception at the Town Hall, by the
Mayor, who spoke in his easy, hearty way we are accustomed to. Two of the gentlemen made answer to the Mayor.
They expressed their admiration for the beautiful city of

22

which he is the first citizen, and they hoped that Antwerp might continue to be prosperous, and that her trade with America might always increase in importance.

We can only hint at the words spoken by these gentlemen on different occasions. They all possess in a masterly way the gift of eloquence. They speak calmly, with feeling, and in choice language. They are all men of ripe years, of strongly built stature, worthy of the powerful forms of the ancient Dutch. They bear on their breasts the antique medal of the *Gueux*, with the joined hands over the beggar's pouch. With the inscription

Fideles au roy jusques à la besace.
(Faithful to the King, till the beggar's pouch.)

The effigy on the other side of the medal is that of King Philip II. In later years this cry became a cruel scoff, by which they no more asked, but required their good rights with sword in hand. The reception at the Mayor's finished, the Town Hall was visited. Afterwards the guests and their guides went to the Museum Plantin Moretus, all the details of which they examined with the greatest attention, writing, before leaving, their names on a page of "The Golden Book." In the afternoon they went to the museum of pictures and the triennial art exhibition. In Antwerp, the last of the American-Dutchmen separated. Two of them are to travel in Europe, and the others to return to America.

We wish them a most happy voyage.

We cannot conclude without a word of praise for the Hollandsche Club, and especially for its chairman, Mr. Bisdom. The members of that association, never permit any occasion to pass without representing the dignity of their native country. Their hospitality is hearty and unrestrained. To Mr. Van Maanen — that popular sea captain, the living link between North and South — we give our most hearty thanks for all he did to uphold the honor of Antwerp.

The Plantin House was of special interest. A complete description of this ancient mansion is published in one of the early numbers of "The Century Magazine" for the year 1888, under the title of "A Printer's Paradise." We were invited to enter our names beneath an appropriate introduction in what is distinguished as the "Golden Book." We here saw a copy of the first Bible and of the first newspaper ever published. We closed the day at the club-house, the front of which was brilliantly illuminated. Here we had the honor of an introduction to the President of the Ancient Society of Beggars. We received a message from the President of the Musical Association, inviting us to the "Garden of Harmony" for Wednesday evening, which would be illuminated in honor of our Society. Our reception by the Burgomaster was exceedingly cordial. His address, partly in English and partly in the French language, flowed from his lips like liquid music. His handsome face and grace of manner enhanced the effect. Drs. Suydam and Hartley made reply. We entertained a few of the committee at luncheon, when it was gravely proposed that members of The Holland Society of New-York should unite with The Holland Society of Antwerp and make a visit to the Trans-Vaal in Africa.

BRUSSELS.

SURELY this is the end! Not so. A gentleman on the street-car, discovering that we were members of The Holland Society of New-York, requested an introduction. He informed us that he was a member of the Dutch Club at Brussels, and invited us to be his guests in that city.

Mr. Ittman, our host, said that he had received too much kindness from Americans while visiting our country, to fail to do his utmost by way of return, as opportunity might be presented. He gave us a royal banquet at the *Restaurant des tous Provenceaux*. At a concert given by the opera company in the evening, we were joined by the ladies of his family.

The next morning he accompanied us to the old and new galleries of art, the *Palais de Justice*, the King's palace, etc. Of special interest to us was the old residence of the Count of Egmont, famous in the Spanish wars. It is now occupied by the family of the Duke of Arenberg, who claims equal standing with the royal house of Belgium. Our interest increased as we saw near-by the building erected on the site of the one destroyed by order of the Duke of Alva, because there the feast was held, upon which occasion the "Society of Beggars" was formed. On the façade was a tablet containing these words: "Here was erected the Palace of Cullenburg, where was held, April 6, 1566, the Banquet of the Beggars. The Council of Blood caused to raze the building in 1568, to scandalize the defendants of liberty of conscience!" Beneath it was a facsimile of the side of our badge containing the Beggars' sack and the inscription,

Jusque a porter la besace.

Napoleon's glorious career culminated in bloody fray and defeat at Waterloo. It was at Waterloo, where, standing on the summit of the mound erected to the memory of the wounded Prince of Orange, the last members representing The Holland Society bade

farewell to each other. Their career had ended with
glory undimmed. The last evening was spent by
one of the members at the beautiful rural home of
Mr. Ittman, to whom our Society is indebted for his
self-sacrificing efforts to do it honor.

HOMEWARD.

The members of The Holland Society and their
guests who returned to America by the steamer
Rotterdam, leaving the city of Rotterdam on the 1st,
and arriving in New-York on the 13th of September,
were as follows:

Hon. EDW. ELSWORTH.	Mr. FRANK HASBROUCK.
Miss MAY ELSWORTH.	Rev. J. ELMENDORF, D. D.
Mr. EUGENE ELSWORTH.	Mrs. J. ELMENDORF.
Dr. JOHN VAN DUYN.	Mr. MENZO VAN VOORHIS.
Mrs. Dr. JOHN VAN DUYN.	Mr. W. H. VREDENBERGH
Mr. PETER V. FORT.	AND SON.
Mr. JAMES A. VAN VOAST.	Hon. L. L. VAN ALLEN.
Mr. ROBERT A. VAN WIJCK.	Miss AGNES VAN ALLEN.
Mr. JAS. H. BLAUVELT.	Mr. GEO. H. HOWARD.
Mr. HARRY R. BLAUVELT.	Mr. LEE W. CASE.
Rev. J. HOWARD SUYDAM, D.D.	Rev. HENRY VAN DIJKE, D. D.
Mr. H. B. GATES.	Mrs. HENRY VAN DIJKE.
Miss GATES.	

The following testimonial was heartily signed by
every member of the Society:

AT SEA, OFF CAPE COD, September 12, 1888.

The undersigned members of The Holland Society of New-
York, returning to America on the S. S. *Rotterdam*, heartily
unite in certifying to the staunch and seaworthy character
of the noble steamship on which we are sailing; and also to
the competency, faithfulness, and courtesy of Captain Van
Der Zee and the officers under his command, to whom we

tender our sincere thanks for their kindness and attention to us on our voyage homeward. And as we near the end of this memorable trip on sea and land, we wish again to express to the officers and managers of the Netherlands-American S. S. Navigation Co. our high appreciation of their generous provision for our comfort and pleasure while embarked on our ocean voyage.

Resolutions offered by Mr. Frank Hasbrouck were also enthusiastically passed by the whole company.

At a meeting of the members of The Holland Society, held on board the steamer *Rotterdam*, in New-York harbor, on the 13th day of September, 1888, it was resolved :

That in view of the magnificent reception of the representatives of The Holland Society by their brothers in Holland, of the unprecedented enthusiasm and royal treatment shown them on their visit, it is fitting that an expression of appreciation of the efforts of the originator, director, and executive head of the excursion should be recorded and conveyed to him,

It was resolved; that the thanks of all the participants in The Holland Society excursion are due and are hereby heartily tendered to Geo. W. Van Sielen, Esq., Secretary, for proposing the excursion, for arranging all details, for conducting a large party successfully through many most pleasant experiences, and for unselfishly devoting all his time and energies during the entire trip to the promotion of the comfort and happiness of all the members of the Society.

With the delightful memories of our visit to the fatherland, the pleasant associations with our hosts and with each other, and our thanks for the distinguished favors conferred, we would especially record our gratitude to God, by whose benignant providence we made our voyage without accident or serious illness.

The historian cannot better close his narrative than by transcribing the valedictory issued by our Secretary on our departure from the country.

Valedictory of the Members of The Holland Society of
New-York on their departure from the Netherlands.
(Inserted in the leading newspapers of Holland.)

To the Editor. AMSTERDAM, Aug. 25, 1888.

Dear Sir : The reception accorded us, as members of The
Holland Society of New-York, on the occasion of our visit
to the Netherlands, was so affecting and remarkable that
we wish most earnestly to express — by means of your
esteemed organ — our sincere thanks : In the first place,
to the Honorable Burgomasters and Committees of Reception at Amsterdam, The Hague, Rotterdam, Utrecht, Leyden,
Delft, Dordrecht, Hoorn, Alkmaar, Leeuwarden, Sneek,
Groningen, Arnhem, Middelburg, Brielle, and Marken; to
the Society *Natura Artis Magistra;* to the Agricultural
Society of the District Alkmaar; to Chevalier van Foreest, at Heilo; to Honorable Levyssohn Norman, at The
Hague; and to the well organized Netherlands-American
Steam Navigation Company ; and also to the people of the
Netherlands, a number of whom showed us great hospitality.
Others would undoubtedly have followed their example, had
not the time at our disposal been so limited.

In a word, we offer our most hearty thanks for the hospitality shown us everywhere; for the brotherly friendship
to be read in the eyes of every one, and expressed in the
hand-shakings on all sides. Indeed, we feel overcome by
these many tokens of kindness, and our hearts are deeply
touched by the demonstrations of welcome especially prepared for us.

Our Society was founded on the sincere love we bore to
Holland, which has been kept alive since 1675, not only by the
names we bear, but also by the throbbing of the blood in our
veins. It was that feeling which impelled us to make this
excursion to the land of our ancestors.

Never can we forget the friendship shown us; and it is
our ardent wish that we also may be remembered by you.

At the close of our too short a visit, we bid a last farewell
to this classic soil of free thought.

THE HOLLAND SOCIETY OF NEW-YORK.

For all the members :

GEO. W. VAN SICLEN, *Secretary.*

THE END.

The "History of Kingston and Its Vicinity," by
Hon. Marius Schoonmaker, published this year, 1888;
and the "Book of American Powder Horns," by Mr.
Rufus A. Grider of Canajoharie, N. Y., were by per-
mission of the trustees, dedicated to The Holland
Society of New-York.

To the committee consisting of Rev. Henry van
Dyke and Messrs. Wm. M. Hoes and Henry S. Van
Duzer, who had charge of the production of the Badge
of the Society, and who carried out with amend-
ments Gen. J. Watts de Peyster's unique design for
a certificate of membership, was entrusted the design
and production of a suitable badge or insignia of
office to be worn by the President of this Society
when representing it upon public occasions. A copy
of the design of this Badge, the result of their labors,
is inserted here.

·FOURTH ANNUAL· DINNER

OF THE

HOLLAND SOCIETY

HOTEL BRUNSWICK.
JANUARY 8th
1889.

R.W.van Boskerck

Eindelijk wordt een Spruit een Boom.

Spijskaart.

De Weleerwaarde Heer Hendrik van Dijke, Th. D. zal aan Tafel voorbidden.

Blauwe Landtongsche Oesters.

Sauterneswijn, 1874.

Soep.

West-Indische Peulen met Kip.
Dikke Zeekreeften Soep.

Topaasche Sereese.

Zijschoteljes.

Selderij. Olijven. Radijs. Kaviaar.
Ansjovis Taartjes.
Garnalen — Pasteitjes, Boheemsche Stijl.

Gekruide Gerechten.

Gestreepte Baars, met Bigarade Saus, in Sint Jacob Schelpen.
Aardappelen, Hollandsche Stijl.
Ossenhaas, Turgot Stijl.
Spruitjes met botersaus.   Aardappelen, Julien Stijl.

Roodewijn.
Pontet Canel.

Voorgerechten.

Krullen van Kapoen, met Perigueux Saus.
Doperwten, Engelsche Stijl.
Land-schildpad in Busjes, Baltimoresche Stijl.

Champagnewijn.
Duminy, buitengewoon prikkelend. Cuvée 1884.
Perrier Jouët, extra Brut.
Irroy, buitengewoon prikkelend.
Roederer, grootwijn, prikkelend.

SORBET, HOLLANDSCHE STIJL.

Gebraad.

Roodkop Eendvogels.
Kwartels op geroosterd Brood.

Ganzenleverpasteitjes met Gelei.
Selderij-sla met citroensaus.

Bourgognewijn.

Zoete Gerechten.

Frambozengelei.   Chateaubriand Ijs.   Zwitsersche Meringue.
    Goudsche Spritsen.   Haarlemsche Roode Letters.
Haagsche Ontbijtkoek.   Pistachio Koek.   Sucadekoek.   Kermiskoek.
    Sint Niklaaskoek.   Witte Janhagel.   Haagsche Hopjes.
Haagsche Moppen.   Utrechtsche Theerandjes.   Genueezen Ijs.

Nagerecht.

Camembert Kaas.   Roquefort Kaas.   Vruchten.
    Nooten en Rozijnen.   Suikerwerk met Deviezen.

Gemonteerde Stukken.

Koffie.

Likeuren, Fransche Brandewijn van Robin, dertig jaren oud. Sigaren.

Pijpen en Tabak.

(Gekronkelde Goudsche Pijpen, gezonden, met de koekjes, uit Holland
door den Nieuw-Amsterdamschen Onder-Voorzitter van het Hollandsche
Genootschaap te New-York, tevens gevolmachtigd Minister en buitengewoon Gezant voor de Vereenigde Staten bij de Nederlandsche Regeering.)

Heil-Dronken.

9

I. Holland.

Holland, the conquest made by man over the sea. The Hollanders made it; it exists because the Hollanders preserve it; it will vanish whenever the Hollanders abandon it.

President Hooper C. van Vorst.

Music. Al is ons Laadje nog zoo klein.

II. Investiture of the President of the Holland Society

With his Badge of Office, on behalf of the Trustees, by

Rev. Henry van Dyke, D. D.

Music. Wien Neêrlandsch Bloed.

III. The "Half Moon."

Push off the boat,
Quit, quit the shore,
The stars will guide us back;
O gathering clouds,
O wide, wide sea,
O waves that keep no track.

Hon. William Waldorf Astor.

Music. De Zilvervloot.

IV. Solidity versus Sensation.

The true grandeur of nations is in those qualities which constitute the true greatness of the individual.

Hon. Thomas F. Bayard.

Music. Noach en de Wijn.

V. The Dutch Masters.

For some must follow, and some command,
Though all are made of clay.

Mr. F. Hopkinson Smith.

Music. Selections from Chimes of Normandy.

VI. Dutch Enterprise.

The Ocean was the birthright of the Dutch. They were the first free nation to put a girdle of Empire around the World.

Hon. William Bourke Cockran.

Music. De Kabels loos.

VII. The Captors of New Netherland.

Our Comrades now; enemies no longer.

Mr. De Lancey Nicoll.

Music. Selections.

Commissie tet regeling van den Maaltijd.

George M. Van Hoesen, Chairman.

George G. De Witt, Jr.   William M. Boes.

Herman W. Vander Poel.   Charles A. Vanderhoof.

Philip Van Volkenburgh, Jr.   Robert W. Van Boskerck.

Holland Society Dinner

AT THE

HOTEL BRUNSWICK, N. Y.

TUESDAY, JANUARY 8, 1889.

BLUE POINT OYSTERS

Sauternes

Potages

CHICKEN WITH OKRA   BISQUE OF LOBSTER

Topaz Sherry

Hors d'oeuvres

CELERY   OLIVES   RADISHES   CAVIAR   ANCHOVY TARTINES
SHRIMP PATTIES BOHEMIENNE

Relevés

ESCALOPPES OF BASS BIGARADE SAUCE
HOLLANDAISE POTATOES

TENDERLOIN OF BEEF TURGOT
BRUSSELS SPROUTS AU BEURRE   JULIENNE POTATOES

Poulet Sauté

Entrées

CREPINETTES OF CAPON, PERIGUEUX
FRENCH PEAS A L'ANGLAISE

TERRAPIN IN CASES A LA BALTIMORE   Champagnes

Holland Sorbet

Duminy Extra dry Cuvee 1884
Perrier Jouet, Special ar Brut
Louis Roederer, Grand Vin Sec
Irroy Extra dry

Rôtis

RED-HEAD DUCK   PALES SUR CANAPES

PATE DE FOIE GRAS TIMBALLS WITH JELLY
CELERY SALAD REMOULADE

Burgundy

Entremets Sucrés

RASPBERRY JELLY
CHATEAUBRIANT ICE CREAM   SWISS MERINGUEES
PETITS FOURS   PISTACHE CAKE
GENOISE GLACEE

Dessert

CAMEMBERT   ROQUEFORT   NUTS AND RAISINS
FRUIT   MOTTOES

Pieces Montées

CAFE

Liqueurs   Cognac Belin, 30 years old   Cigars

·

ANNUAL DINNER OF

THE HOLLAND SOCIETY OF NEW-YORK,

JANUARY 8, 1889.

HE Society sat down to its annual dinner January 8, 1889, at the Hotel Brunswick. The dinner was excellent, and well served, but the Society had increased so in membership that the room was overcrowded. There was at this time no convenient room in the city at which a full dinner or banquet could be properly served for so many guests at one time.

Among the many works of art which were kindly lent by their owners to decorate the dining-hall were copies of pictures by Rembrandt made by Mr. Thos. W. Shields, and one copied by Mr. J. Carroll Beckwith, a Frans Hals which hangs in the Town Hall at Haarlem and represents the banquet of the officers of the St. George's Archers in 1627; also a companion Frans Hals hanging in the same gallery, a group of old Dutch women representing the governing board of some charity, copied by Mr. Wm. M. Chase.

GUESTS OF MEMBERS OF THE HOLLAND SO-
CIETY AND ITS MEMBERS AT THE ANNUAL
DINNER, JANUARY 8, 1889.

W. W. ASTOR,
JAMES H. BAILEY,
CHARLES H. BECKETT,
HERMAN S. BERGEN,
HENRY AUGUSTUS BOORAEM,
NICHOLAS BREWER,
CHARLES BRAY,
MORGAN B. BLYDENBERGH,
JACOB A. CANTOR,
HOWARD CARROLL,
WILLIAM BOURKE COCHRAN,
E. BEACH CROWELL,
Rev. WESLEY REID DAVIS,
    D. D.,
PETER DE BAUN,
THOMAS DIMOND,
WM. J. DUFFY,
FRANK L. FROMENT,
Col. EDWARD GILON,
ALMON GOODWIN,
ROBERT B. HIGHT,
A. J. G. HODENPYL,

L. ISRAELS,
JOHN JAY,
LYMAN A. JACOBUS,
JOHN V. JEWELL,
Lieut. T. B. M. MASON,
    U. S. A.,
GEORGE W. McGOWN,
EDWARD B. MERRILL,
EDWARD MITCHELL,
JACOB F. MILLER,
DE LANCY NICOLL,
EDWARD S. RAPALLO,
CHARLES L. RICKERSON,
McKENZIE SEMPLE,
EDWARD F. SLAYBACK,
F. HOPKINSON SMITH,
GEORGE M. SNYDER,
ROBERT M. STREBEIGH,
M. B. STREETER,
FREDERICK C. WAGNER,
JOSIAH L. WEBSTER, Jr.,
SPENCER WHITEHEAD.

SPEECH OF PRESIDENT VAN VORST.

Gentlemen of The Holland Society:

SOME person has said, perhaps the wish was father to the thought, that The Holland Society in selecting this evening, the 8th of January, for its annual dinner, designed to pay some special honor to the battle of New Orleans, and to General Jackson, who won that great victory, under the belief on the part of Dutchmen that General Jackson was a Dutchman. If he was a Dutchman, gentlemen, he certainly was not one on his father's side.

But this is an entire mistake. We had no idea of appropriating General Jackson to ourselves. He was a distinguished man, undoubtedly, and possessed many of the distinctive traits in the Dutch character. General Jackson was a courageous man, and he was decided in his action to the very last degree. These are Dutch qualities, undoubtedly. But we, the Dutch, have had our own victories upon the land and upon the sea, and we have no occasion to appropriate to ourselves either New Orleans or General Jackson. General Jackson and his victory belong to us as

American citizens, and we honor him as a great statesman and a great soldier.

But it was a happy coincidence, undoubtedly, which led the Committee to select this 8th of January for its dinner, a day which chronicles an action highly honorable to American courage, and highly honorable to its soldiers. In fact, gentlemen, it would be exceedingly difficult to select any day in the year in which it would not appear that some heroic action has been performed either by our own countrymen or by our Holland ancestors.

It has been the custom of The Holland Society, gentlemen, to hold its annual dinner in the early days of the new year, when there are bright thoughts in the mind, and when we are forming new plans for the future. We are not now seated amidst the ashes of dead enterprises, but we are lifted up by the inspiration of our future, which is holding out bright promises to us. It is allowable for us, as the descendants of the Dutch settlers upon these shores of the New World, in the beginning of the new year, to have our thoughts directed to our ancestry, men who have accomplished so much for their posterity, and so much for mankind in every department which ennobles life and distinguishes action.

The evidence, gentlemen, of the patient and intelligent industry of the Dutch is written all over the face of that land which they wrested with strong hands from the ocean, and which they have secured from the approaches of the sea, and its terrible assaults, by strong walls. Napoleon, when he had taken Holland, said: " Why, Holland belonged to our empire once ; the soil with which the Dutchmen have made their land was torn from France by its rivers, the Scheldt and the Meuse, and borne down there, and these Dutchmen have made Holland of it." That was his justification for his conquest of Holland.

The faithful historian, gentlemen, with an impartial and eloquent pen, must tell of the great sacrifices which our ancestors have made through many years to resist the oppression of tyranny and to establish law and liberty.

We have met at this hour, my friends, to reflect with pleasure upon the hospitality of our ancestors, extended to exiles from foreign lands, driven by the cruelty of men and of society to more congenial shores — to a grander hospitality and a grander treatment which they received in Holland. In times of war their courage was invincible, and their resources equal to any emergency; but when war was over and peace proclaimed, they cultivated science, scholarship, literature, and the arts, every department of which they have illustrated with immortal works.

Holland is a country in area very much smaller than the State of New-York, yet it presents to the world as a statesman and a soldier, William the Silent; as a scholar, Erasmus; as a student in law, Grotius; and in the arts, Rembrandt. We say to other lands as a whole, surpass them if you can.

Now, gentlemen, although Holland (and that is my text according to the programme which the Committee has presented), with its cities and its people, should be swallowed by the sea from which it was captured, as many of its cities and hundreds of thousands of its people in past centuries have been, yet the influence of the Dutch upon mankind cannot be lost. Its memorial will always be found indelibly written in the history and experience of all civilized States. Here upon these shores, upon this Manhattan Island, in this great city of New-York, and State of New-York, upon their institutions and upon their laws are to be found the impress of the intelligent and liberty-loving mind of the first Dutch settlers.

Although generations of men have come and have passed away, although they may appear in the future and disappear, yet the influence of the early Dutch settlers of the State of New-York will never be lost. It is so written in the lives of these men. It is so written in our institutions that it can never be lost.

Gentlemen, I congratulate you to-night upon the progress made by The Holland Society. During the past year its membership has greatly increased. This is not a mutual admiration society. We are here, my friends, from all parts of the country; our membership extends from Maine to California, from the Atlantic to the Pacific. All the large cities of the land furnish members for The Holland Society, and although the heart is here in the city of New-York, it has not become corrupted; it is a good, sound, and solid heart, my friends, and it sends out its warm, living current through all extremities of its body. Its blood is neither cold nor thin. The interest taken in our organization and work shows itself in all parts of the country where descendants of the Dutch are found. The people of Holland regard our organization with great interest. It could not well be otherwise. They observe with pleasure the just pride which we take in our common ancestors and our common interest in all great things which Holland has accomplished.

Faithfully yours
W. S. Ogden Hegeman

During the past summer many members of The Holland Society visited Holland, where they received gracious welcome, and experienced from communities and from the people everywhere the sincerest expressions of a generous hospitality. Nothing was withheld. I had not the pleasure of being one of that company, but, from the reports brought to us, there was no limit to the expressions of kindness and generous hospitality on the part of our Dutch friends on the other side. Nothing was omitted to make the visit attractive and pleasant.

Now, my friends, I would not willingly cast a cloud over the joy of this occasion. I would not willingly call before you anything which could cause any feeling of sorrow or sadness to arise in your hearts. I cannot but allude to a loss which we have sustained in the last hours of the year just passed away. I allude to the death of William A. Ogden Hegeman, a man endeared to us by his many virtues. I speak feelingly upon this subject. He has always been at our dinners; he was a charter member of this Society, and one of its first trustees. His death was sudden, but his life was a well-rounded one; it was equally useful and honorable.

Now, gentlemen, I bid welcome in your name to the representatives from our sister cities, to the St. Nicholas Society, the St. George Society, the New England Society, the Martin Luther Society, and all other societies who may have representatives with us. We have no ground of complaint to make with the New England Society now, I believe. Those severe conflicts, of which the great historian Irving has written, between the Dutch and the Yankees, have gone away; they have passed, and we are at

peace with them. We are now here together, united
by blood and by friendship, and our occupation of
this part of the country, the Dutch and the New
Englanders, is a joint one. If we have any enemy at
all, if we have any unpleasantness at all, from any
source, it may be from the countrymen of our friend
Mr. Bourke Cockran, who is seated there beside the
Mayor, or from the Germans. But we mean to stick;
we mean to stay here as long as we possibly can,
although we are surrounded by water, and with
water, gentlemen, the Dutch are familiar.

I have said to you that the peace between ourselves
and the New England Society is a lasting one, and I
trust that it will never be broken. I will state a
remarkable instance of it. I was reading within a
very few days an article descriptive of the celebration
of the New England Society in Charleston, South
Carolina, and I noticed the eloquent addresses that
were made there on that occasion. It was to my
mind a striking incident that the New England
dinner should be presided over by a Dutchman, the
Reverend Doctor Vedder, who was born in the State
of New-York, on the Mohawk River. I recall with
pleasure the speech he made on that occasion, in the
course of which he accounted for the singular fact
that a Dutchman had been elected President of the
New England Society in the State of South Carolina.

Now, the Dutch are rather persuasive, not only
with the gun, but with the tongue, also. They can
wield that with very great power, and Dr. Vedder
seems to have acquired that art, for he persuaded
the New England people in South Carolina that the
New Englanders, in fact, the Old Englanders, also,
were all Dutchmen; that they were descended from

the Jutes, Saxons, and Angles of Old Netherlands.
The argument, gentlemen, would seem to have been
sufficient, for it secured his election to be President
of the New England Society.

But I must bring my remarks, which are but the
prelude to the real enjoyment of the evening, to a
close. With the speaking which is yet to come, I
am sure you are to be delighted.

SPEECH OF REV. HENRY VAN DYKE, D. D.

May it please the Court :

THE duty with which I have been charged to-night is one which does not need very much explanation, or any apologies; in fact, so superficial is my speech, your Honor, that you may be justified in using to me the language of an Irish Judge, who said : "Prisoner at the bar, I want you to understand that we want nothing out of your mouth, and mighty little of that." But it is hardly in human nature, and certainly not in American human nature, after dinner to scorn the opportunity of making a few remarks, and it certainly is not in my power to perform silently the task which awakens sentiments of respect, friendship, and affection. In fact, I may say, I have been charged by the honorable trustees of this Society not to be dumb, but to make you understand distinctly that there is not a man in this room who is guilty of contempt of Court, but that, on the contrary, this ceremony expresses a very sincere and cordial sentiment of regard and esteem from every member of The Holland Society.

Faithfully Yours

Henry J. van Dyke Jr.

Four years ago, sir, you were called upon to preside over the destinies of this Society, and since that time you have held that office to our great satisfaction. Even your native bashfulness cannot keep us from saying that you are the most truthful, the most honorable, the most wise, the most agreeable President that The Holland Society has ever had. Through all these years, sir, you have borne your honors meekly; you have assumed no airs of superiority, and have not claimed any insignia of authority. No blatant cock crows before you on the table; you do not wear an immense Holman liver pad to aid your digestion; no, sir. You take your chance with the rest of us, and you appear quite simple in your personal dignity, and in the comparative nakedness of a modern dress coat. In this, sir, you prove your modesty, and your true Holland descent. My friends, sons of Dutchmen are modest, and we are proud of it. While the descendants of other lands have been making "Much ado about nothing," claiming credit for everything; while St. George has laid his hand upon all the style, and St. Andrew claimed all the prudence, and St. Plymouth Rock has claimed all the piety, and St. Patrick has expressed a desire to paint the City Hall green, the descendants of the men who discovered this island and founded this city, have impressed their character upon its civic life and institutions, and have mainly kept quiet and minded their own business. Stolid and phlegmatic? Perhaps so; but indifferent? No. If we reckon it a higher honor than royal courts or heralds can confer to be able to trace a direct descent in the male line to those true, brave, straightforward, honest, highminded, big-hearted men, who fought the battles of liberty in the Old World, and gave the New World her freest and her grandest State, we believe in their type of republicanism which does not mean license, but liberty, secured by law, to every man. We believe in their type of civilization, which is orderly, conservative, and makes haste slowly. We believe in their type of piety, which is broad, generous, cheerful, and accords to others the same freedom of faith which they claim for themselves.

Gentlemen, we look back to those old Hollanders, and we are convinced in a quiet but rather firm way that we have shown the greatest possible wisdom in the choice of our ancestors. Now, gentlemen, please do not let any one misunderstand our sentiments upon this point. It is not modern Holland to which we look with these feelings of reverence and affection. She is an admirable nation. Those gentlemen who visited her in the summer season found her in many respects an amiable country, but she is not our Motherland, only a cousinland about eight or nine generations removed, and you know you can take liberties with a cousin of about eight or nine generations which would not be allowable to take with persons who are not so closely connected.

We rejoice that our blood is drawn from the United Netherlands in the days of their brightest glory and of their highest power; drawn, mark you, not left to stagnate in the congested veins of the Old World, but transfused into the heart of this new and nobler Republic. This is an American Society, and don't you forget it. Why, there is not a man here who cannot trace his family name and fortune through two hundred and fourteen years of this country's history. We hold our Americanism by a title older than many an English duke holds his dukedom, and with a greater pride. I do not believe in those societies which are intended to perpetuate class distinctions, arouse enmities in this country of ours, and split up the broad continent of national feeling into little islands of unnaturalized foreigners, but I do believe in a society which emphasizes the honor of pure republican descent, and reminds us that we are bound of all men to defend against anarchists, against aristocrats, and against socialists, those laws and liberties which were established on the shores of this New World by the free spirit and daring courage of our Dutch forefathers. Of such a society, sir, you are the worthy President, and I do not know but that all compliments and praise will seem small and weak beside such words as these. It is fitting that you should be presented with this badge, which is no gaudy, glaring, and meretricious emblem, but simple and plain, and made of pure gold. It bears upon it the emblems which remind us of the past, of the present, and of the future. Here below hangs that Beggar's Penny, which was the first token of amity and concord among the liberty-loving sons of the United Netherlands. Here above, stands the Lion of the Netherlands; perhaps to remind you that your only "lyin'" should be done on this badge. On the other side, on the left, stands the Arms of Old Amsterdam; on the right hand side the Arms of New Amsterdam, and between them is the *Mayflower* with her bow pointed west. At the bottom stands a green and flourishing tree, with this inscription: " Eindelijk wordt een spruit een Boom." "Every sprout in time has its ' boom.'"

It is fitting, sir, that you should be presented with this badge. No man ever made a mistake when he called you "Your Honor." You have presided over

these meetings of ours with the dignity of a judge,
and with the temperance of an archbishop, in a
manner which we can assure you has sent a warm
and cheerful glow through all our hearts. We rejoice
to do you honor. We arise, and, as I place this
insignia upon your neck, we all drink long life,
health, and honor to President Van Vorst of The
Holland Society.

To which the President, JUDGE VAN VORST, responded:

I CANNOT value too highly this honor which has
been conferred this evening, but I beg you to understand that all that it implies is official, and not
personal. This badge, according to the eloquent
statement of our friend, symbolizes honesty, patriotism, virtue, everything, really, that dignifies man, and
makes life noble, and I trust that this badge may
have the power of communicating to whoever may
wear it some of these distinguishing virtues. We
will now proceed with the other exercises.

At this point the President read communications
from the following persons expressing their regret at
their inability to be present:

> The PRESIDENT OF THE UNITED STATES.
> General BENJAMIN HARRISON, President-elect.
> His Excellency the GOVERNOR OF THE STATE
> OF NEW-YORK.
> The REPRESENTATIVE OF THE GOVERNMENT OF
> HOLLAND in this country.
> Hon. CHAUNCEY M. DEPEW.
> Mr. ROOSEVELT, American Minister at The
> Hague.

Mr. Roosevelt, in his telegram, says he dines to-night at The Hague with the Diplomatic Corps, and that on that occasion he will toast The Holland Society. Mr. Roosevelt, our distinguished representative, who takes a deep interest in this Society, represents our Government there, and we have sent an answer to his cablegram in these words: "Holland forever."

Now, gentlemen, we will proceed to another part of this entertainment. We all remember that some two years ago a gentleman of this city, Mr. Astor, was here with the sword of William the Silent before him, and he addressed us on that occasion. We have not forgotten his speech, and it will be long before we can forget it. The sword is here to-night, and we have also an offering from Mr. Astor in this floral vessel, the *Half Moon*, of which he is to speak; so you see the interest that he takes in your organization, and I beg now to present to you Mr. William Waldorf Astor.

SPEECH OF

MR. WILLIAM WALDORF ASTOR.

T is two hundred and eighty years since the *Half Moon* anchored off Manhattan Island. She was a storm-tossed little vessel after her long exploration through Arctic seas, and we can imagine the delight with which Hendrik Hudson looked about him on that memorable September morning. The enchantment of the bay and of the river, the imposing line of the Palisades, the forests in their brilliant autumnal tints, the fragrance of the breeze and the sparkle of the sunshine on the water — all these, the *Half Moon's* journal describes with a vividness that brings the scene before us like a flower of yesterday. The picturesque and silent shores along which the *Half Moon* sailed soon beheld the rise of villages, and the building of New Amsterdam. The colonists prospered because they brought habits of industry and thrift, and, above all, because they possessed the rare intelligence to understand that in dealing with the Indians, the honest way was always the best.

W. WALDORF ASTOR.

But the Dutch came not merely as traders. Their great nation had expanded in its small country, and had been so tempered and hardened in the fire of the war of its independence, that Holland stood first for the noble and generous qualities that make her nation a guide, a leader, and a founder of others. By a valor whose steadfastness not all the blood shed by Alva, nor the faggots and chains of Spanish persecution could dismay, nor even the tears of their own helpless and suffering ones could dishearten, the Dutch established for all mankind the principles of religious toleration and of constitutional government. This was the gift of Holland to the human race, and this it was that made the triumphant flag of the States General, flying at the masthead of the *Half Moon*, a harbinger of salvation and freedom to the New World.

The pioneers to this region were men of truth and courage. Their example influenced the character and destiny of New-York in revolutionary times, and their spirit has lived among us ever since, helping to make us what we are to-day. New Amsterdam long since outstripped its ancient namesake of the Zuyder Zee. From a struggling settlement we have come to be the third city in the world; where the *Half Moon* cast anchor is now a roadstead for the iron steamships of modern science; where a puny stockade was raised on the line of Wall street against the Indians, George Washington took the oath of office one hundred years ago as the head of the American Republic, and on that same spot next April, his successor, Benjamin Harrison, will receive the same commission from fifty millions of people. The *Half Moon* has left but a name and a memory; she has vanished

like the savages that came out to meet her, bearing
in their hands the green boughs of peace and of
good-will.

But the glory of that heroic period, when her splendid blows were struck for the emancipation of mankind, grows brighter as we look back to it, and the
story of that adventurous vessel is one that we
cherish for ourselves, and for our children, forever.
In our imagination, the *Half Moon* still sails, a fairy
and a phantom ship, across the stormless seas. Her
memory is one that we rejoice to honor to-night with
the attributes your ancestors loved so well, and in
which the Dutch poets delighted:

> The music of the lute,
> The flower of the crimson rose,
> The wine-cask emptied to the lees.

THE PRESIDENT: We had expected at our last dinner to have had the pleasure of hearing Mr. Bayard,
the Secretary of State, but he was unable to be
present. He was one of our very first members;
his name in the first catalogue of The Holland Society
stands first, and I have the pleasure to announce
now, although it is said "Hope deferred maketh
the heart sick," that we have him here to-night, and
shall listen to him with very great pleasure.

THOS. F. BAYARD.

SPEECH OF

HON. THOMAS F. BAYARD.

HEN I heard him who is fitly called "Your Honor" read to-night the excuses of men in Washington that they could not come here, I felt a little self-accused that I had run away from my duty to follow the dictates of my heart, and the lines of Gray came back, of the truants from Eton College:

> "Still as they run they look behind,
>   And hear a voice in every wind,
>   And snatch a fearful joy."

I wish to thank you greatly for the kindness of your reception, and to say it has been my misfortune not before to receive it, but no descendant of a Dutchman will blame a man who stays away from any place when duty detains him. I am rejoiced to come among my countrymen whose homes are somewhat distant from my own, and yet who nourish sympathies and admirations which they hold in common with me. Do not let us, in what are termed the practical affairs of life, forget that obscure memories and vague traditions are powerful forces in our social fabric. The value of societies like this is that they seek the fountains of history from which men of Holland descent and connection drew their traditions. Every community depends for its real strength upon the number of men and women of individual worth that it contains. No society, my friends, can be strong merely because it is large, for the more fools or the more knaves that you get together so much the worse. In the last analysis the strength of a country will be found in the personal character and individual conscience that happen to exist within its borders.

There are few Americans to whom we owe a greater debt for his literary charm, poetic talent, the gentle humor that blends wisdom with wit, than to Dr. Oliver Wendell Holmes. Some one asked him a while ago when you should begin the education of a child, and he said: "About one hundred years before the child was born." We of The Holland Society can "see" the good Doctor, and, if I may speak profanely, "go him a little better." We go back pretty nearly three hundred years before any man in this room was born to find the sources of that which has educated us to come here. We claim for our godfather Count Brederode, in 1566. "Water beggars" we are, at least water seems to go begging to-night, but "water beggars" were the society that he formed at that time upon his famous compromise, and we are here to-night to thank him for doing it. He was our godfather, and our education then commenced. Perhaps we do not take the water quite as straight as they may have taken it, although I have great respect for their judgment, and I do not think when they begged for water that they did not put something in it, but, gentlemen, as "Man shall not live by bread alone," nor by water alone, we drink in something to-night in the example of those men that is better than wine or water; we drink in to-night the example of the solid virtues of those early times, and I hope we shall avoid the frothy sensationalism of times nearer to us. The virtues of Holland were solid. This mute sword now before us has its history; under William the Silent, the good Father William, "the Dutch Washington," inquisition into private affairs was forbidden, and that was an essential step to civil and religious liberty. Have we nothing to-day in laws that propose to instruct men what they shall drink, and what they shall wear, that will not indicate to us the value of that edict three centuries old that you shall not inquire into the personal habits of men? This was a solid virtue and it made Holland the asylum of men and women from whom I draw my name and blood, who, after religious liberty became impossible in France, and the troubles and bloody contentions of the time of the massacre of St. Bartholomew, found in Holland an asylum for a conscience that could worship God at the altar of its own choice. Every year the English people meet to commemorate the defeat of the Spanish armada. I wish they could find time in their rejoicing to remember that it was the courage of the plain Dutchman that kept in the Holland ports the Spanish ships that were intended for the destruction of the liberties of England. Let justice be done. Has ever the like been seen in history of a race who conquered the ocean, except the one in whose honor our Society is named? If King Canute had been a Dutchman and had lived on the

shores of Holland he could have sat in his chair at
ease and forbidden the waves to approach. I ask you
whether in all the solid reality of history was there
ever a case before where the area of a kingdom was
formed as to one-third of its extent by man's power
over the sea? Ah, gentlemen, there was skill, there
was patient endurance, there was simple, unpro-
claimed industry that win our admiration, but there
was something even finer than these, for the patient,
plodding industry, and engineering skill, that kept the
ocean at bay, and sent it back so that men might live
in plenty and comfort upon the ground that was so
gained; that same skill, that same force, had the
courage to call back the ocean when liberty was at
stake, and bid it preserve the liberties of the men and
their posterity who had built the dykes. To these
plain burghers was it given to beckon the Atlantic
to and fro, to retire when it was not needed, and to
come again when liberty called it.

Can you suppose that the man who built those
dykes for the purposes of honest industry, and destroyed them for the nobler purposes of human
elevation and liberty, could have the horizon of their
ideals narrowed by possessions of wealth, or by the
easy satisfaction of living at home in comfort? Oh,
no! One solid quality begets another, and so the
same force and courage that gained for these people
land where land was not, and made the ocean their
tributary for further gain or for their defense, made
them the pioneers of navigation, of enterprise, of commercial potency in the civilized world. And there
was something better than that. They were not small
men, and, so far as I can read their annals, the successes of the Dutch in commerce were not acquired

by sharp bargains, much less by trickery. They taught, as it seems to me, a lesson that might well be engraved over the portals of every Chamber of Commerce, that solid honesty is the soul of commerce.

I knew well Judge Jeremiah Black, of Pennsylvania, who, in delivering from the Bench a eulogy upon Chief-Justice Gibson, said: "He was an honest man; by that I do not mean a man who had that negative honesty that it is a disgrace to want, but who had that positive honesty that enforces itself in every transaction and in every conversation of life."

There is a difference, gentlemen, between the negative honesty that permits a fraud and the positive honesty that strikes it wherever it is found. The Dutch settlers on this island — did they not bring with them this positive honesty, these solid qualities, and is there not within the knowledge of every man who lives upon Manhattan Island the fact that they planted the seeds, the fruits of which we enjoy to-day?

New-York is a great city; it is vast in wealth, it is vast in population, and in its material strength; vast in its intellectual strength, and countless are the business transactions daily in this great city. Incalculable are the amounts that are embraced within them. The pulsations of your vigor are felt throughout this continent, almost throughout the world. Think over them all, and take comfort in the reflection that so few of all these transactions are questionable. How few, how infinitesimal is the proportion of trickery as compared to honest dealings. It is not just to-day, my pessimistic friend, wherever you may be found, to doubt the strength of this Republic. It is safe to-day to say that honesty and honor are the

prevailing forces in the government and in the transactions of the city of New-York. They are the rule,
and not the exception, and, if it were not so, the business of New-York could not be conducted for a single
week. Gentlemen, these qualities are not noisy;
they are not self-proclaiming; they do not advertise
themselves, simply because they are solid, and not
sensational, and who will deny or depreciate the good
Dutch soil of manners, and morals, and law, of which
the natural fruits are seen around us to-day.

> "Sensation asks for what is new,
> Solidity asks for what is true."

Sensation prefers a new fiction dressed in the clothes
of a pantaloon, political or religious, as the case may
be; solidity prefers truth, well tested, in its most
sober garb.

Physicians know—and there are wise ones here—
that health has no symptoms. Physicans know that
disease has nothing else. And here is the difference
between solidity and sensationalism. We breathe the
pure air of heaven insensibly; it is only when it is
contaminated and vitiated that we recognize the
offense, and experience a sensation. Solidity considers both cause and effect; sensation rejoices in
effect alone. Gentlemen, unquestionably, our lot is
cast in a remarkable age, and a most remarkable
country. Properly understood, fairly appreciated,
our institutions are the noblest in the world. They
are founded upon the equities of humanity. I, with
you, love them, admire them. I seek to serve them.
I joined this Society as a brotherhood with the same
end in view. The Holland Society is an agency to
bring forth every attribute and every tradition of

worth and honor, no matter on what soil it originated, no matter in what accents its early voice was heard. It is their object, it is my object, that all that is brave, honorable, and just shall be brought into the service of the great American Republic. Let us be eclectics as to that. But as I would build the tower high, so I would have it strong. I would ask that its base be solid and not sensational.

May I close by a parallel between something that was the product of American life, of American institutions, and a genius wholly distinct. May I take a homespun lawyer-farmer from the State of Virginia, and compare him to that meteor that lit, but also scorched, the continent of Europe. May I compare Thomas Jefferson with Napoleon Bonaparte, and use the words of another in describing the difference, even as to the possibilities of ambition, between the man that was solid and the man that was sensational. I read from the words of a contemporary of both, the late Charles J. Ingersoll, a grown man when Napoleon was made the First Consul of France, and who long outlived him and Thomas Jefferson. He, writing of the election of 1801, at the time that the "Louisiana Purchase," so-called, was consummated, said: "If the President had then been Aaron Burr, as was near being the case, instead of Thomas Jefferson, immediate armament and forcible occupation would have, no doubt, been the executive policy, and, with executive influence, why not the legislative will? But Jefferson, inflexible in his resolution to govern without physical force, exerted all his official influence and personal popularity to deprive his office of patronage, and his country of military organization. The results as they came to pass in Jefferson's and

26

Napoleon's respective reigns and regions may perplex and confound history, but the facts are of recent and of universal familiarity of knowledge. Napoleon with superhuman intelligence, by stupendous armaments crushed several enormous coalitions, putting many millions of men to death in convulsive warfare, closed his prodigious career with no considerable change of dominion, leaving the boundaries of his country less than when, by such means, he undertook their enlargement. Jefferson's country, during the same period, his administration conducted with hardly a soldier or a tax, was in profound peace, extended over more world than Napoleon won or lost by conquest. Patience, mostly more effectual than violence, has sometimes been called genius."

There may be something in our time, my friends and fellow-countrymen, to make this retrospect of value to the American people. There is a haste, there is an ambition, there is a sensationalism, which is the worst product of both, and generally shallow, superficial, unreal, and unmanly. Our duty is plain in our day and generation, to promote the growth of those solid qualities that make a man, that make a city, that make and keep a nation. They are not noisy, but they are profound, and enduring in their results.

The President then read a message from Dr. Vander Veer, of Albany, sending greeting to the Society and wishing all a joyful evening, after which he introduced the next speaker, who responded to the toast of the "Dutch Masters."

SPEECH OF F. HOPKINSON SMITH.

A DUTCH friend of mine engaged in the laudable occupation of selling beer to his countrymen during the summer months in his back-yard, with the first breath of spring bared his head to the breeze, and said to his attendant: "Hans, the summer is come; the garden is open, bring out the trees." And when the tables were set, and his hungry and thirsty guests by slow syphonic processes were transferring the high-water mark of the keg to the low-water mark of their stomachs, he would caution Hans with: "Pull that mug lower down, the profit is in the boobles."

I always look forward, my friends, to the annual dinner of The Holland Society as a sure sign that the summer has come, and that the garden of good cheer and good fellowship is open wide to the sallies of wit, the sparkles of humor, and flashes of eloquence which surround the tree after it is out.

The Dutch Masters — the toast covers as much ground as a pasture in Holland. If success waits on perseverance, and perseverance is twin sister to obstinacy, the Dutch should be masters of the world. It is true that they are the tortoises of the nationalities. They may not have the legs of the French hare, nor the wings of the American eagle, yet, with the persistency of an insect that in summer flesh is heir to, they get there all the same. Scratch a New Yorker, one who has lifted his head high enough to be seen, and who has won for himself something of a name in the arts, literature, science, the law, politics, or trade, and, nine chances out of ten, way down below the surface you will find some of the blood that was spilled in the immortal days of Alva, at Haarlem and Leyden, by a people that would rather give their land to the sea than have it violated by an enemy. The only thing that I ever heard of that staggered a Dutchman, when he ran right against it so hard that he had to sit down and catch his breath, was a big block of Missouri, Kansas, and Texas sixes. But the end is not yet, gentlemen, and a settlement may still have to be made with many in Amsterdam instead of one only in New York.

Dutch Masters — masters of what? Of the sea that never was kept within bounds before. "Here shall ye come, and no further," said a Dutchman, "and here shall your proud waves be stayed. Here will we live and our little ones, and you can gnash your teeth and growl along the white sands of our dykes." Of the soil; the land is a garden from Meridan to the sea. Of the arts; search the museums of the Old World. We have the priceless volumes printed in that early time, and bound in the vellum of Leyden. What workers in metal they were. Preserved to-day in the kitchens, surrounded by their porcelain and china, is their tile-work of Amsterdam dating back two centuries. Of the cutting of gems, bringing to an exact mathematical precision the reduction of the shape of the glitterless pebble until it is only rivaled by a sunbeam bathed in a dew drop. Of working in iron, and the carving of wood, and the cutting and engraving of fine glass.

I am led to believe that by the Dutch Masters you mean that type of men who sprang into prominence in the early part of the seventeenth century; you refer to that king of painters, whose pictures have belonged to the civilized world for two centuries. Grand as he is, grand master and all, his influence to-day is stronger over the minds of the artistic world than any other painters of modern time — Rembrandt. And there are many others.

These, gentlemen, were not Dutch Masters because they were masters in their Dutch land alone; they are masters by their skill, by their genius, by their power to create, by their sagacity, which has brought the arts of all men to what is considered a high order of genius, so that we can even read the words of your toast, not as you have written it, simply Dutch Masters, but " The Dutch Master."

THE PRESIDENT: The next speaker certainly needs no introduction to you. He is our eloquent advocate, who will speak to you of that nation which put the girdle of empire around the world.

SPEECH OF HON. W. BOURKE COCKRAN.

Mr. Chairman and Gentlemen of The Holland Society:

THESE proceedings were opened to-night with a reference to the battle of New Orleans, the glorious anniversary which is being celebrated in many cities of this country at this hour; and I remembered an invitation to one which I had myself received. For a moment, I was disposed to regret that I had not accepted it, but as I reflected upon the subject which was assigned to me, as I listened to the speeches which were delivered from this desk, I became convinced that there is nothing creditable to American valor, nothing glorious in American history that can be more fitly celebrated anywhere than in a meeting of The Holland Society.

The toast which has been assigned to me certainly opens up a subject of the widest amplitude. I do not believe that I am flattering your hereditary pride when I state as my deliberate judgment that the enterprise of the Dutch was the vehicle in which modern civilization was borne around the globe. Modern civilization is distinguished by the fact that it possesses the earth. That possession we owe to the enterprise and courage of the Dutch navigators. When the barbarians of the North Forest took possession of the fertile plains of Europe, and shattered the Roman civilization which the Roman legions were unable to defend, the system of feudalism sprang up as the legitimate outcome of force triumphant. The serf was the natural product of the feudal system. The man who never moved from the fields on which he was born, unless to follow some military standard upon an incursion of war, saw no other force than the petty king to whom he owed allegiance, who cared for him, sheltered him from the heat and the storm. The king, the prince, the baron, upon whose lands he dwelt, was to him the embodiment of power, the beginning and the end of all authority.

But when men learned to move across the surface of the globe; when they yearned to see the wonders which were in the world around them, they began to think. With thought came uneasiness, and that ripened into revolt. They either became independent or else sank into a submission which was abject because it was conscious.

Along the mouth of the Rhine there were a number of communities that, in the language of the Secretary of State, wrestled closely with the sea for the possession of their soil, and redeemed it from the embrace of the ocean. That ocean, familiar to them, had no terrors for them. They launched their barks upon it; they penetrated every quarter of the then known globe. They visited Britain; they went over to the shores of Italy. As they saw the wealthy cities and the palaces in which their citizens dwelt; as they realized that all this wealth and luxury was due to the security of property within the walls of an independent city, they returned home, and told their neighbors of what they had seen.

The little castle of the baron shrank into meanness as they compared it with the magnificent palace of the Florentine merchant. The flocks, the herds, the hawks, the hounds, their visible wealth, shrank into insignificance compared with the gold and silver, and the superb palaces, with marble stairways, which distinguished the cities of Italy. Then that spirit of invention, which we celebrate here to-night, awakened in the minds of the Dutch. They learned to weave; they learned to spin; they learned to build. Their communities grew rich. They were able to purchase liberty of the feudal lord. The barons gave charters to the city, and the chartered city became the foe before which feudalism and absolutism were shattered forever.

As we recall the history of the Dutch cities, as we note their growth in wealth, we are struck by the fact that as soon as their material wants were secured, their minds became expanded to the cultivation of the beautiful and of the sublime as well as the practical.

The eulogy which has just been pronounced upon the Dutchmen does but scant justice to their merits, eloquent as it is. The lesson that the Dutch learned was that liberty was at the foundation of prosperity, and that lesson bore its fruit. It bore its fruit when the Spaniard sought to strike at the independence of the Dutch cities.

Like the Italian cities, they had no trained but expensive armies, and their wealth every day increased. But they defended the homes that were dear to them, and, though men despised as beggars

by the opprobrious epithets of Spanish pride, they
beat in a contest the chivalry and the trained armies
of all the forces by which the Spanish tyrant sought
to demolish their walls and destroy their future.

There was no force too strong for Dutch resistance.
The proud Protector, before whose nod every throne
in Europe trembled, met the Dutch fleets upon the
sea. They knew not how to fly. English sailors
learned that Dutch courage was a force with which
even English valor was unable to successfully cope.
And the geographical discoveries of that age were due
more to these hardy adventurers who had conquered
the sea than to English desire to penetrate its unknown regions.

They launched their barks and trimmed their sails
to every breeze. They pointed their prows in every
direction. No land was so distant that they did not
dare to sail for it; no shore so rugged that they
feared to approach it; no harbor that they did not
dare to enter.

The winds that chilled, and the suns that burned,
were unable to check them; the atrocities of the
North American Indians did not deter them, and
they despised the fevers of the tropics. They gave
the ancient name of their country to an eastern
island; in the western hemisphere, where they founded
a settlement which prospered, until to-day it stands
the third city of the world, and destined, within a
generation, to outstrip all other competitors for the
proud post of the capital of modern civilization.

We would do faint justice to Dutch enterprise if
we but spoke of its achievements. Grander and
better even than the bravery which they displayed
was the spirit by which they were animated. The

27

colonies which they founded were established as lamp posts on the pathway of civilization. They were the legitimate outcome of the efforts of a mighty people, whose cities were unable longer to contain that organizing, arousing enterprise which, like a tide, swept away every obstacle by which it was confronted.

The men who established their settlements did not fly from cruel and oppressive laws which rendered their lot at home intolerable. They bore the torch of civilization into quarters of the globe which had been hitherto undiscovered. The foes with which they contended were the forces of nature, the curses of undiscovered lands. Under the hot sun, or in the biting frost, they searched in the bosom of the earth for undiscovered treasures. Wherever they went, their labors show to-night the interests of civilization were inspired by a love of humanity.

They have, indeed, in the language of this toast, placed a girdle around the globe. But it was not a pathway of blood; it was a shining zone of light. Here upon this island, the chief result of that enterprise, we rejoice to-night in the possession of blessings which are ours because the spirit of the Dutch settlers has survived through centuries. That tolerance of religious belief, that disposition to dwell peaceably with one's neighbors — these are distinctive inheritances from the Dutch settlers.

We have not a single memory which we would wish to forget; there is not an act which a loyal Dutchman or his descendants would wish to obliterate from the pages of history. We have no cruel laws to apologize for, and claim that they were the result of the bigoted spirit of the age. No cruel fires were lit under helpless women on this island. The Puritan himself, when he came down here to join with you and to take the best chair of your ancestors, was fashioned into a new man by contact with the descendants of the Dutchmen. Sons of Dutch sires, bearers of Dutch names, descendants of Dutchmen, well may you claim for your Society the foremost place amongst all her sisters this spirit which animated the Dutch burgher who drew his sword in defense of the liberties of the Dutch cities. Within twenty-five years, at the call of duty, their descendants cast down the implements of toil and girded on those of war when the safety of this country was imperiled, the same spirit, living again, inspired those descendants, and they went to the scene of carnage, toil, and battle to meet their foes.

Other nations have achieved a commercial supremacy, but never while the tide ebbs and flows in the harbor which Hudson discovered, never while favoring winds waft to our shores the argosies of foreign commerce, never while this city stands at the mouth of the Hudson, the metropolis of this continent, the envy of all her sisters, with both her arms outstretched, the one across the continent, and the other across the sea, for the profits and the pleasures of the world, never while the history of daring deeds and solid traits remains recorded, can be forgotten the courage, perseverance, and indomitable skill which were the essential features and the living elements of the Dutch enterprise which has reduced the universe to the possession of mankind.

PRESIDENT VAN VORST: It gives me peculiar pleasure to announce to you the next speaker, who is known to you all. He has done the State some service, and we know it. It is a quality that the Dutch have of finding out good people, and bringing them forward at the proper time, and it gives me pleasure to introduce to you Mr. Delancey Nicoll.

SPEECH OF DELANCEY NICOLL.

Mr. President and Members of The Holland Society:

OF all the invited guests at this banquet, I ought most to appreciate the compliment, for, in inviting me to your feast, your committee have unconsciously violated one of the traditions of those admired ancestors whose progeny you are.

It is recorded in that history of New-York, from the beginning of the world to the fall of the Dutch dynasty, which was written by the late lamented Diederich Knickerbocker, that, although upon the surrender to the English commander in August, 1664, the Dutch were permitted to remain in peaceable possession of their houses and property, yet, such was their inveterate hatred of the British, that, at a meeting of the leading citizens of New Amsterdam, it was solemnly resolved never to invite any of the detested conquerors or their descendants to dinner.

In one of the ships which composed the British expedition, and acting as secretary to his uncle, who commanded the fleet, was that poor but honest gentleman to whom, in aristocratic assemblages like

this, I am accustomed to point with pride as my
ancestor, and it is indeed a gratifying illustration of the softening influences of time that you
have permitted me, the descendant of one of your
conquerors, to sit at this feast, to eat your hardtack,
and drink your foaming ale. And while it is difficult
for me to suppress the exultant emotions which rise
in my bosom when I recall that late unpleasantness in the harbor of New-York, in the month of
August, 1664, I shall endeavor, in the language of the
toast, to convince you that we are "comrades now,"
and "enemies no longer."

It is very evident that the excellent committee who
selected me to speak to the toast, "The Capture of
New Amsterdam," paid little respect to the political
history of this city, and its present political condition.
The English did make a capture of New Amsterdam; but what, after all, did it amount to? At that
time the city had only fifteen hundred inhabitants,
and not more than one hundred houses. Not only
that, but the English respected the rights of the
Dutch inhabitants, and even permitted the burgomasters to retain their offices. Indeed, Englishmen
became Dutchmen. Those who remained in this
country became so fascinated by the rosy cheeks
and rounded forms of the Dutch ladies that they
became your great, great, great-uncles by taking in
marriage your great, great, great-aunts, and sharing
some of that respectable patrimony which your great,
great, great, great, grandfathers had been accumulat-
ing. Such was the capture of New Amsterdam by
the English. But they were not the real captors of
New Amsterdam. A century elapsed before the real
captors came. They came — a witty and a warlike

race from the land of the shamrock, from the home of St. Patrick, from Limerick, Cork, and Killarney. When they came they made a clean sweep. They drove the burgomasters out, and, notwithstanding the compliments which have been showered upon you by their sole representative at this banquet, such has been their indomitable energy that neither you Dutchmen, nor myself, Englishman, nor all of us together, have been able to wrest any offices from them since.

When I view before me the numerous progeny of the founders of New Amsterdam, many of whom are conspicuous in the life of this city, and consider the perils to which their ancestors, huddled together upon the point of Manhattan Island, were exposed, I am filled with admiration for a race which of all races on the face of the earth could have survived the perils which encircled them and escape utter extermination. Consider for yourselves the unparalleled danger of the situation of the founders of New Amsterdam upon the point of Manhattan Island. In the year 1664 they numbered only 1500. They had no stores of ammunition; they had no system of fortifications; there was no way of escape except the sea, and they had few vessels; they were surrounded by hordes of savages whose natural enmity was liable at any moment to be inflamed into a passionate desire to exterminate them altogether, and yet, notwithstanding the hazard of that situation they grew, multiplied, and prospered, and appropriated to themselves the choicest of the Indian possessions, this lovely island of Manhattan. How was it accomplished? How did they achieve it? It was a triumph of Dutch enterprise, a marvel of Dutch thrift, a tribute to the genius of the Dutch race for commerce. It is the most notable illustration in history of the saying that "Peace hath her victories not less renowned than war." They accomplished it because they were traders and not warriors. Instead of antagonizing the noble red man they invited him to their homes, they took him to their bosoms, they stimulated his desire for beads, they encouraged his taste for Holland pottery, and cultivated his appetite for Holland gin. The noble red man could beat them at the game of war, but he was no match for them at the game of commerce. So they taught him the game of commerce, and then they beat him at it. When he was a loser they gave him a few presents, and he came back and played the game again. It was a game which even the redoubtable Stuyvesant did not despise, for of him it is recorded that upon one occasion, when returning from an expedition against the struggling colony at the mouth of Chesapeake Bay, he found the Indians in revolt, he deliberately took the money of your ancestors, and purchased from the savages miles of land with a few barrels of Holland pottery and a few hogsheads of Holland gin.

The Dutch were the only race that could have founded New Amsterdam. No other race could have succeeded under the conditions which surrounded the founders. What, gentlemen, think you, would the warlike Irish have done under such circumstances? What would the impetuous French or even the martial English have accomplished? They would have waged against the Indians unremitting war until the colony was exterminated. It required something higher, something better, and more intelligent than mere brute force to establish a colony upon this island. It required a genius for trading, for bargaining, and buying. It required the peculiar genius of your ancestors.

In the month of August, 1664, when the English fleet sailed up the bay and anchored off the Battery, the infant city was the scene of unusual activity. While there were few buildings above Wall street, all below was bustle and excitement. On the great farms which stretched from Wall street up to the Harlem River, your industrious progenitors were engaged in tilling the soil, in fattening the hog, and in dodging the occasional arrow from the Indian bow. In Harlem all was quiet except at the tavern called "The Waiting Place" where your progenitors repaired every noon to slake their thirsts with bowls of ale. In the city the various officers were immersed in the cares of state. Stuyvesant was in the City Hall engaged in writing a message to the burgomasters upon the surplus; the burgomasters were speculating upon the profits of a combine to sell the franchise for a soda-water fountain on the Bowery; the elder Van Vorst, who was the magistrate of that period, was engaged in trying for sedition two Englishmen who had spoken disrespectful words of Stuyvesant, and Van Dyke, the elder, who had been appointed prosecutor by Stuyvesant, was trying to convict them. The elder DeWitt was engaged in cornering the market on flour; the elder Van Siclen had just entered the office of his trust company; Van Slyck and Van Wyck were getting up a trust in Indian corn, and the elder DePeyster was vainly endeavoring to learn the English language in order to qualify himself for the position of deputy mayor. Such was the peaceful condition of New Amsterdam on that summer morning in 1664 when the English fleet sailed through the Narrows.

28

No suspicion of invasion disturbed the peaceful bosom of the city. The English commander at once sent a demand for unconditional surrender. Stuyvesant summoned the burgomasters. They were for peace, he was for war; but on listening to their arguments, he sent a hurried note to the English admiral. When the latter discovered that there was a division in the public sentiment of the town, he industriously circulated through his agents the most alluring promises of protection to your ancestors, and succeeded in seducing them from the government. He promised to every man who should voluntarily submit to his Britannic majesty that he should enjoy undisturbed the possession of his houses, his flower beds, and his cabbage garden; that he should be permitted to speak the Dutch language, to smoke his pipe, and wear as many breeches as he pleased, and that he should be permitted to import from Holland his jugs and bowls instead of manufacturing them upon the spot. He also promised that they should never be compelled to learn the English language, nor to adopt other system of counting than by adding up on their fingers, and inscribing the result upon their hats; promised that every man should be permitted to inherit from his grandfather, his coat, his hat, his pipe, and his shoe buckles, and that under no circumstances should they be obliged to conform to any modern innovations, but, on the contrary, be permitted to manage their farms, to conduct their business, to rear their hogs, and till their soil as had been done from time immemorial.

It is not surprising that with such alluring promises, your thrifty progenitors fell an easy prey to the English commanders. And so New Amsterdam was captured without a drum being sounded, a gun discharged, or a drop of blood spilt. On the next morning after its capture, your thrifty progenitors went about as usual, and succeeded at the close of the day in adding something to that substantial pile which their grateful descendants are spending this evening in riotous living.

The capture of New Amsterdam by the English, in 1664, was the beginning of that commingling of races which is not only the distinct characteristic of its civilization, but the cause of the present unparalleled growth of the city of New-York. It is that which distinguishes the Empress of the West from her older sisters in Europe. London is the product of England, Paris is the creation of France, Berlin is the work of Germany, but New-York is not the achievement of any one race of people. This magnificent city, with its miles of streets, its hundreds of acres of parks, its avenues of palaces and stores, adorned with churches and cathedrals, with libraries, with temples of art and song, with monuments of private and public charities, is not the work of any one race. In the veins of New-York flow the blood of all the great nations of the earth; all have contributed to her matchless growth. And yet, of all the contributions, the greatest came from the founders of New Amsterdam, your progenitors. England contributed her laws, her customs, and her love of liberty. France contributed taste and art; Germany, music and liberal living; but Holland contributed that spirit of freedom and religious tolerance, that genius for industry, that extraordinary capacity for rapid development which have already made this city rich beyond the dreams of avarice, and entitled her to the foremost place among the cities of the earth.

DINNER OF

THE HOLLAND SOCIETY IN ALBANY,

FEBRUARY 14, 1889.

T HE members of The Holland Society resident in Albany and its vicinity determined that, as many of them were unable to attend the annual dinner on January 8th, they would have a dinner of their own where all could attend, on February 14, 1889. The President, Secretary, and Treasurer were invited from New-York. Judge Van Vorst was, unfortunately, unable to get away, and thus missed the charming hospitality of the Albanians. The following account of the dinner appeared in the "Albany Journal":

The good old Dutch folk were a hospitable people, and tradition has it that when they did undertake to give a feast it was a royal one; fortunate indeed was he whose lot it was to live in those days, and to partake of the good things set before them by the fathers of Albany. But it would have broken the heart of old Jeronemus Van Vlieren, whose "lott containing in breadth thirty-four foot and in length one hundred

The Holland Society of New York.

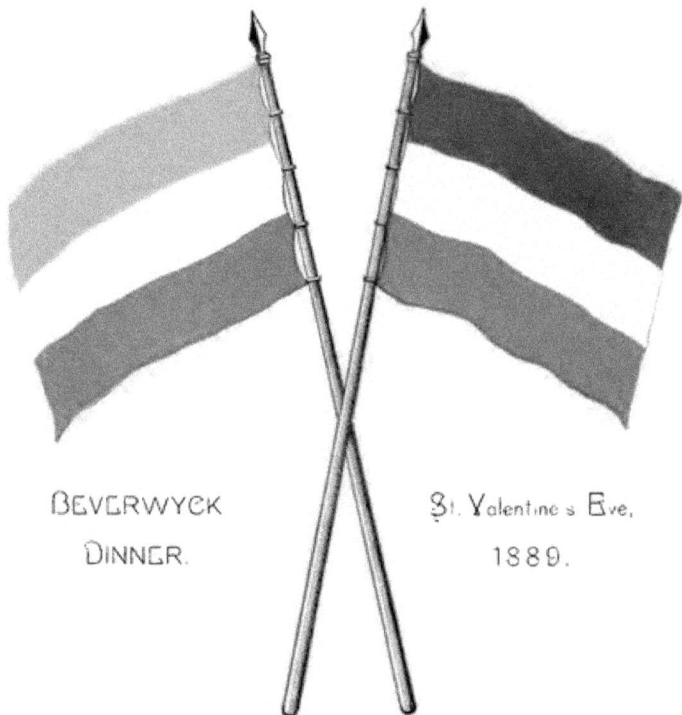

BEVERWYCK
DINNER.

St. Valentine's Eve,
1889.

ALBANY,

DELAVAN HOUSE.

THE HOLLAND SOCIETY

OF NEW YORK.

FLAGS.

The flag to the left, on the first page (orange, white and blue) was adopted by the United Netherlands in 1582. It floated from the mast head of the "Half Moon" when Henry Hudson visited the present site of our venerable city, on the 22d of Sept., 1609. In 1650, after the death of "William II," a red stripe was substituted in place of the orange; this is the present flag of Holland, and is represented to the right.

The flag to the left, on the last page (white with coat of arms in center), is the flag of the State of New York, promulgated in the "Military Regulations, 1859." This flag, by act of the Legislature, "Shall be displayed from the Capitol during the hours when the Legislature is in session." The flag to the right is our glorious "Star Spangled Banner," the unsullied emblem of the United States.

The coat of arms of the city (at top of left hand corner of last orange page), was copied from a map bearing date prior to 1700.

The seal, at the lower corner, was copied from a deed from the city of Albany, signed by Peter Schuyler, Mayor, bearing date of December, 1686, and was the first seal of the city.

GEORGE WEST VAN SICLEN.

Treasurer,
ABRAM VAN SANTVOORD.

Vice-President,
For Albany,
ALBERT VANDER VEER.

BERT VANDER VEER, V P.

DERRIK VARICK DE WITT,

JAAP HENRIK TEN EYCK,

KOBUS TEN EYCK,

JOHANNES VAN SCHAAICK LANSING PRUYN

KAREL HENRIK VAN BENTHUYSEN,

MELLIS WOODWARD VOSBURGH, Sec'y,

Committee.

SEAL OF ALBANY, 1686.

CHAS VAN BENTHUYSEN & SONS PRINT
OLDEST STEAM PRINTING HOUSE IN AMERICA 1827

and twenty foot wood measure," is spoken of in a resolution of the "comon councill" July 14, 1719, if he had found his way into the Delavan House dining-room last night, and seen how his progeny were putting away good things material, and introducing good things mental at a rate calculated to induce a stare in one unaccustomed to such doings. There were Dutchmen from Beverwyck, and Dutchmen from Esopus, and Dutchmen from New Amsterdam; with Dutchmen from every point between and within a radius of a good many miles on every side. There were good wishes from San Francisco and from New-York, and there was no sort of doubt but that the spirits of the fine old mynheers of two Dutch centuries ago hovered over the gathering with pride, and gave schnapp, perhaps, to their wine, and brightness to their already sparkling wit.

It was only a few minutes after 7 o'clock when Dr. Albert Vander Veer, wearing the badge of the President of The Holland Society of New-York hung about his neck with an orange ribbon, took the arm of Secretary Geo. W. Van Siclen, and led the way to the dining-hall. The 112 gentlemen who sat down to the table followed in twos, and when the President and Secretary reached the door the orchestra struck up "William of Nassau," the score being by Prof. Ehrmann. The seating was accomplished with little or no difficulty. A card bearing the name of each person rested on a glass at his place. The members and their guests were soon in their places, as follows:

Cross table at the north: James Ten Eyck, the Hon. T. Low Barhydt, Samuel D. Coykendall, the Hon. F. H. Woods, the Hon. A. T. Clearwater, John V. L. Pruyn, Dr. Albert Vander Veer, Secretary G. W. Van Siclen, the Hon. Abraham Lansing, Trea-

surer Abram Van Santvoord, the Rev. Dr. Prall, Prof.
H. P. Warren, W. L. Van Denberg.

East table: J. H. Van Antwerp, H. E. Sickles,
John W. Vrooman, John M. Bailey, T. C. Callicot, T.
J. Van Alstyne, S. T. Schermerhorn, Alfred De Graff,
John Schermerhorn, President Webster of Union
College, M. Van Voorhis, W. B. Van Rensselaer, Dr.
Henry Hun, Teunis M. Post, John G. Myers, John
Van Schaick, Clinton Ten Eyck, E. P. Durant, W. W.
Newcomb, A. V. DeWitt, John Wolff, Martin Van
Buren, John E. Voorhees, James Voorhees, W. C.
Groesbeck, E. A. Groesbeck, Jacob W. Clute, W. M.
Horton, J. B. Schuyler, J. B. Sanders, Dr. C. C.
Schuyler, Dr. James P. Boyd, Dr. Van Vleck, D. H.
Van Auken, Dr. Van Slyke, Dr. Marselius, W. F.
Winship, J. B. Visscher, I. D. F. Lansing, Ira L.
Wales, George N. Southwick, M. H. Griffin, Richard
Varick DeWitt.

West table: Charles B. Lansing, Abraham Van
Vechten, T. E. Vermilye, G. A. Van Allen, John
Van Voorhis, G. W. Van Slyke, J. A. Sleicher, Wm.
M. Van Antwerp, E. L. Judson, H. S. Van Santford,
W. H. Van Wormer, Jasper Van Wormer, R. H.
Southwick, M. E. Viele, M. W. Vosburgh, J. E.
McElroy, J. Townsend Lansing, J. A. Lansing, Wm.
Kline, A. V. V. Benson, S. M. Van Santvoord, Charles
H. Van Allen, Chas. H. Van Benthuysen, Leonard
Kip, James MacNaughton, P. V. B. Hoes, Charles V.
Winne, Charles L. Pruyn, B. R. Heyward, Peyton F.
Miller, P. V. Fort, F. Van Ness, E. Y. Lansing, Fletcher
Vosburgh, E. D. Jennison, Jacob H. Ten Eyck.

The dinner was served in ten courses, and the
spiced rum was not reached until past 9 o'clock. The
serving of the meal was prefaced with a prayer by
the Rev. William Prall, the announcement on the

menu being made in this fashion: "De Weleerwaarde
Heer Willem Prall, Ph. D. zal aan Tafel voorbidden."
Though the dishes were known to the participants
under French, Italian, and English names, the menu
was printed in this fashion:

SPIJSKAART.

BLAAUWE LANDTONGSCHE OESTERS.

Sauterne Wijn.

SOEP.

Dikke Zeekreeften Soep.

ZYSCHOTELTIES.

Pasteitjes in Koninklijke Stijl. *Sherry Wijn.*

VISCH.

Gekookte Kennebec Zalm, Ansjovis Saus.
Aardappelen in Hollandsche Stijl.

GEKRUIDE GERECHTEN.

Ossenhaas met Champignons.
Spinage met Room Saus.
Aardappelen in Julien Stijl *Pontet Canet.*

TUSSCHEN GERECHTEN.

Gekruide Kalkoen met Truffles in vormen.
Gekookte Land-Schilpad in Arlington Stijl.
Sorbet, Hollandsche Stijl. *Champagne.*

GEBRAAD.

Roodkop Eendvogel met Gelei.
Selderij Sla.

ZOETE GERECHTEN.

IJs in Mandjes.
Champagne Gelei in vormen.   Verschillende Koekjes.
Charlottes in bijzondere vormen.   Oliekoeken.

NAGERECHT.

Roquefort, Edam en Engelsche Kaas.
Vruchten.

KOFFIJ.

Gekruide Rum.
Cigaren, Goudsche Pijpen en Tabak.

The pipes were filled with fragrant tobacco when the meal was done, and each Dutchman, and his guests leaned back and in true Dutch style enjoyed the solace of a smoke, while the "feast of reason and flow of soul" went on. Dr. Vander Veer, surrounded by the persons on whom he called for responses, looked exceedingly happy when he rapped the assemblage to order and announced the first toast: "The New Netherlands—the New Netherlands wherein our forefathers established their principles of civil liberty and order." Dr. Vander Veer said: "Gentlemen, the first respondent to our toasts this evening is one in whom the members of this society feel a brotherly interest. In county, State and national legislative halls he has exhibited that progressive, but conservative spirit, so characteristic of his forefathers, that record in which we all take a just pride. We find him to-day in charge of one of the most important financial bureaus of his native State. It may be justly said that he fully represents the New Netherlands. I call upon Edward Wemple, the Comptroller of the State to respond. In his absence Mr. Garret A. Van Allen will read his response." Mr. Van Allen did so in his happiest vein, and would have astonished even the Comptroller had he been present. The response contained these thoughts: The most imaginative day-dreamer among the Frisians and the Batavii, a century and a half before our Christian era, in the wildest flight of his half-savage fancy, could not have had even a glimmer of imagination that, away to the west, nearly a thousand leagues beyond the dark waters of the North Sea, waters that broke, advanced, and retreated among the lowlands that made his home, there lay a continent whose shores should be inhabited, whose political and religious institutions should, in a great measure, be shaped and controlled by descendants from the land of his birth. That over 2000 years from that time, representatives from the same blood, or from the same land as his, should gather here to-night to commemorate in feast, song, speech, and story that same land that gave him his birth and home. No thought could have come to this same ancestor, perhaps of some of us, that over 1700 years after the commencement of this era, a white-winged, sea-going vessel should leisurely float in upon the waters where the Hudson weds the sea, and like her namesake in the blue vault of the sky, as quietly sail slowly up the blue waters that came then from unknown sources, until the advancing voyage was ended at a spot not more than cannon-shot distant from where we are assembled now. Yet all this came to pass. My topic is "The New Nether-lands," yet I would fain linger a moment over the memories of history that gather round the land of our ancestors that I might with clearer light approach my theme; might linger over pages that tell of times from the time the Netherland contingent, as allies of Rome, by their cavalry charge gave the battle and the day of Pharsalia to the Roman Empire and unto Cæsar. The New Netherlands, that land whose waters the good ship *Half Moon* first entered upon, and that land that as a geographical division of this continent exists no more by metes and bounds, but lives in history, romance, poetry, tradition, and song. Within these bounds our ancestors built their homes, made treaties with the great Indian tribes, ranged them in kindness under the banner of the Dutch Re-public. Yes, even upon this very ground, almost

29

upon the spot where we meet to-night, the great Iroquois, "Romans of the Western World," made a treaty with our fathers that was never violated, but stood a bulwark of defense against the French from Canada, and the savage tribes of the North and West. Fifty-four years the Dutch reign lasted; fifty-four years of almost peace and prosperity; fifty-four years was it the New Netherlands. Then the flag of the Dutch Republic was hauled down, the red cross of St. George raised over Fort Amsterdam, and the New Netherlands became New-York. Nine years later the Dutch flag again floated from the same fort, floated there for five hundred days; for five hundred days was there a New Netherlands again; then for the last time descended in power that flag of the United Provinces upon Manhattan Island, and the New Netherlands as a geographical division of the world passed away never to return. In some respects the government and people of this Dutch land of ours were far advanced in their ideas for the education of the masses through the education of their children; children who should grow to become the State. They were the first upon American soil to make education a public charge, a matter of the State and not of individuals. The first step taken toward a system of public schools was under the direction of the government of the New Netherlands, and the common school system of our great Republic sprung first into life in the land under the fostering care of the Dutch of the New Netherlands. The days of the New Netherlands passed away two centuries and a quarter ago, but the influence, spirit, and work of the men who inhabited and ruled that land are with us to-day.

The orchestra struck up "The Star-Spangled Banner," and, as the music concluded, Toastmaster Vander Veer proposed this sentiment: "The President of The Holland Society —

"An upright and fearless judge, whom the members of this society delight to honor.

"All our town in peace awaits you,
All our doors stand open for you;
You shall to our *stockade enter*,
And the heart's right hand we give you."

Then he added: "I wish I had the ability to express in words becoming this occasion the love, loyalty and affection we bear towards him who was to respond to this toast. There are many hearts in this city and vicinity who remember him kindly during his residence here in early life. There are those who will recollect him as president, in 1847, of that most flourishing institution, the Young Men's Association of this city, and who have watched with interest his progress onward and upward to success in the great metropolitan city. Just at this moment it is fitting that I express the wishes of the members of The Holland Society resident in Albany and vicinity in extending to your invited guests this night a hearty and earnest welcome." Then Dr. Vander Veer read a letter from Judge Hooper Van Vorst, President of the Society, who was to respond to the toast, in which the judge said that an important trial detained him, and concluded: "This is a great disappointment to me. I have many friends in Albany who are very dear to me, and I am always glad to meet them. The Holland Society has a large and highly-esteemed membership at Albany. We are always glad to see them in New-York, at our meetings and our social gatherings."

In the absence of President Van Vorst, Secretary George W. Van Siclen was called upon, without notice, to respond to the toast to the former; he said:

"Oh, that I were worthy to be the Elisha upon whose shoulders the mantle of that Elijah might fall!

"Mr. President Vander Veer and gentlemen, I seem to find myself again in Holland, as in August last; this superb banquet, this hospitality, the suddenness with which I am called on to speak, the many friends who look upon me with such kindly eyes, the handsome and noble-looking men, six feet three in their stockings, who look down upon me as I speak to them, all combine to bring back to me the atmosphere of the fatherland, as well they may in this old Dutch city.

"This is a fortunate Society—unlike the Democratic party at the last election, it confronts a theory and not a condition—it is founded upon an idea, the memory of our ancestors. And such ancestors. Honest, religious, hospitable to all nations, and to all creeds, and faithful unto death in the performance of duty, whether it led to death by burning at the stake, or by blowing up a warship to prevent its falling into the hand of the enemy; or by calmly launching in a storm at sea the life-boat that could never return from the vain attempt to save life from a drifting, shipwrecked hulk. They call the rope-ladder over a ship's side, 'Jacob's Ladder'; those Dutch sailors who, not long ago, near the channel, went down that ladder to realize the almost certain death in their hope to save others, were angels as much as any that Jacob of old saw in his vision.

"This Society, Mr. President, was formed to bring together the descendants of such men. And, looking for an ideal President, this Society chose Hooper C. Van Vorst. For nearly three-score years and ten his walk and conversation have been known of all men. Upright, pure, genial, the friend of all, his white hair is a crown of glory, and he well deserves to be made the perpetual President of this Society, and to lead us into heaven, that stockade to which, no doubt, you, our Albany friends, refer in the lines which you have coupled with this toast to his name. A Dutchman is nothing if he be not religious. Our ancestors built a church in the corner of each fort, and each stockade, and while you say to him,

> All our town in peace awaits you,
> All our doors stand open for you ;
> You shall *to our stockade enter,*
> And the heart's right hand we give you ;

you also feel that before very many years that 'dome with wisdom silvered o'er' shall lead you into the stockade with walls of gold and gates of pearl, the home not made with hands eternal in the heavens."

"Wien's Neerlandsch Bloed" was rendered by the orchestra, and Vice-President Vander Veer announced : "The Dutchmen of Beverwyck.—'Ah ! blissful and never-to-be-forgotten age. When everything was better than it ever has been since or ever will be again—when the shad in the Hudson were all salmon, and when the moon shone with a pure and resplendent whiteness,'" and said: "Gentlemen, the committee considers itself especially fortunate in having one to respond to this toast who so well represents the Dutch families of Albany and vicinity. I have the pleasure of calling upon the Honorable Abraham Lansing." Mr. Lansing gave one of his scholarly and able addresses, tracing the lineage of the Dutch back to the Roman Empire. He said he would be cut and slashed all to pieces by those who were to follow him, especially Mr. Clearwater, and the next time wanted to have the last speech. Mr. Lansing told much of Albany's past history; of the habits and customs of the Dutchmen who first settled here, and were content to live, trade, and die here; and the development in every manner of the place that was dear to every Hollander. "De Zilver Vloot" broke the applause which followed Mr. Lansing's taking his seat, and then Toastmaster Vander Veer was seen to rise above the tobacco smoke. His lips parted and he said: "I move that a cable message be sent to our minister at The Hague." This was adopted with a cheer and a rising vote, and Minister Roosevelt's health was drunk. The cablegram was penned by Mr. G. A. Van Allen, and sent in these words:

"R. B. ROOSEVELT,

"*Am. Legation, The Hague, Netherlands:*

"The Albany banquet of The Holland Society greets the fatherland. VANDER VEER.
VAN SICLEN."

Then he proposed the toast: "The Mayor of Albany. In our early days a Dutch Dongan governed us. To-

day a like Dutchman, with the same blood in his
veins, controls our destinies." Dr. Vander Veer said :
"Gentlemen, if the orderly doing of all things, the
proper appreciation of the responsibilities of official
trusts, and thorough honesty of purpose in discharg-
ing public duties were characteristic of the early
Dutchmen of this city, then it may be truly said that
he who is to respond to this toast to-night is in reality
a Dutchman. For we know that in his official career he
has presented all these good qualities. I was to have
had the pleasure of calling upon the Mayor of Albany,
but he has sent this regret by the hand of his chief
clerk : 'The Mayor looked forward with pleasant anti-
cipations, and deplores the ill-health which enforces
his absence. He is very sorry that his non-attendance
will affect the excellent programme. As to delegating
some one in his stead, he would suggest either Alderman Pruyn or Alderman Van Allen — they being city
officials.'" Alderman-at-large Pruyn said he had been
in the habit of sitting by and letting others do the
talking. He preferred to vote rather than to talk, and
thought that Alderman Van Allen should have responded, as Van Allen was in the first Board of Aldermen. He said : "It is an interesting fact that the
charter of this Dutch city was granted by an Irishman,
and that an Irishman is the mayor of the city to-day.
It is deeply to be regretted that the mayor is not with
us to-night. Dutchmen that we are, it is a great
satisfaction to us to know that the city is presided
over by its present excellent executive. And when
we say excellent executive, we mean it in the Dutch
sense. Municipal government received its greatest
impulse and development in the cities of the Netherlands, and the city governments were remarkable

for their honesty and efficiency. These principles of
sound government have been fully developed in the
government of Albany, from Pieter Schuyler down
to Edward A. Maher, who is a worthy successor of
our. Dutch mayors. In the ancient Dutch cities it
was a high honor to be a schepen or alderman, and a
burgomaster or mayor, and it may not be indelicate
for me as a Dutchman to claim that similar positions
are equally honorable in our American cities. This
city has an interesting history—in some ways the
most interesting of American cities. Founded by the
Dutch, in whom were innate the principles of liberty,
it was fitting that in 1754 a convention should be
held here looking toward the peaceful union of the
colonies. Without bringing politics to a social gathering, I may be permitted to remark that this ancient
burg was Democratic in its best sense. Any one who
has read Miss Grant's 'American Lady' will understand this, and any one who knows Dutch character will understand it better. Liberty, equality,
and fraternity, the mottoes of the French Republic,
were in reality Dutch. To be out of Florence was
exile to Dante. Socrates never cared to go beyond
the bounds of Athens. May every true Albanian,
wherever he may roam, how greatly he may be
attracted elsewhere, nevertheless feel that Albany is
good enough for him." Before Col. Pruyn could
retake his seat the orchestra struck up "De Nederlandsche Vlag."

Little did Dr. Vander Veer dream of the mine he
was about to spring when he called upon A. T. Clearwater, of Kingston, to respond to the toast: "Our
Esopus ancestors. They gathered from the East,
from the West, but from the South came the pure

and sparkling spring of life. 'Paddles none he had,
or needed, for his thoughts as paddles served him.'"
Then the good doctor presented Mr. Clearwater in
this fashion : " I know, gentlemen, that you have in
store a rich treat. The bones of our ancestors, in the
lovely and pure language for which our vice-president
of Kingston is noted, will be presented to us in a
manner entertaining and instructive." Mr. Clearwater broke the ice with an anecdote about that
good old Dutchman, Timothy J. Campbell, and Mrs.
Secretary Whitney. Ten days ago he had received a
note from the doctor asking if he would attend the
dinner, and, with a Dutchman's anxiety for a free
lunch, he immediately accepted. When asked if he
would respond to a toast, he had responded that, for
a Society with such views of high license as The
Holland, he thought it had clear water enough.
He was placed under a Scotch title to respond to a
Dutch toast. His friend Pruyn might be an Irish-
Dutchman, but he was not a Scotch-Irishman, or a
Scotch-Dutchman. The true statement of facts is
that an attribute of a genuine Dutchman is that he
tells the whole truth, and the Dutchmen of Esopus
are typical in this respect. It was only such Irish-
Dutchmen as Pruyn and Lansing that could exaggerate, he said. Of all Dutchmen those of Esopus
stood head. It was the Dutch of Esopus who held
the first popular election; it was they who swung
the State of New-York into line when it was waver-
ing, and elected the federation of the American
Colonies; it was they who signed the first Constitution of New-York; it was among them that Governor
Clinton, New-York's first Governor was inaugurated,
and it was at Esopus that the first Constitution of the

30

States in 1775 was signed, "And, gentlemen, let me state right here with becoming modesty," he added, "that my friend on the left, Mr. Coykendall, cultivates the great Dutch virtue of hospitality on behalf of the Dutchmen of Esopus. At Esopus we have the incarnation of Dutch hospitality, as any of you will find if you come down and call on the Esopus representative, Mr. Coykendall."

The orchestra played "Oranje boven al."

"Our Brother Nationalities. And others were there who, by reason of their noble work, became true and worthy companions," was announced by the Toastmaster, who added: "Some of us who are gathered here to-night have been more fortunate than others. Some of us know full well how many a banquet has been enriched by the clean, clear-cut sentences, filled with wit and wisdom, of him who is about to speak. All of us will now have our minds enriched by him whom I have the honor to call upon." Surrogate Francis H. Woods responded amid much merriment. He had enjoyed listening to the rivalry between the Dutch of Esopus and Beverwyck. "Here it must be confessed," he said, "there were but two nationalities contending for supremacy. After 200 years the Irish smilingly climb to the top. If Dr. Vander Veer had not been so busy he could have patched up our mayor so that he might have been here to-night. The Dutchman shrewdly saw the commercial advantage of this place, and settled here, establishing a trade with the Indians that lasted. The Dutchman found the Yankee too much for him, and fenced the town in. Some say the fences are still up." He had followed in the cavalcade with Mayor John Boyd Thacher when he opened the South gate three years ago, and bade the world enter; but he did not notice any great increase in the population save that noted in the vital statistics. "The North gate was opened, 'leading to the North and ye Canadas'; yet our exclusiveness still continues. Not a head of a bank or any city official has since passed through that gate. In 1749 Peter Kalm, a Swede, came here, and said that all the inhabitants were Dutch, and that nothing but the Dutch language was spoken; that the Dutch on returning home at night would silently sit, and smoke, and look at their wives. When they did break the silence they would indulge in endearing terms. The coming of other nationalities here is best indicated by the growth of denominational congregations. The most gracious incident in our early history was the welcoming of Father Jonges, as he fled from the Hurons, by Dr. Megapolensis and his people. As the population grew it brought together men and women who believed they had souls to be saved. On every Sunday morning, from an hundred belfrys deep-mouthed bells call men of all nationalities to prayer with glad and not discordant notes, and true religion advances as we better understand the injunction of the Prince of Peace. 'Love one another,'" he said. The wise men of the East came here, captured the Dutchmen's daughters, opened banks, and new ways of trade. The preserver and translator of our Dutch records was Dr. O'Callaghan. In 200 years no man had been mayor except a Dutchman or the husband of a Dutch wife, except an Irishman, named Nolan, who built a brewery near the banks of the American Rhine which he called Beverwyck, and if it were n't for this he still would sign from Clare and not from Albany. "The spirits of the first settlers hover about us. May turmoil, nor strife, nor sectarianism, nor foul civic methods ever drive them weeping away from us."

The orchestra finished off "The Groves of Blarney" in a scientific style, and apparently to Judge Woods's satisfaction, before Toastmaster Vander Veer proposed the final one of the stated toasts —"The Holland of to-day," this sentiment standing for introduction:

> "Sing for us your merry song,
>   Sing the beggar's song to please us;
>   That the feast may be more joyous,
> That the time may pass more gayly,
>   And our guests be more contented."

"Gentlemen," said Dr. Vander Veer, "I am sure in calling upon him who is to respond to this, the last toast of the occasion, we have much to rejoice in. He comes from an atmosphere of mirth and merry-making, filled with boyhood's happy dreams and expectant successes. He represents one of the oldest institutions in the city; an institution founded, nurtured, and sustained by Dutchmen, and from whose halls have graduated generation after generation of the sons of Dutchmen, and yet, not contented with this affiliation, he has recently visited old Holland, and can tell us now of Holland of to-day. I know you will all join with me as I call upon him who at the present time has our dear ones still in charge. I call upon Professor Henry P. Warren." Professor Warren was most happy in his response, which, embodying every point of interest possible in so brief a time, was applauded till the tables fairly danced. The strife of the Dutch against the Zuyder Zee, and the prophesy that another generation will see Holland without a drop of water within her dykes were the main points.

The set toasts finished, Dr. Vander Veer called upon Charles H. Van Benthuysen to respond to "Our flags." He said, referring to the ornamented menu: The flag to the left, on the first page (orange, white, and blue) was adopted by the United Netherlands in 1552. It floated from the mast head of the *Half Moon*, when Henry Hudson visited the present sight of our venerable city on the 22d of September, 1609. In 1650, after the death of " William II," a red stripe was substituted in place of the orange; this is the present flag of Holland, and is represented to the right. The flag to the left, on the last page (white with coat of arms in center), is the flag of the State of New-York, promulgated in the "Military Regulations, 1859." This flag, by Act of the Legislature, "shall be displayed from the capitol during the hours when the Legislature is in session." The flag to the right is our glorious "Star-Spangled Banner," the unsullied emblem of the United States. The coat of arms of the city (at top of left-hand corner of last orange page), was copied from a map bearing date prior to 1700. The seal, at the lower corner, was copied from a deed from the city of Albany, signed by Pieter Schuyler, mayor, bearing date of December, 1686, and was the first seal of the city.

Professor Webster, of Union College, was next called upon as a representative of the Mohawk Indian. He denied any Mohawk lineage, but said he longed to be a Dutchman. For that matter, he would not mind being part Irish, or Scotch-Dutch; but as it was, be was obliged to be satisfied with being a Yankee. His opinion wasn't asked when the question of his lineage was decided, so he must be content with what he was. In the history of the college of which he was honored as being president, there was much of Dutch—lots of Vans. The Dutch beauty is proverbial, and if the gathering there present was representative, the proverb was a sound one. He had been thoroughly entertained, both as to the body and mind, and had only one fault to find. He had had an envelope there in which to carry off the literary spoils. Somebody had stolen it, and he was uneasy as to how he should convince his wife without the documents, that he had been with so respectable a crowd of Dutchmen.

Theodore V. Van Heusen had a few words to say about a club he encountered while abroad last season and proposed a toast to The Holland Club of London. He said: " In number not many as yet, but I found them of rare quality. I am sure that a better representation of men never put their feet under mahogany. They were considerate of us, representatives of The Holland Society of New-York, sent a cordial letter of welcome to our secretary, Mr. Van Siclen, at Amsterdam, inviting any of us who should get to London, to make themselves at home at the club-rooms. At the request of Secretary Van Siclen we answered this in person, with due thanks, and I now make report to him of the result. The president of the club was prompt to call on us, and it was arranged that my son and I should receive a club dinner."

Miles W. Vosburgh received the following telegrams, which Dr. Vander Veer read:

NEW-YORK.— I deeply regret that other engagements will prevent my celebrating with The Holland Society to-night. No place in the state or country so naturally becomes the home of a Holland society as Albany. If Diederich Knickerbocker's ghost comes down from Schaghticoke to shake your festivities, he may be surprised at your costumes, but will recognize in your manners and capacity the unimpaired vigor of the original stock. CHAUNCEY M. DEPEW.

SAN FRANCISCO.—Invitation too late. Accept cordial greetings. I wish the members of The Holland Society good health, perfect contentment, plenty of schnapps, and many merry reunions. WILLIAM ALVORD.

[Mr. Alvord is a graduate of the class of 1848, Albany Academy, is ex-mayor of San Francisco, and president of the Bank of California, the largest institution of its kind in the United States.]

At the north end of the dining hall, forming a fitting background for the speakers, the decoration consisted of a screen, the center of which was formed with an elegant, rare, Dutch rug, the property of Mrs. John V. L. Pruyn. This had woven into it the Dutch coat of arms, and a border of brilliant tulips. On either side of the rug were drapings of garnet cloth, the ends being finished off with draperies of American and Dutch flags. Across the top were broad bands of red, white, and blue festooned, and surmounted by American and Dutch flags. The chandeliers had wreaths of smilax about them, and the Albany City band orchestra was hidden behind a hedge composed of palms and longiflorum lilies. Along the entire length of the tables at the inner edge of the plates was a row of smilax, which partially hid long-stemmed clay pipes of the old Dutch fashion around whose slender stems were tied dainty bows of blue ribbon. Opposite each plate was a slender glass of water over which nodded a tulip. At each end of the tables were beds of tulips, and through the center of the table were potted plants, azaleas and bunches of calla lilies and hyacinths. Toastmaster Vander Veer, his face beaming with smiles, was hidden while he sat at the dinner by a large epergne. But he towered grandly above this as he rose to announce the toasts.

The scores of the Dutch pieces played were set by Professor Ehrmann.

Even the charlotte russe was encircled with orange ribbon.

The bulbs which furnished the tulips were imported from Holland.

The cigars were distributed in pairs, each pair being held together with orange ribbon.

Alderman Pruyn referred to the fact that we had an Irish mayor who is painting the City Hall roof red.

Heer Karel Henrick Van Benthuysen wore his medal after the French mode, pendant from his shirt collar.

Last night was the first time in America that the tulip was publicly recognized as the distinctly Dutch flower.

Dr. Van Buren, of Kinderhook, a descendant of President Martin Van Buren, spoke of the Dutch history of Kinderhook.

Much of the success of the affair — and there was nothing to mar the occasion — was due to the untiring efforts of James Ten Eyck.

There were some oliekocks. These were made by Miss Van Vechten, a descendant of one of Albany's mayors, Teunis Van Vechten. They were pronounced *à la mode* of 1614.

"You will have to wear the orange to-night," said Mr. DeWitt, as he placed a tulip into the buttonhole of Surrogate Woods's coat. "This is the only occasion I would wear it," returned Judge Woods.

31

ANNUAL MEETING OF
THE HOLLAND SOCIETY OF NEW-YORK,

AT the annual meeting of The Holland Society of New-York, held June 11, 1889, a committee consisting of Messrs. Egbert L. Viclé, Edgar M. van Winkle, and Giles Y. van der Bogert, was appointed to represent the Society, February 2, 1890, at the bicentennial of the massacre of Schenectady, N. Y.

On motion of Mr. Theo. M. Banta, it was determined to begin the publication of the records of the old Dutch churches of America, nearly all of which have now been copied by the Society.

A proposed increase of the initiation fee and annual dues was defeated.

On motion of Mr. Geo. W. Van Siclen, it was resolved that the President and Secretary of this Society be requested to send greeting to our kinsmen, the descendants of the Dutch settlers in South Africa; that the sentiments of warm friendship so happily revived with our fatherland may be extended to our more distant relatives, brave and worthy descendants of the old Batavii.

On motion of Mr. Geo. W. Van Siclen, it was resolved that this Society tender to the venerable the Hon. Marius Schoonmaker, author of the "History of Kingston," its congratulations that his noble son, our fellow-member, Commander Cornelius Marius Schoonmaker, U. S. N., had the opportunity to die with honor at the post of duty, at the Island of Samoa, March 15, 1889.

It was also determined, on motion of Rev. J. Howard Suydam, to offer a Holland Society cup for the yacht races at Sneek, on the Zuyder Zee, Holland, one of the places where the members of The Holland Society were so handsomely entertained on their pilgrimage last summer.

After ordering an oil portrait of its President, Judge Van Vorst, the Society proceeded to sing in chorus:

> I 'm a Van, of a Van, of a Van, of a Van,
>   Of a Van of a way back line;
> On every rugged feature
>   Ancestral glories shine;
> And all our band in kinship stand
>   With all that 's old and fine;
> I 'm a Van, of a Van, of a Van, of a Van,
>   Of a Van of a way back line.

Necrology

FROM PINKSTER, 1888, TO PINKSTER, 1889.

W. A. OGDEN HEGEMAN,
OF NEW-YORK.

EDWARD YATES LANSING,
OF ALBANY, N. Y.

ABRAHAM LOTT,
OF BROOKLYN, N. Y.

HENRY R. LOW,
OF MIDDLETON, N. Y.

Capt. CORNELIUS MARIUS SCHOONMAKER, U. S. N.,
OF KINGSTON, N. Y.

GARRET LANSING SCHUYLER,
OF NEW-YORK.

GARDINER BAKER VAN VORST,
OF NEW-YORK.

BENJAMIN STEVENS VAN WYCK,
OF NEW-YORK.

THEODORE CHARDAVOYNE VERMILYE,
OF TOMPKINSVILLE, N. Y.

Necrology.

FROM PINKSTER, 1889, TO PINKSTER, 1890.

WILLIAM BROSS,
OF CHICAGO, ILLS.

AUGUSTUS A. HARDENBERGH,
OF JERSEY CITY, N. J.

LOUIS V. D. HARDENBERGH,
OF BROOKLYN, N. Y.

JAMES RIKER,
OF WAVERLY, N. Y.

HENRY EVERITT ROOSEVELT,
OF NEW-YORK.

HENRY JACOB SCHENCK,
OF NEW-YORK.

GEORGE WASHINGTON SCHUYLER,
OF ITHACA, N. Y.

JOHN SCHERMERHORN,
OF SCHENECTADY, N. Y.

THOMAS STORM,
OF NEW-YORK.

Necrology.

———

JOHN H. SUYDAM,
OF NEW-YORK.

JOHN BARENT VISSCHER,
OF ALBANY, N. Y.

JOHN ENDERS VOORHEES,
OF AMSTERDAM, N. Y.

WILLIAM VOORHIS,
OF NYACK, N. Y.

ABRAM BOVEE VAN DUSEN,
OF NEW-YORK.

HOOPER CUMMING VAN VORST,
OF NEW-YORK.

JOHN WALING VAN WINKLE,
OF PASSAIC, N. J.

JOHN VOORHEES VAN WOERT,
OF NEW-YORK.

THE HOLLAND SOCIETY.

Officers.

PINKSTER, 1890.

President.

ROBERT BARNWELL ROOSEVELT.

Vice-President.

New-York City.

MAUS ROSA VEDDER, M. D.

Brooklyn, N. Y.

HARMANUS BARKALOO HUBBARD.

Jersey City, N. J.

GEORGE CLIPPENGER VARICK.

Albany, N. Y.

ALBERT VAN DER VEER, M. D.

Kingston, N. Y.

SAMUEL DECKER COYKENDALL.

Kinderhook, N. Y.

PETER VAN SCHAACK PRUYN, M. D.

Rockland County, N. Y.

GARRET VAN NOSTRAND.

Westchester County, N. Y.
Rev. CHARLES KNAPP CLEARWATER.

Catskill, N. Y.
Rev. EVERT VAN SLYKE, D. D.

Schenectady, N. Y.
GILES YATES VAN DE BOGERT.

Amsterdam, N. Y.
WALTER L. VAN DENBERGH.

Newtown, L. I.
JOHN E. VAN NOSTRAND.

New Brunswick, N. J.
Rev. WILLIAM HOFFMAN TEN EYCK, D. D.

Bergen County, N. J.
GEORGE FREDERICK SCHERMERHORN.

Passaic County, N. J.
JOHN HOPPER.

Cobleskill, N. Y.
JOHN VAN SCHAICK.

Poughkeepsie, N. Y.
FRANK HASBROUCK.

Monmouth County, N. J.
D. AUGUSTUS VAN DER VEER.

Somerset County, N. J.
LAWRENCE VAN DER VEER.

Minisink, N. Y.
AMOS VAN ETTEN, Jr.

Buffalo, N. Y.
SHELDON T. VIELE.

Philadelphia, Pa.
EUGENE VAN LOAN.

Yonkers, N. Y.
WILLIAM L. HEERMANCE.

Lansingburgh, N. Y.
WILLIAM C. GROESBECK.

Camden, N. J.
PETER L. VOORHEES.

North Hempstead, L. I., N. Y.
ANDREW J. ONDERDONK.

Staten Island, N. Y.
Rev. WILLIAM PRALL, Ph. D., LL. D.

Vice-President for the Army.
Brevet Major-General STEWART VAN VLIET, U. S. A.

Vice-President for the Navy.
Commander DELAVAN BLOODGOOD, Medical Director, U. S. N.

Secretary.

GEORGE WEST VAN SICLEN.
Secretary's address, 7 Wall Street, New-York.

247

Committees.

1889.

Committee on Finance.

GEORGE G. DE WITT, Jr.
WILLIAM M. HOES.
W. W. VAN VOORHIS.

Committee on Genealogy.

GEORGE M. VAN HOESEN.
THEODORE M. BANTA.
AUGUSTUS VAN WYCK.

Committee on History and Tradition.

Rev. HENRY VAN DYKE, D. D.
JOHN L. RIKER.
WILLIAM J. VAN ARSDALE.

List of Members.

CONSTITUTION. ARTICLE III.

Section 1. No one shall be eligible as a member unless he be of full age, of respectable standing in society, of good moral character, and the descendant in the direct male line of a Dutchman who was a native or resident of New-York or of the American colonies prior to the year 1675. This shall include those of other former nationalities who found in Holland a refuge or a home, and whose descendants in the male line came to this country as Dutch settlers, speaking Dutch as their native tongue. This shall also include descendants in the male line of Dutch settlers who were born within the limits of Dutch settlements, and descendants in the male line of persons who possessed the rights of Dutch citizenship within Dutch settlements in America, prior to the year 1675; also any descendant in the direct male line of a Dutchman, one of whose descendants became a member of this Society prior to June 16, 1886.

ACKER, CHARLES LIVINGSTON . . . . New-York City.

ACKER, * DAVID DEPEYSTER . . .   "   "

ACKER, Jr., DAVID DEPEYSTER . .   "   "

ACKER, FRANKLIN . . . .   "   "

ADRIANCE, FRANCIS HENRY . . . . . Poughkeepsie, N. Y.

ADRIANCE, HARRIS ELY . . . . . . Pelham Manor, N. Y.

ADRIANCE, ISAAC REYNOLDS . . . . . Poughkeepsie, N. Y.

ADRIANCE, JOHN ERSKINE . . . . . .   "   "

ADRIANCE, JOHN PETER . . . . . .   "   "

ADRIANCE, WILLIAM ALLEN . . . . .   "   "

AMERMAN, BENJAMIN LAUDER . . . . . New-York City.
AMERMAN, FREDERICK HERBERT . . . . .   "   "
AMERMAN, NEWTON . . . .   "   "
AMERMAN, WILLIAM H. . . . .   "   "
AMERMAN, WILLIAM LIBBEY . . . . . .   "   "
ANTHONY, RICHARD AMERMAN . . . . . .   "   "

BANTA, CORNELIUS VREELAND . . . New-York City.
BANTA, GEORGE A. . . . .   "   "
BANTA, JOHN . . . .   "   "
BANTA, THEODORE MELVIN . . . . . .   "   "
BARHYDT, GEORGE WEED . . . . Plainville, Conn.
BARHYDT, THOMAS LOW . . . . Schenectady, N. Y.
BAYARD, THOMAS FRANCIS . . . . Wilmington, Del.
BEEKMAN, GEORGE CRAWFORD . . . . . Freehold, N. J.
BEEKMAN, GERARD . . . . New-York City.
BEEKMAN, HENRY M. T. . . . . Jersey City, N. J.
BEEKMAN, HENRY RUTGER . . . . New-York City.
BEEKMAN, J. WILLIAM . . . .   "   "
BEEKMAN, JOHN WOODHULL . . . . . Perth Amboy, N. J.
BENSEN, ALBERT VAN VOAST . . . . Albany, N. Y.
BERGEN, FRANCIS H. . . . . Brooklyn, N. Y.
BERGEN, FRANK . . . . Elizabeth, N. J.
BERGEN, HERMAN SUYDAM . . . . New-York City.
BERGEN, JAMES J. . . . . Somerville, N. J.
BERGEN, TUNIS G. . . . . Brooklyn, N. Y.
BERGEN, VAN BRUNT . . . . Bay Ridge, L. I.
BERGEN, ZACCHEUS . . . . New-York City.
BERRY, RICHARD J. . . . . Flatbush, L. I.
BLAUVELT, ALONZO, M. D. . . . . . . New-York City.
BLAUVELT, Rev. CORNELIUS RYCKMAN . . . Nyack, N. Y.
BLAUVELT, JAMES HENRY . . . .   "   "
BLAUVELT, WILLIAM OSCAR . . . .   "   "
BLEECKER, JAMES . . . . New-York City.
BLEECKER, Jr., JAMES . . . .   "   "
BLEECKER, Jr., THEOPHYLACT BACHE . . .   "   "
BLOODGOOD, Dr. DELAVAN Med. Dir. U.S.N., Brooklyn, N.Y.
BLOODGOOD, FRANCIS . . . . Milwaukee, Wis.
BLOODGOOD, HILDRETH KENNEDY . . . . New-York City.
BLOODGOOD, JOHN . . . .   "   "
BLOODGOOD, JOSEPH FRANCIS, M. D. . . .   "   "
BLYDENBERGH, BENJAMIN B. . . . . . .   "   "

BLYDENBERGH, JOHN B.	New-York City.
BOGARDUS, ABRAHAM	Brooklyn, N. Y.
BOGART, JOHN	New-York City.
BOGART, JOSEPH HEGEMAN, M. D.	Roslyn, N. Y.
BOGERT, ALBERT GILLIAM	New-York City.
BOGERT, ANDREW DEMAREST	Englewood, N. J.
BOGERT, CHARLES EDMUND	New-York City.
BOGERT, Dr. EDWARD STRONG, Med. Inspector U. S. N	Brooklyn, N. Y.
BOGERT, HENRY A.	Flushing, L. I.
BOGERT, HENRY L.	New-York City.
BOGERT, JOHN G.	" "
BOGERT, PHILIP E.	" "
BOGERT, STEPHEN GILLIAM	" "
BOGERT, STEPHEN VAN RENSSELAER, M.D.,	NewBrighton, S. I.
BOORAEM, HENRY LIENAU	Jersey City, N. J.
BOORAEM, JOHN VAN VORST	Brooklyn, N. Y.
BOORAEM, LOUIS VACHER	Jersey City, N. J.
BOORAEM, THEODORE BURGES	New Brunswick, N. J.
BOOROM, Rev. SYLVESTER DALEY, Chaplain, U. S. N	Horseheads, N. Y.
BREVOORT, JAMES RENWICK	Yonkers, N. Y.
BRINCKERHOFF, ALEXANDER GORDON	Brooklyn, N. Y.
BRINCKERHOFF, ELBERT ADRAIN	New-York City.
BRINCKERHOFF, HENRY WALLER	Brooklyn, N. Y.
BRINCKERHOFF, JOHN HENRY	Jamaica, L. I.
BRINCKERHOFF, VAN WYCK	New-York City.
BRINK, BENJAMIN M.	Saugerties, N. Y.
BRINKERHOFF, WARREN MONTGOMERY	Auburn, N. Y.
BROSS,* WILLIAM	Chicago, Ills.
BROUWER, GEORGE HOWARD	New-York City.
BROUWER, THEOPHILUS ANTHONY	" "
BROWER, ABRAHAM GILES, M. D.	Utica, N. Y.
BROWER, ABRAHAM THEW HUNTER	Chicago, Ill.
BROWER, BLOOMFIELD	New-York City.
BROWER, CHARLES DE HART	" "
BROWER, JOHN	" "
BROWER, JOHN LEFOY	" "
BROWER, JACOB VREDENBURG	St Paul, Minn.
BROWER, WILLIAM LEVERICH	New-York City.
BRUYN, AUGUSTUS HASBROUCK	Kingston, N. Y.
BURHANS, CHARLES	" "
BURHANS, Jr., SAMUEL	New-York City.

CADMUS, CORNELIUS ANDREW . . . . Paterson, N. J.
CANTINE, PETER . . . . Saugerties, N. Y.
CLEARWATER, ALPHONSO TRUMP- } Kingston, N. Y
  BOUR . . . .
CLEARWATER, Rev. CHARLES KNAPP . . Mt. Vernon, N. Y.
CLUTE, JACOB WINNE . . . . Schenectady, N. Y.
CLUTE, M. D., WILLIAM TELLER . . .   "   "
COLE, D. D., Rev. DAVID . . . . Yonkers, N. Y.
COLE, FRANK HOWARD . . . .   "   "
CONOVER, ALONZO EDWARD . . . . . . New-York City.
CONOVER, CHARLES EDWIN . . . . . Middletown, N. J.
CONOVER, CHARLES E. . . . . Wickatunk, N. J.
CONOVER, FRANK BRUEN . . . . Freehold, N. J.
CONOVER, FRANK EDGAR . . . . New-York City.
CONOVER, GARRET B. . . . . Englishtown, N. J.
CONOVER, JAMES C. . . . . Freehold, N. J.
CONOVER, JAMES SCOTT . . . . . . New-York City.
CONOVER, JOHN BARRICLO . . . . . . Freehold, N. J.
CONOVER, JOHN S. . . . . Wickatunk, N. J.
CONOVER, RICHARD STEVENS . . . . South Amboy, N. J.
CONOVER, STACY PRICKETT . . . . . . Wickatunk, N. J.
COOPER, EBENEZER LANE . . . . New-York City.
COOPER, JAMES C. . . . .   "   "
COOPER, WASHINGTON LAFAYETTE . . .   "   "
CORTELYOU, LAWRENCE VAN VOORHEES . Brooklyn, N. Y.
COWENHOVEN, CHARLES TIEBOUT . . New Brunswick, N. J.
COWENHOVEN, JOHN . . . . Bath Beach, L. I.
COYKENDALL, SAMUEL DECKER . . . . . Rondout, N. Y.
COYKENDALL, THOMAS CORNELL . . . .   "   "
CRISPELL, CHARLES WINEGAR, M. D. . .   "   "
CRUM, GEORGE LATHAM . . . . New-York City.
CRUSER, MATTHIAS VAN DYKE . . . . . Brooklyn, N. Y.
CUYLER, CORNELIUS C. . . . . New-York City.
CUYLER, Rev. THEODORE LEDYARD, D. D. . Brooklyn, N. Y.
CUYLER, THOMAS DE WITT . . . . . . Philadelphia, Pa.

DE BEVOISE, GEORGE PINE . . Steinway, L. I., N. Y.
  DE BEVOISE, ISAAC C. . . . . . . Brooklyn, N. Y.
  DE GRAAF, HENRY PEEK . . . . New-York City.
DE GRAFF, ALFRED . . . . Fonda, N. Y.
DE GROOT, ALFRED . . . . Port Richmond, S. I.
DE GROOT, WILLIAM . . . . New-York City.

De Kay, Sidney . . . . New Brighton, N. Y.
Delamater, Ezra Doane . . . . Hudson, N. Y.
De Lamater, George Beckwith . . . . New-York City.
Demarest, John . . . . Newark, N. J.
Denise, David Demarest . . . . Freehold, N. J.
Depew, Chauncey Mitchell . . . . . New-York City.
De Peyster, Frederic J. . . . .   "   "
De Peyster, Col. Johnston Livingston . . Tivoli, N. Y.
De Peyster, John Watts . . . . . . New-York City.
Devoe, Frederick William . . . . . .   "   "
De Witt, Abraham van Dyck . . . . . Albany, N. Y.
De Witt, Alfred . . . . New-York City.
De Witt, Cornelius . . . . Norfolk, Va.
De Witt, George Gosman . . . . Nyack, N. Y.
De Witt, Jr., George G. . . . . New-York City.
De Witt, Henry Clinton . . . . . .   "   "
De Witt, Jerome . . . . Binghamton, N. Y.
De Witt, Rev. John, D. D. . . . . Chicago, Ills.
De Witt, John Evert . . . . Portland, Me.
De Witt, Moses J. . . . . Newark, N. J.
De Witt, Peter . . . . New-York City.
De Witt, Richard Varick . . . . Albany, N. Y.
De Witt, Sutherland . . . . Elmira, N. Y.
De Witt, Thomas Dunkin . . . . Pelham Manor, N. Y.
De Witt, William Cantine . . . . . Brooklyn, N. Y.
De Witt, William G. . . . . New-York City.
Deyo, Jacob . . . . New Paltz, N. Y.
Deyo, Jerome Vernet . . . . . . Poughkeepsie, N. Y.
Deyo, Peter . . . . West Superior, Wis.
Dillenbeck, Morris H. . . . . New-York City.
Ditmars, Abram Douwe . . . .   "   "
Ditmars, Edward Wilson . . . .   "   "
Ditmars, Isaac Edward . . . .   "   "
Douw, Charles Gibbons . . . . . · Poughkeepsie, N. Y.
Du Bois, Coert, M. D. . . . . New-York City.
Du Bois, Cornelius . . . .   "   "
Du Bois, Elijah . . . . Kingston, N. Y.
Du Bois, Eugene . . . . . . West New Brighton, N. Y.
Du Bois, Dr. Francis Latta, Med. } Portsmouth, N. H.
   Inspector U. S. N. . . . . . . }
Dumond, Cornelius J., M. D. . . . . . . New-York City.
Duryea, Joseph W. . . . .   "   "
Duryea, Samuel B. . . . . Brooklyn, N. Y.

DURYEE, GUSTAVUS ABEEL . . . . Newark, N. J.
DURYEE, Rev. JOSEPH RANKIN, D. D. . . . New-York City.
DURYEE, Rev. JOSEPH T., D. D. . . . . . . Omaha, Neb.
DURYEE, WILLIAM B. . . . . Freehold, N. J.
DURYEE, Rev. WILLIAM RANKIN, D. D. . Jersey City, N. J.

CKERSON, PETER Q. . . . . New-York City.
    ELMENDORF, DWIGHT L. . . . . .   "   "
    ELMENDORF, Rev. JOACHIM, D. D. .   "   "
ELMENDORF, JOHN AUGUSTUS . . . . . .   "   "
ELMENDORF, JOHN B . . . .   "   "
ELMENDORF, NICOLL FLOYD . . . .   "   "
ELTING, E. J. . . . . Yonkers, N. Y.
ELTING, IRVING . . . . Poughkeepsie, N. Y.
ELTING, JACOB . . . . Clintondale, N. Y.
ELTING, JESSE . . . . New Paltz, N. Y.
ELTING, PETER J. . . . . Yonkers, N. Y.
ELSWORTH, EDWARD . . . . Poughkeepsie, N. Y.
ESSELSTYN, EVERETT JAMES . . . . . . New-York City.
ESSELSTYN, HERMAN VEDDER . . . . . . Hudson, N. Y.
ESSELSTYN, JACOB BROADHEAD . . . . . Claverack, N. Y.

ONDA, DOUW HENRY . . . . Albany, N. Y.
    FORT, PETER VAN VRANKEN . . . .   "   "
    FRYER, ROBERT LIVINGSTON . . . . Buffalo, N. Y.
FRYER, WILLIAM JOHN, Jr. . . . . New-York City.

ARRETSON, GARRET JAMES . . . . New-York City.
    GARRISON, WILLIAM DOMINICK . .   "   "
    GOELET, OGDEN . . . .   "   "
GOELET, ROBERT . . . .   "   "
GROESBECK, EDWARD ANSON . . . . . . Albany, N. Y.
GROESBECK, HERMAN JOHN . . . . . . Cincinnati, Ohio.
GROESBECK, LEONARD H. . . . . . . Lansingburgh, N. Y.
GROESBECK, WILLIAM CHICHESTER .   "   "
GULICK, ALEXANDER R. . . . . New-York City.
GULICK, C. R., M. D. . . . .   "   "
GULICK, ERNESTUS SCHENCK . . . . . . Brooklyn, N. Y.
GULICK, JAMES C. . . . . New-York City.
GULICK, JAMES IZAAK . . . .   "   "
GULICK, JOHN CALLBREATH . . . .   "   "
GULICK, Rev. URIAH DE HART . . . . . .   "   "

33

HARDENBERGH, ABRAM JANSEN . . . Brooklyn, N. Y.
HARDENBERGH,* AUGUSTUS A. . Jersey City, N. J.
HARDENBERGH,* LOUIS V. D. . . . Brooklyn, N. Y.
HARING, GEORGE T. . . . .   "   "
HARING, ISAAC CORNELIUS, M. D . . . . Mont Moor, N. Y.
HASBROUCK, Jr., ALFRED, U. S. A. . . Poughkeepsie, N. Y.
HASBROUCK, FERDINAND, M. D. . . . . . New-York City.
HASBROUCK, FRANK . . . . Poughkeepsie, N. Y.
HASBROUCK, GEORGE WICKES . . . . . . New-York City.
HASBROUCK, ISAAC EDGAR . . . . Brooklyn, N. Y.
HAS BROUCK, JACOB D. P. . . . . . . High Falls, N. Y.
HASBROUCK, JOHN CORNELIUS . . . . . . New-York City.
HASBROUCK, JOSEPH EDWIN . . . . Modena, N. Y.
HASBROUCK, OSCAR . . . .   "   "
HASBROUCK, SAYER, M. D. . . . . Providence, R. I.
HEERMANCE, DE WITT . . . . Rhinebeck, N. Y.
HEERMANCE, MARTIN . . . .   "   "
HEERMANCE, WILLIAM L. . . . . Yonkers, N. Y.
HEERMANS, FORBES . . . . Syracuse, N. Y.
HEERMANS, THOMAS BEEKMAN . . . . .   "   "
HEGEMAN, JOHNSTON NIVEN . . . . New-York City.
HEGEMAN, JOSEPH PEROT . . . . . . New London, Conn.
HEGEMAN,* W. A. OGDEN . . . . New-York City.
HOAG, PIERRE CLUTE, M. D. . . . .   "   "
HOES, PIERRE VAN BUREN . . . . . . Kinderhook, N. Y.
HOES, Rev. ROSWELL RANDALL, Chap- } Washington, D. C.
   lain U. S. N. . . . . }
HOES, WILLIAM MYERS . . . . New-York City.
HOOSE, JAMES HARMON . . . . Cortland, N. Y.
HOPPER, JOHN . . . . Paterson, N. J.
HOPPER, JOHN HENRY . . . .   "   "
HOPPER, ROBERT IMLAY . . . .   "   "
HOUGHTALING, DAVID HARRISON . . . . Brooklyn, N. Y.
HOYSRADT, ALBERT . . . . Hudson, N. Y.
HOYSRADT, JACOB WARREN . . . .   "   "
HUBBARD, HARMANUS BARKALOO . . . . Brooklyn, N. Y.
HUBBARD, SAMUEL McKAY . . . . . . Brooklyn, N. Y.
HUBBARD, TIMOTHY INGRAHAM . Flatlands, Kings Co., N. Y.
HULST, Rev. GEORGE DURYEE . . . . . Brooklyn, N. Y.
HUN, HENRY . . . . Albany, N. Y.
HUN, LEONARD GANSEVOORT . . . . .   "   "
HUN, THOMAS . . . .   "   "
HUYCK, EDMUND NILES . . . .   "   "
HUYCK, FRANCIS CONKLIN . . . .   "   "

JACOBUS, ARTHUR MIDDLETON, M. D. New-York City.
 JACOBUS, JOHN WESLEY . . . . . " "
 JACOBUS, RICHARD MENTOR . . . " "
JANSEN, Rev. JOHN NATHANIEL . . . . . . Newark, N. J.
JOHNSON, Jr., JEREMIAH . . . . New-York City.

KETELTAS, HENRY . . . . New-York City.
 KIP, CLARENCE VAN STEENBERGH . " "
 KIP, GEORGE GOELET . . . . . . " "
KIP, IRA ANDRUSS . . . . " "
KIP, LEONARD . . . . Albany, N. Y.
KIP, WILLIAM F. . . . . Buffalo, N. Y.
KNICKERBACKER, DAVID BUEL . . . . . Indianapolis, Ind.
KNICKERBACKER, JOHN . . . . Troy, N. Y.
KNICKERBACKER, THOMAS ADAMS . . . . . " "
KNICKERBOCKER, EDGAR . . . . New-York City.
KOUWENHOVEN, FRANCIS DURYEE . . Steinway, L. I. City.

LANSING, ABRAHAM . . . . Albany, N. Y.
 LANSING, CHARLES . . . . . Lansingburgh, N. Y.
 LANSING, CHARLES B. . . . . Albany, N. Y.
LANSING,* EDWARD YATES . . . . " "
LANSING, ISAAC DE FREEST . . . . " "
LANSING, JOHN . . . . Watertown, N. Y.
LANSING, JOHN TOWNSEND . . . . Albany, N. Y.
LANSING, JOSEPH ALEXANDER . . . . . . " "
LE FEVRE, DE WITT C. . . . . Buffalo, N. Y.
LEFFERTS, JOHN . . . . Flatbush, L. I.
LEFFERTS, JOHN, Jr. . . . . " "
LEGGETT, Rev. WILLIAM JAMES . . . . . Belleville, N. J.
LODEWICK, CHARLES CASPER . . . . . . Greenbush, N. Y.
LONGSTREET, HENRY H. . . . . Matawan, N. J.
LONGSTREET, JACOB HOLMES . . . . . Bordentown, N. J.
LOTT,* ABRAHAM . . . . Brooklyn, N. Y.
LOTT, JAMES VAN DER BILT . . . . " "
LOW,* HENRY R. . . . . Middletown, N. Y.
LOW, JOHN W. . . . . " "
LYDECKER, CHARLES EDWARD . . . . . . New-York City.

MARSELIUS, WILLARD CHARLES, M. D. . Albany, N. Y.
 MARSELLUS, JOHN . . . . . . Syracuse, N. Y.
 MARSELLUS, MAX DE MOTTE . . . . Passaic, N. J.
MESEROLE, WALTER MONFORT . . . . . Brooklyn, N. Y.

MESSLER, REMSEN VARICK . . . . Pittsburgh, Pa.
MESSLER, THOMAS DOREMUS . . . .   "   "
MILLER, PEYTON FARRELL . . . . Albany, N. Y.
MILLER, THEODORE . . . . Hudson, N. Y.
MONTANYE, GEORGE EDWARD . . . . . . New-York City.
MONTANYE, LEWIS FOSTER . . . .   "   "
MONTANYE, WILLIAM HENRY . . . .   "   "
MORRIS, JOHN JACOB . . . . Paterson, N. J.
MOTT, HOPPER STRYKER . . . . New-York City.
MYER, ALBERT JAMES . . . . Buffalo, N. Y.
MYERS, ANDREW GORMLY . . . . New-York City.
MYERS, GEORGE TOBIAS . . . . Portland, Oregon.
MYERS, JOHN GILLESPY . . . . Albany, N. Y.
MYNDERSE,* BARENT AARON, M. D. . . Schenectady, N. Y.
MYNDERSE, HERMAN V., M. D. . . . .   "   "
MYNDERSE, WILHELMUS . . . . New-York City.

NOSTRAND, GEORGE E. . . . . . . Bath Beach, L. I.
NOSTRAND, FREDERICK WILLIAM . New-York City.
NOSTRAND, JOHN LOTT . . . . . Brooklyn, N. Y.
NOSTRAND, WARNER HATCH . . . . . Dobb's Ferry, N. Y.

ONDERDONK, ANDREW JOSEPH . . . . New-York City.
ONDERDONK, THOMAS WILLIAM, M. D.   "   "
ONDERDONK, WILLIAM MINNE . .   "   "
OOTHOUT, JOHN WEBSTER . . . . Rochester, N. Y.
OSTERHOUDT, HOWARD . . . . Kingston, N. Y.
OSTRANDER, Rev. ANGELO . . . . Catskill, N. Y.
OSTRANDER,* STEPHEN MELANCTHON . . . Brooklyn, N. Y.

PAULISON, JOHN PAUL . . . . Tenafly, N. J.
PENTZ, ARCHIBALD MACLAY . . . New-York City.
PERRINE, DAVID VAN DER VEER . . Freehold, N. J.
POLHEMUS, ABRAHAM . . . . New-York City.
POLHEMUS, HENRY DITMAS . . . . . . Brooklyn, N. Y.
POLHEMUS, HENRY MARTIN . . . . . . New-York City.
POLHEMUS, Rev. ISAAC HEYER . . . . . .   "   "
POLHEMUS, JAMES SUYDAM . . . .   "   "
POUCHER, JOHANNES WILSON, M. D. . Poughkeepsie, N. Y.
PRALL, JOHN HOWARD . . . . Newton, L. I.
PRALL, Rev. WILLIAM, Ph. D., LL. D. . South Orange, N. J.
PRALL, WILLIAM M. . . . . St. Louis, Mo.

PROVOOST, GEORGE B. . . . . Dubuque, Iowa.
PROVOOST, JOHN MOFFAT . . . . Buffalo, N. Y.
PRUYN, CHARLES LANSING . . . . Albany, N. Y.
PRUYN, ISAAC . . . . Catskill, N. Y.
PRUYN, JOHN KNICKERBOCKER . . . Mechanicsville, N. Y.
PRUYN, JOHN VAN SCHAICK LANSING . . . . Albany, N. Y.
PRUYN, PETER VAN SCHAICK, M. D. . . Kinderhook, N. Y.
PRUYN, ROBERT CLARENCE . . . . Albany, N. Y.

QUACKENBUSH, ABRAHAM . . . . . . New-York City.
QUACKENBUSH, ABRAHAM C. . . .   "   "
QUACKENBUSH, CEBRA . . . . . . Albany, N. Y.
QUACKENBUSH,* JAMES WESTERVELT . Hackensack, N. J.
QUACKENBUSH, JOHN . . . . Mahwah, N. J.

RAPELYE, AUGUSTUS . . . . New-York City.
RAPELYE, CORNELIUS . . . . Astoria, N. Y.
RIKER, CHARLES EDGAR . . . . . New-York City.
RIKER,* JAMES . . . . Waverly, N. Y.
RIKER, JOHN HANCOCK . . . . New-York City.
RIKER, JOHN JACKSON . . . .   "   "
RIKER, JOHN LAWRENCE . . . .   "   "
ROMAINE, DE WITT C., M. D. . . . . . .   "   "
ROMER, J. L. . . . . Los Angeles, Cal.
ROOSA, DANIEL BENNETT ST. JOHN, M. D. . New-York City.
ROOSA, DE WITT . . . . Rondout, N. Y.
ROOSEVELT, CHARLES HENRY . . . . . New-York City.
ROOSEVELT,* CORNELIUS VAN SCHAICK South Orange, N. J.
ROOSEVELT, FREDERICK . . . . New-York City.
ROOSEVELT,* HENRY EVERITT . . . . . .   "   "
ROOSEVELT, JAMES . . . . Hyde Park, N. Y.
ROOSEVELT, NICHOLAS LATROBE . . . . . New-York City.
ROOSEVELT, ROBERT BARNWELL . . . . .   "   "
ROOSEVELT, ROBERT BARNWELL, Jr. . . .   "   "
ROOSEVELT, SAMUEL MONTGOMERY . . .   "   "
ROOSEVELT, THEODORE . . . .   "   "
ROOSEVELT, WILLIAM EMLEN . . . . . .   "   "
ROSA, HYMAN, M. D. . . . . Kingston, N. Y.
ROSEVELT, GEORGE W. . . . . New-York City.
ROSEVELT, WARREN . . . .   "   "
RYERSON,* MARTIN JOHN . . . . . . Bloomingdale, N. J.
RYERSON, ROBERT COLFAX . . . . Caldwell, N. J.

SANDERS, JACOB GLEN . . . . Albany, N. Y.
SANDERS, JAMES BLEECKER . . . . .   "   "
SCHANCK, SAMUEL M. . . . . . Hightstown, N. J.
SCHENCK, ABRAHAM VOORHEES . . . New Brunswick, N. J.
SCHENCK, CASPAR, Pay Director U. S. N. . . . Norfolk, Va.
SCHENCK, EDWARD . . . . New-York City.
SCHENCK, Rev. FERDINAND SCHUREMAN . . . Hudson, N. Y.
SCHENCK, FREDERICK BRETT . . . . New-York City.
SCHENCK,* HENRY JACOB . . . .   "   "
SCHENCK, PETER L., M. D. . . . . Brooklyn N. Y.
SCHENCK, TEUNIS, M. D. . . . . New Utrecht, L. I.
SCHERMERHORN, GEORGE FREDERICK . . Rutherford, N. J.
SCHERMERHORN, JACOB MAUS, Jr. . . . . Syracuse, N. Y.
SCHERMERHORN,* JOHN . . . . Schenectady, N. Y.
SCHERMERHORN, JOHN EGMONT . . . . New-York City.
SCHERMERHORN, SIMON J. . . . . . Schenectady, N. Y.
SCHOONMAKER, ADRIAN ONDERDONK . . . New-York City.
SCHOONMAKER, AUGUSTUS . . . . Kingston, N. Y.
SCHOONMAKER,* Capt. CORNELIUS MARIUS, } Kingston, N. Y.
    U. S. N. . . . .
SCHOONMAKER, FREDERICK WILLIAM . . . New-York City.
SCHOONMAKER, GEORGE BEEKMAN . . . . New-York City.
SCHOONMAKER, HIRAM . . . .   "   "
SCHOONMAKER, JAMES M. . . . . Pittsburgh, Pa.
SCHOONMAKER, JOHN . . . . Newburg, N. Y.
SCHOONMAKER, JOSEPH S. . . . . Uniontown, Pa.
SCHOONMAKER, LUCAS ELMENDORF . . . . New-York City.
SCHOONMAKER, SYLVANUS L. . . . . Pittsburgh, Pa.
SCHOONMAKER, WILLIAM DAVIS . . . . . New-York City.
SCHUYLER, ARENT HENRY . . . .   "   "
SCHUYLER, CHARLES E. . . . .   "   "
SCHUYLER, CLARKSON CROSBY, M. D. . . . . Troy, N. Y.
SCHUYLER,* GARRET LANSING . . . . . . New-York City.
SCHUYLER,* GEORGE WASHINGTON . . . . . Ithaca, N. Y.
SCHUYLER, GERALD LIVINGSTON . . . . . New-York City.
SCHUYLER, HERMAN PHILIP . . . .   "   "
SCHUYLER, MONTGOMERY ROOSEVELT . . .   "   "
SCHUYLER, PERCIVAL RAYMOND . . . . . Paterson, N. J.
SCHUYLER, STEPHEN . . . . West Troy, N. Y.
SICKELS, DAVID BANKS . . . . New-York City.
SICKELS, HIRAM EDWARD . . . . Albany, N. Y.
SICKELS, ROBERT . . . . Davenport, Iowa.
SKILLMAN, FRANCIS . . . . Roslyn, N. Y.

SMIDT, ALLEN LEE . . . . New-York City.
SMIDT, FRANK BISHOP . . . . "   "
SOMARINDYCK, JOHN WILLIAM . . . . . . Glen Cove, L. I.
STARIN, JOHN HENRY . . . . Fultonville, N. Y.
STEVENS, JOHN BAKER . . . . New-York City.
STEVENS, JOHN BRIGHT . . . . "   "
STORM, EDWARD . . . . Poughkeepsie, N. Y.
STORM,* THOMAS . . . . New-York City.
STORM, WALTON . . . .
STRYKER, General WILLIAM SCUDDER . . . Trenton, N. J.
STRYKER, WM. H. H. . . . . Paterson, N. J.
STUYVESANT, HENRY . . . . New-York City.
STUYVESANT, JOHN READE . . Tapley, Osborne Co., Kans.
STUYVESANT, PETER J. . . . . New-York City.
SUTPHEN, JOHN SCHUREMAN . . . . . "   "
SUTPHEN, JOHN S., Jr. . . . . "   "
SUTPHIN, JOHN HENRY . . . . Jamaica, L. I.
SUYDAM, CHARLES CROOKE . . . . . . Elizabeth, N. J.
SUYDAM, JAMES . . . . New-York City.
SUYDAM, Rev. J. HOWARD, D. D. . . . . Jersey City, N. J.
SUYDAM, JOHN FINE . . . . New-York City.
SUYDAM,* JOHN H. . . . . "   "
SUYDAM, JOHN RICHARD . . . . Sayville, L. I.
SUYDAM, LAMBERT . . . . New-York City.
SUYDAM, WILLIAM FARRINGTON . . . . . Hawley, Pa.
SWARTWOUT, GEORGE ALBERTINE . . . . Pasadena, Cal.
SWITS, JOHN LIVINGSTON . . . . . . Schenectady, N. Y.

APPEN, FREDERICK D. . . . . . . New-York City.
TELLER, Rev. HENRY W. . Pompton Plains, N. J.
TEN EYCK, CLINTON . . . . Albany, N. Y.
TEN EYCK,* HENRY JAMES . . . . "   "
TEN EYCK, JACOB H. . . . . "   "
TEN EYCK, JAMES . . . . "   "
TEN EYCK, SANDFORD ROWE . . . . . . New-York City.
TEN EYCK, STEPHEN-VEDDER, M. D. . . . "   "
TEN EYCK, Rev. WM. HOFFMAN, D. D. New Brunswick, N. J.
TERHUNE, Rev. EDWARD PAYSON, D. D. . Brooklyn, N. Y.
TERHUNE, HENRY STAFFORD . . . . . . Matawan, N. J.
TRAPHAGEN, HENRY . . . . Jersey City, N. J.
TRUAX, CHARLES HENRY . . . . New-York City.
TRUAX, CHAUNCEY SHAFFER . . . . . . "   "
TRUAX, JAMES R. . . . . Schenectady, N. Y.

AN ALEN, WILLIAM K. . . . . San Francisco, Cal.
VAN ALLEN, CHARLES H. . . . . Albany, N. Y.
VAN ALLEN, GARRET ADAM . . . " "
VAN ALLEN, LUCAS L. . . . . New-York City.
VAN ALSTYNE, ANDREW . . . . Chatham Centre, N. Y.
VAN ALSTYNE, RICHARD H. . . . . Troy, N. Y.
VAN ALSTYNE, WILLIAM . . . . New-York City.
VAN ALSTYNE, WILLIAM CHARLES . . . . . Albany, N. Y.
VAN ANTWERP, CORNELIUS HENRY . . . . " "
VAN ANTWERP, DANIEL LEWIS . . . . " "
VAN ANTWERP, JOHN HENRY . . . . " "
VAN ANTWERP, THOMAS IRWIN . . . . . . " "
VAN ANTWERP, WILLIAM MEADON . . . . . " "
VAN ARSDALE, WILLIAM JAMES . . . . . New-York City.
VAN AUKEN, DAVID H. . . . . Cohoes, N. Y.
VAN AUKEN, EDWIN ELECTUS . . . . . New-York City.
VAN AUKEN, JAMES A. . . . . " "
VAN AUKEN, MYRON WILBER . . . . Utica, N. Y.
VAN AUKEN, WILLARD J. . . . . New-York City.
VAN BENSCHOTEN, EUGENE . . . . . . " "
VAN BENSCHOTEN, J. C. . . . . . . Middletown, Conn.
VAN BENSCHOTEN, SAMUEL . . . . . New-York City.
VAN BENTHUYSEN,* CLARENCE ROMNEY . " "
VAN BENTHUYSEN, CHARLES F. . . . . . . Albany, N. Y.
VAN BENTHUYSEN, CHARLES H . . . . . " "
VAN BENTHUYSEN, EDGAR . . . . . . New Orleans, La.
VAN BENTHUYSEN, WARNER . . . . New-York City.
VAN BEUREN, FREDERICK T. . . . . " "
VAN BEUREN, HENRY SPINGLER . . . . . " "
VAN BLARCOM, GEORGE GREEN . . . . . . Nyack, N. Y.
VAN BLARCOM, JACOB CRAIG . . . . . . St. Louis, Mo.
VAN BOSKERCK, ROBERT WARD . . . New-York City.
VAN BRUNT, ARTHUR HOFFMAN . . . . " "
VAN BRUNT, CHARLES . . . . Fort Hamilton, N. Y.
VAN BRUNT, CORNELIUS . . . . New-York City.
VAN BRUNT, CORNELIUS BERGEN . . . . Bay Ridge, N. Y.
VAN BRUNT, JOHN HOLMES . . . . . . " "
VAN BRUNT, WILLIAM HALLIDAY . . . . New-York City.
VAN BUREN, JOHN DASH . . . . Newburg, N. Y.
VAN BUREN,* JOHN D. . . . . " "
VAN BUREN, MARTIN . . . . Amsterdam, N. Y.
VAN BUSKIRK, AMZI HATHAWAY . . . . New-York City.
VAN BUSKIRK, DE WITT . . . . " "

VAN BUSKIRK, JOHN R. . . . . New-York City.
VAN CAMPEN, GEORGE . . . . Olean, N.Y.
VAN CLEAF, JOHN COUWENHOVEN . . . . New-York City.
VAN CLEEF, AUGUSTUS . . . .   "   "
VAN CLEEF, JACOB CHARLES . . . New Brunswick, N. J.
VAN CLEEF, JAMES HENRY . . . .   "   "   "
VAN CLEEF, Rev.·PAUL DURYEA, D. D. . Jersey City, N. J.
VAN COTT, ALEXANDER HAMILTON . . . . New-York City.
VAN COTT, CORNELIUS . . . .   "   "
VAN COTT, JOSHUA MARSDEN . . . . . .   "   "
VAN COTT, LINCOLN . . . . Brooklyn, N. Y.
VAN DE BOGERT, GEORGE OHLEN . . . . New-York City.
VAN DE BOGERT, GILES YATES . . . . Schenectady, N. Y.
VAN DE GRIFT, LEWIS CASS . . . . . . Wilmington, Del.
VAN DENBERGH, WALTER L. . . . . . Amsterdam, N. Y.
VAN DER BEEK, FRANK I. . . . . Jersey City, N. J.
VANDERBEEK, GEORGE HOWARD . . . . . Allentown, N. J.
VAN DER BEEK, ISAAC I. . . . . Jersey City, N. J.
VAN DER BEEK, ISAAC PAULIS . . . .   "   "
VAN DER HOOF, CHARLES ALBERT . . . . New-York City.
VAN DER HOOF, ELISHA W. . . . .   "   "
VANDERPOEL,* AARON J. . . . .   "   "
VANDERPOEL, AUGUSTUS GIFFORD . . . .   "   "
VANDERPOEL, AUGUSTUS H. . . . . . .   "   "
VAN DER POEL, HERMAN WENDELL . . .   "   "
VAN DER POEL, JOHN, M. D. . . . . . .   "   "
VAN DER POEL, SAMUEL OAKLEY, M. D. .   "   "
VAN DER POEL, WALDRON BURRITT, M. D.   "   "
VAN DER POOL, EUGENE . . . . Newark, N. J.
VAN DER VEER, ALBERT, M. D. . . . . . Albany, N. Y.
VAN DER VEER, BENJAMIN BEEKMAN . . . New-York City.
VAN DER VEER, DAVID AUGUSTUS . . . Manalapan, N. J.
VAN DER VEER, FRANK FILLMORE . . . . New-York City.
VAN DER VEER, JOHN REEVE . . . . . .   "   "
VAN DER VEER, LAWRENCE . . . . . . Rocky Hill, N. J.
VAN DER VEER, MATHEW N. . . . . . Somerville, N. J.
VAN DER VEER, PETER LABAGH . . . . Santa Fé, N. M.
VAN DER VOORT, WILLIAM LEDYARD . . New-York City.
VAN DEUSEN, ALMON AUGUSTUS . . . . Mayville, N. Y.
VAN DEVENTER, CHARLES HENRY . . . . New-York City.
VAN DEVENTER, GEORGE MATHER . . . .   "   "
VAN DEVENTER, HUGH BIRCKHEAD, M. D. Sands Point, L. I.
VAN DEVENTER, JAMES T. . . . . Knoxville, Tenn.

34

VAN DEVENTER, Rev. JOHN CORNELIUS . . . Nyack, N. Y.
VAN DE WARKER, ELY, M. D. . . . . . . Syracuse, N. Y.
VAN DE WATER, Rev. GEORGE ROE, D. D. New-York City.
VAN DE WATER, JOHN WALKER . . . . . " "
VAN DOREN, LOUIS OTIS . . . . " "
VAN DOREN, P. A. V. . . . . Pasadena, Cal.
VAN DORN, DANIEL POLHEMUS . . . . Marlborough, N. J.
VAN DUSEN,* ABRAM BOVEE . . . . New-York City.
VAN DUYN, JOHN, M. D. . . . . Syracuse, N. Y.
VAN DUZER, HENRY SAYRE . . . . . . New-York City.
VAN DUZER, SELAH REEVE . . . . Newburg, N. Y.
VAN DUZER, SELAH . . . . New-York City.
VAN DYCK,* HENRY H. . . . . " "
VANDYCK, HENRY LEFLER RICE . . . . Jersey City, N. J.
VAN DYKE, HERBERT . . . . New-York City.
VAN DYKE, Rev. HENRY JACKSON, SR., D. D. . B'klyn, N. Y.
VAN DYKE, Rev. HENRY, D. D. . . . . . New-York City.
VAN DYKE, THOMAS KITTERA . . . . . . Lewisburgh, Pa.
VAN EPPS, EVERT PEEK, M. D. . . . . Schenectady, N. Y.
VAN ETTEN, AMOS . . . . Port Jervis, N. Y.
VAN ETTEN, EDGAR . . . . Buffalo, N. Y.
VAN ETTEN, SOLOMON . . . . Port Jervis, N. Y.
VAN GAASBEEK, LOUIS BEVIER . . . . . Kingston, N. Y.
VAN GIESON, Rev. ALMON PULASKI, } Poughkeepsie, N. Y.
  D. D. . . . . }
VAN HEUSEN, THEODORE VAN WYCK . . . Albany, N. Y.
VAN HOESEN, GEORGE M. . . . . New-York City.
VAN HOESEN, JOHN WILLIAM . . . . . . " "
VAN HOEVENBERGH, HENRY, M. D. . . . . Kingston, N. Y.
VAN HOEVENBERG, JAMES D. . . . . Tompkinsville, N. Y.
VAN HORN, CHARLES FRENCH . . . . . Philadelphia, Pa.
VAN HORN, FRANCIS CHARLES . . . . . Dedham, Mass.
VAN HORNE, JOHN G. . . . . Jersey City, N. J.
VAN HORNE, STEPHEN VAN ALEN . . . . New-York City.
VAN HOUTEN, D. B. . . . . " "
VAN INWEGEN, CHARLES FRANCIS . . . Port Jervis, N. Y.
VAN KEUREN, CORNELIUS, M. D. . . . . New-York City.
VAN KLEECK, EDWARD . . . . Poughkeepsie, N. Y.
VAN KLEECK, FRANK . . . . " "
VAN KLEECK, THEODORE . . . . . . " "
VAN KLEECK, WILLIAM HENRY . . . . . New-York City.
VAN KLEECK, JOHN JAMES . . . Owego, Tioga Co., N. Y.
VAN LOAN, EUGENE . . . . Philadelphia, Pa.

VAN LOAN, HENRY FAIRBANK . . . . . . New-York City.
VAN LOAN, JOHN . . . .   "   "
VAN MATER, JOSEPH I. . . . . Holmdel, N. J.
VAN NAME, CALVIN DECKER . . . . . . New-York City.
VAN NESS, EUGENE . . . . Baltimore, Md.
VAN NESS, FRANCIS . . . . Kinderhook, N. Y.
VAN NESS, RUSSELL . . . . New-York City.
VAN NESS, SHERMAN, M. D. . . . . . .   "   "
VAN NESS, Lieut. WILLIAM PERCY, } Fort Hamilton, N. Y.
   U. S. A. . . . . }
VAN NEST, ALEXANDER T. . . . . New-York City.
VAN NEST, FRANK ROE . . . . Newark, N. J.
VAN NEST, GEORGE WILLETT . . . .   "   "
VAN NORDEN, WARNER . . . .   "   "
VAN NOSTRAND, CHARLES B. . . . . . . Brooklyn, N. Y.
VAN NOSTRAND,* DAVID . . . . New-York City.
VAN NOSTRAND, GARDINER . . . . Newburg, N. Y.
VAN NOSTRAND, GARRET . . . . Nyack, N. Y.
VAN NOSTRAND, HENRY DUNCAN . . . . Jersey City, N. J.
VAN NOSTRAND, JOHN EVERITT . . . . . New-York City.
VAN NOSTRAND,* JOHN J. . . . . Brooklyn, N. Y.
VAN NOSTRAND, MARSHALL R. . . . . . . Elizabeth, N. J.
VAN NOSTRAND, SEYMOUR, ...   "   "
VAN OLINDA, JAMES EDGAR . . . . . . Brooklyn, N. Y.
VAN ORDEN, CHARLES HOPKINS . . . . . Catskill, N. Y.
VAN ORDEN, EDWARD . . . . New-York City.
VAN ORDEN, HENRY DE WITT . . . . . .   "   "
VAN ORDEN, PHILIP VERNON . . . . . . Catskill, N. Y.
VAN ORDEN, WILLIAM . . . .   "   "
VAN PELT, GILBERT SUTPHEN . . . . . . New-York City.
VAN PELT, JOHN VAN DER BILT . . . . Bath Beach, N. Y.
VAN PELT, TOWNSEND CORTELYOU . . .   "   "   L. I.
VAN PETTEN, JOHN BULLOCK . . Claverack, Col. Co., N. Y.
VAN RENSSELAER, CORTLANDT SCHUYLER . New-York City.
VAN RENSSELAER, KILIAEN . . . .   "   "
VAN RENSSELAER, JOHN . . . . Blackwell's Island, N. Y.
VAN RENSSELAER, Rev. MAUNSELL, } New-York City.
   D. D., LL. D. . . . . }
VAN RENSSELAER, WILLIAM BAYARD . . . Albany, N. Y.
VAN REYPEN, CORNELIUS C. . . . . . . Jersey City, N. J.
VAN REYPEN, GARRET DANIEL . . . . .   "   "
VAN REYPEN, Dr. WILLIAM KNICKER- } Washington, D. C.
   BOCKER, Med. Inspector, U. S. N. . }

VAN RIPER, CORNELIUS, M. D. . . . . Passaic, N. J.
VAN SANTVOORD, ABRAHAM . . . . New-York City.
VAN SANTVOORD, Rev. CORNELIUS . . . . Kingston, N. Y.
VAN SANTVOORD, HENRY STAATS . . . . . Albany, N. Y.
VAN SANTVOORD, RICHARD, M. D. . . . . New-York City.
VAN SANTVOORD, SAMUEL McCUTCHEON . . Albany, N. Y.
VAN SANTVOORD, SEYMOUR . . . . Troy, N. Y.
VAN SCHAICK, EUGENE . . . . New-York City.
VAN SCHAICK, HENRY . . . .   "   "
VAN SCHAICK, JENKINS . . . .   "   "
VAN SCHAICK, JOHN . . . . Cobleskill, N. Y.
VAN SICKLE, JOHN WADDELL . . . . . Springfield, Ohio.
VAN SICLEN, ARTHUR . . . . New-York City.
VAN SICLEN, FERDINAND . . . . Brooklyn, N. Y.
VAN SICLEN, GEORGE WEST . . . . New-York City.
VAN SINDEREN, ADRIAN . . . . Brooklyn, N. Y.
VAN SINDEREN, W. LESLIE . . . .   "   "
VAN SLYCK, ANDREW WEBSTER, M. D. . . Coxsackie, N. Y.
VAN SLYCK, GEORGE WHITFIELD . . . . . New-York City.
VAN SLYCK, NICHOLAS . . . . Providence, R. I.
VAN SLYCK, WILLIAM HENRY . . . . . . New-York City.
VAN SLYKE, Rev. EVERT, D. D. . . . . . . Catskill, N. Y.
VAN SLYKE, EUGENE, M. D. . . . . Albany, N. Y.
VAN SLYKE, GEORGE W. . . . .   "   "
VAN SLYKE, Rev. JOHN GARNSEY, D. D. . Kingston, N. Y.
VAN SYCKEL, BENNETT . . . . Trenton, N. J.
VAN VALEN, JAMES MONROE . . . . . Hackensack, N. J.
VAN VALKENBURGH, JOHN L. . . . . Albany, N. Y.
VAN VECHTEN, ABRAHAM . . . .   "   "
VAN VECHTEN, ABRAHAM VAN WYCK . . New-York City.
VAN VECHTEN, HENRY CLAY . . . . .   "   "
VAN VECHTEN, SCHUYLER . . . . . South Orange, N. J.
VAN VLACK,* GEORGE W. . . . . . Palatine Bridge, N. Y.
VAN VLECK, ABRAHAM KIP . . . . . . New-York City.
VAN VLECK, CHARLES KING, D. D. S. . . . Hudson, N. Y.
VAN VLECK, FRANK . . . . San Diego, Cal.
VAN VLECK, J. M. . . . . Middletown, Conn.
VAN VLECK, JASPER . . . . New-York City.
VAN VLECK, ROBERT BARNARD . . . . .   "   "
VAN VLECK, WILLIAM DAVID . . . . . .   "   "
VAN VLIET, BENSON . . . . Poughkeepsie, N. Y.
VAN VLIET, DE FOREST . . . . Ithaca, N. Y.
VAN VLIET, DEUSE M. . . . . New-York City.

Van Vliet, Frederick Christian, M. D. Shrewsbury, N. J.
Van Vliet, Frederick Gilbert . . . . New-York City.
Van Vliet, Purdy . . . .   "   "
Van Vliet, Brevet Major-General } Washington, D. C.
   Stewart, U. S. A. . . . .
Van Vliet, William Downs . . . . Goshen, N. Y.
Van Voast, Col. James, U. S. A. . . . . Cincinnati, Ohio.
Van Voast, James Albert . . . . . Schenectady, N. Y.
Van Volkenburgh, Edward . . . . . New-York City.
Van Volkenburgh, Philip, Jr. . . . .   "   "
Van Volkenburgh, Thomas Sedgwick .   "   "
Van Voorhis,* Bartow White . . . .   "   "
Van Voorhis, Bartow White, Jr. . . .   "   "
Van Voorhis, Elias William . . . . .   "   "
Van Voorhis, John . . . . Rochester, N. Y.
Van Voorhis, Menzo . . . .   "   "
Van Voorhis, William Walgrove . . . New-York City.
Van Vorst, Abraham, A. . . . . . . Schenectady, N. Y.
Van Vorst, Frederick Boyd . . . . . . New-York City.
Van Vorst,* Gardiner Baker . . . . . . Albany, N. Y.
Van Vorst,* Hooper Cumming . . . . . New-York City.
Van Vorst,* John, M. D. . . . . Jersey City, N. J.
Van Vranken, Adam Tunis, M. D. . . . West Troy, N. Y.
Van Vranken, Edward Wheeler . . . Brooklyn, N. Y.
Van Vranken, George Williamson . Schenectady, N. Y.
Van Vranken, Josiah . . . . New-York City.
Van Vredenburgh, Wm. Townsend, M. D.   "   "
Van Wagenen, Bleecker . . . .   "   "
Van Wagenen, George . . . .   "   "
Van Wagenen, Gerrit Hubert . . . . Rye, N. Y.
Van Wagenen, Henry William . . . . . New-York City.
Van Wagenen, Hubert . . . .   "   "
Van Wagenen, John Richard . . . . . Oxford, N. Y.
Van Wagner, Albert . . . . London, England.
Van Wagner, John Nelson . . . . Troy, N. Y.
Van Winkle, Edgar Beach . . . . Paris, France.
Van Winkle, Frank O. . . . . Jersey City, N. J.
Van Winkle, Rev. Isaac, A. M. . . . Cold Spring, N. Y.
Van Winkle, John Albert . . . . Paterson, N. J.
Van Winkle,* John Waling . . . Passaic Bridge, N. J.
Van Winkle, Stephen . . . . Paterson, N. J.
Van Woert, James Burtus . . . . . . New-York City.
Van Woert,* John Voorhees . . . . .   "   "

Van Woert, John Voorhees, Jr. . . . . . New-York City.
Van Wormer, Jasper . . . . Albany, N. Y.
Van Wormer, John Rufus . . . . New-York City.
Van Wyck, Augustus . . . . Brooklyn, N. Y.
Van Wyck,* Benjamin Stevens . . . . . New-York City.
Van Wyck, Jacob Southart . . . . . .   "   "
Van Wyck, Jacob Theodorus . . . . .   "   "
Van Wyck,* John Thurman . . . . . .   "   "
Van Wyck, Robert Anderson . . . . .   "   "
Van Wyck, Samuel . . . . Brooklyn, N. Y.
Van Wyck, Stephen . . . . Roslyn, N. Y.
Van Wyck, Stephen Miller . . . . . Rhinebeck, N. Y.
Van Wyck, William Edward . . . . . New-York City.
Van Wyck, William Harrison, M. D. . .   "   "
Van Wyck,* William . . . .   "   "
Van Zandt, Maxey Newell . . . . . . Rochester, N. Y.
Van Zandt, Milton Burns . . . . . . New-York City.
Van Zandt, Sigourney . . . .   "   "
Varick, Edgar Fitz-Randolph . . . . .   "   "
Varick, George Clippinger . . . . Jersey City, N. J.
Varick, John Barnes . . . . Manchester, N. H.
Varick, John Leonard . . . . New-York City.
Varick,* Theodore Romeyn, M. D. . . Jersey City, N. J.
Varick, Theodore Romeyn, Jr. . . . . New-York City.
Varick, William Woolsey, M. D. . . . Jersey City, N. J.
Vedder, Rev. Charles Stuart, D. D. . Charleston, S. C.
Vedder, Commodore Perry . . . . . Ellicottville, N. Y.
Vedder, Maus Rosa, M. D. . . . . . . New-York City.
Vedder, Ransom Hollenback, M. D. Chatham Centre, N. Y.
Veeder, Andrew Truax . . . . . . Schenectady, N. Y.
Veeder, Harman Wortman . . . .   "   "
Veeder, Lieut. Ten Eyck De Witt, U. S. N. "   "
Vermeule, Adrian, Sr. . . . . . . New Brunswick, N. J.
Vermeule, Adrian, Jr. . . . . . .   "   "   "
Vermeule, Cornelius C. . . . . New-York City.
Vermeule, John D. . . . .   "   "
Ver Meulen, Edmund C., M. D., U. S. N. Philadelphia, Pa.
Vermilye, Edward L. . . . . New-York City.
Vermilye, Jacob Dyckman . . . . . .   "   "
Vermilye, Marion Hoagland . . . . .   "   "
Vermilye,* Theodore Chardavoyne Tompkinsville, N. Y.
Vermilye, Thomas Edward, Jr. Brick Church, Orange, N. J.
Verplanck, Philip . . . . Yonkers, N. Y.
Ver Planck, Samuel Hopkins . . . . . Geneva, N. Y.

VERPLANCK, WILLIAM EDWARD . . . . New-York City.
VER PLANCK, WILLIAM GORDON . . . .   "   "
VIELE, EGBERT LUDOVICUS . . . .   "   "
VIELE, JOHN JAY . . . .   "   "
VIELE, MAURICE A. . . . .   "   "
VIELE, MAURICE EDWARD . . . . Albany, N. Y.
VIELE, SHELDON THOMPSON . . . . . . Buffalo, N. Y.
VISCHER, JOHN HAYDEN . . . . Brooklyn, N. Y.
VISSCHER,* JOHN BARENT . . . . Albany, N. Y.
VOORHEES, ALFRED M. . . . . Brooklyn, N. Y.
VOORHEES, ANSON AUGUSTUS . . . . . . Verona, N. J.
VOORHEES, ALBERT VAN BRUNT . . . . Bath Beach, N. Y.
VOORHEES, CHARLES HENRY . . . . . . New-York City.
VOORHEES, CHARLES HOLBERT . . New Brunswick, N. J.
VOORHEES, CHARLES H. . . . . Rocky Hill, N. J.
VOORHEES, FRANK S. . . . . Brooklyn, N. Y.
VOORHEES, FREDERICK NICHOLAS . . . . Somerville, N. J.
VOORHEES, JAMES . . . . Amsterdam, N. Y.
VOORHEES,* JOHN ENDERS . . . . . .   "   "
VOORHEES, JOHN HUNN . . . . Washington, D. C.
VOORHEES, JOHN H. . . . . Amsterdam, N. Y.
VOORHEES, JOHN JACOB . . . . Jersey City, N. J.
VOORHEES, JOHN NEWTON . . . . . . Flemington, N. J.
VOORHEES, PETER L. . . . . Camden, N. J.
VOORHEES, PETER V. . . . .   "   "
VOORHEES, JUDAH BACK . . . . Brooklyn, N. Y.
VOORHEES, LOUIS A. . . . . . . New Brunswick, N. J.
VOORHEES, THEODORE . . . . New-York City.
VOORHEES, WARDER . . . . Washington, D. C.
VOORHEES, WILLARD PENFIELD . New Brunswick, N. J.
VOORHEES, WILLIAM DILWORTH . . . Bergen Point, N. J.
VOORHEES, WILLIAM K. . . . . Brooklyn, N. Y.
VOORHIS, AUGUSTUS MARVIN . . . . . . Nyack, N. Y.
VOORHIS, JACOB . . . . Greenwich, Conn.
VOORHIS, JAMES . . . . Pompton Plains, N. J.
VOORHIS, JOHN R. . . . . New-York City.
VOORHIS, JOHN . . . . Greenwich, Conn.
VOORHIS,* WILLIAM . . . . Nyack, N. Y.
VOSBURGH, BENJAMIN FREDENBURGH, M.D. New-York City.
VOSBURGH, FLETCHER . . . . Albany, N. Y.
VOSBURGH, MILES WOODWARD . . . . .   "   "
VREELAND, JOSIAH PIERSON . . . . . . Paterson, N. J.
VREDENBURGH, ALFRED . . . . . . Bergen Point, N. J.
VREDENBURGH, ALFRED PURDY . . . . "   "   "

VREDENBURGH, EDWARD LAWRENCE . . Bergen Point, N. J.
VREDENBURGH, FRANK . . . .   "   "   "
VREDENBURGH, JAMES B. . . . . Jersey City, N. J.
VREDENBURGH, WILLIAM H. . . . . . . Freehold, N. J.
VROOM, GARRET DORSET WALL . . . . . . Trenton, N. J.
VROOM, Capt. PETER DUMONT, U. S. A. San Antonio, Texas.
VROOMAN, ISAAC HENRY . . . . Albany, N. Y.
VROOMAN, JOHN WRIGHT . . . . Herkimer, N. Y.

ANDELL, TOWNSEND . . . . New-York City.
    WEMPLE, EDWARD . . . . . . Fultonville, N. Y.
    WENDELL, BURR . . . . Cazenovia, N. Y.
WENDELL, BENJAMIN RUSH . . . . . . New-York City.
WENDELL, EVERT JANSEN . . . .   "   "
WENDELL, FREDERICK FOX . . . . . Fort Plain, N. Y.
WENDELL, GORDON . . . . New-York City.
WENDELL, JACOB . . . .   "   "
WENDELL, JACOB IRVING . . . . Albany, N. Y.
WENDELL, JOHN DUNLAP . . . . Fort Plain, N. Y.
WENDELL, MENZO EDGAR . . . . Troy, N. Y.
WENDELL, TEN EYCK . . . . New-York City.
WENDELL, WILLIS . . . . Amsterdam, N. Y.
WESSELL, CHARLES . . . . New-York City.
WESTBROOK,* THEODORIC ROMEYN . . . Kingston, N. Y.
WESTERVELT, JOHN CALVIN . . . . New-York City.
WHITBECK, ANDREW J. . . . .   "   "
WILLIAMSON, HENRY VEIGHT . . . . . .   "   "
WINNE, CHARLES V. . . . . Albany, N. Y.
WITBECK, CLARK . . . . Schenectady, N. Y.
WORTMAN, Rev. DENIS, D. D. . . . . . Saugerties, N. Y.
WYCKOFF, GEORGE HENRY . . . . New-York City.
WYCKOFF, Rev. JOHN HENRY . . . . . . Claverack, N. Y.
WYCKOFF, PETER . . . . Brooklyn, N. Y.
WYCKOFF, WILLIAM FORMAN . . . . . .   "   "
WYNKOOP,* AUGUSTUS W. . . . . . . Kinderhook, N. Y.
WYNKOOP, GERARDUS HILLES, M. D. . . New-York City.
WYNKOOP, JAMES DAVIS . . . .   "   "

ABRISKIE, Rev. ALBERT A. . . . Jersey City, N. J.
   ZABRISKIE, ALBERT STEPHEN . . Sufferns, N. Y.
   ZABRISKIE, ALBERT S. . . . . . . Allendale, N. J.
ZABRISKIE, ANDREW CHRISTIAN . . . . . New-York City.

* Deceased.

This is to Certify that

is a Member of

THE HOLLAND SOCIETY OF NEW YORK

In testimony whereof the names of the proper
officers and the seal of the Society are here
unto affixed this   day of   18